Publications of the

CENTER FOR EDUCATION IN LATIN AMERICA
INSTITUTE FOR INTERNATIONAL STUDIES

Teachers College, Columbia University

Lambros Comitas,
General Editor

We Wish to Be Looked Upon
A Study of Aspirations of Youth in a Developing Society
VERA RUBIN AND MARISA ZAVALLONI

Guidelines to Problems of Education in Brazil
A Review and Selected Bibliography
MALVINA R. MCNEIL

Black Images
WILFRED G. CARTEY

The Middle Beat
A Correspondent's View of M
El Salvador
PAUL P. KENNEDY

Telling Tongues
Language Policy in Mexico, Colony to Nation
SHIRLEY B. HEATH

Politics and the Power Structure
A Rural Community in the Dominican Republic
MALCOLM T. WALKER

Malcolm T. Walker

POLITICS
AND THE
POWER STRUCTURE

A Rural Community
in the Dominican Republic

TEACHERS COLLEGE PRESS

Teachers College, Columbia University
New York and London

To my parents

Editor's Note

Over the past several decades, the systematic study of the peoples of the Caribbean has grown and fluorished to the degree that this small part of the world is now considered by many to be a significant as well as a distinctive region for social scientific exploration. For diverse historical and political reasons, however, not every Caribbean or West Indian land has received equally intensive professional attention. A case in point is the island of Hispaniola, which contains within its boundaries both Haiti and the Dominican Republic—two nations of longstanding independent status that differ in language, social structure, and culture. On the one hand, Haiti is comparatively well known to anthropology and other social sciences. One need only mention Rémy Bastien, Harold Courlander, Melville J. Herskovits, Alfred Métraux, Jean Price-Mars, and Sidney W. Mintz among the many who have contributed to our understanding of the Haitian existence. On the other hand, the Dominican Republic is an anthropological *terra incognita*, a society on whose contemporary lifeways virtually no serious studies have been made. If for no other reason then, Malcolm Trafford Walker's monograph, *Politics and the Power Structure: A Rural Community in the Dominican Republic*, would be a most welcome addition to this series. There are, however, other compelling reasons for its inclusion. We have, in the following pages, a sensitive but nonetheless objective view of the sources of power in a mountain town of a highly centralized country together with descriptions and analyses of the ways in which this power is exercised and the ways in which decisions are made that affect the daily lives of people. These are questions of theoretical as well as practical import that, on the community level, have been little studied and little understood. Walker's examination of politics and power manipulation, placed as it is in the context of local history, economic life, social aggregations, life cycle, and family system, gives us the realities of rural life in a basically agricultural country. It is this context that is so pertinent to those in education and other fields concerned with the welfare of Dominicans now that thousands, in a wave that started with the death of Trujillo, have settled in the United States to work, to compete, and to live in an American urban setting.

Dr. Walker is a former Research Associate of the Center for Education in Latin America and one of the first graduates of the Teachers College-Columbia University Joint Program in Applied Anthropology. His monograph is the sixth volume in this series sponsored by the Center,

vii

which attempts, in its publications, to bring forth the specifics of formal education and to offer materials and analyses that place the educational process in meaningful context. Geographically, the series concentrates on those political units, those nations, territories, and colonies south of The Rio Grande, commonly referred to as Latin America and the Caribbean. These constituent societies form a complex sphere that, with considerable theoretical difficulty, can be ordered into three culturally distinctive segments, a tripartite scheme that illuminates the heterogeneity of the area. Within each subdivision, uniformities in historical development, similar patterns of economic exploitation, and indigenous populations of roughly equal size and complexity have led to structurally homologous forms of social organization and articulation. Social institutions in each of these subdivisions, including those related to education, have developed distinctively regional forms and carry specific social significance.

One subdivision includes the territories and countries of the Antilles and the Circum-Caribbean. Characteristically, these societies contain institutions that bear the imprint of a long colonial heritage and a social legacy from forced connection with the metropoles of Western Europe. The populations of many of these societies have been derived primarily from Africa, but they also include important pockets of people with origins in Europe, the Indian subcontinent, China, and the Middle East. *We Wish to Be Looked Upon* and *Black Images* and now *Politics and the Power Structure* are books in this series that concentrate on these island and coastal polities. A second subdivision includes those countries, most often located in the highlands of South and Central America, that contain large, culturally viable populations of Amerindians and in which the process of social and cultural integration of native peoples has dramatically influenced the course and form of nation building. *The Middle Beat* and *Telling Tongues* deal with nations in the subdivision, a region sometimes referred to as Indo-America. The third subdivision encompasses the societies of the southern, temperate zones of the Western Hemisphere, which demographically and culturally are dominated by the descendants of migrants from Europe. *Guidelines to Problems of Education in Brazil* focuses on this region.

Lambros Comitas

Acknowledgments

The material for this work was originally gathered for my Ph.D. dissertation in Anthropology at Columbia University. The research was funded by the Research Institute for the Study of Man, New York, the Institute of Latin American Studies, Columbia University, and the Center for Education in Latin America, Teachers College, Columbia University. I wish to express my appreciation to these foundations for making the research possible.

I owe a great deal to a number of men who were on the faculty at Columbia while I was a student—Professors Lambros Comitas, Morton Klass, Charles Wagley, A. P. Vayda, Conrad Arensberg, and Solon T. Kimball. Those familiar with the contributions of Arensberg and Kimball to community studies will recognize their influence on this work. Professors Norman E. Whitten, Jr., Milton Altschuler, and Jerome Handler read earlier drafts of the manuscript. I am grateful for their helpful criticisms. I also wish to thank Dr. Glenn Hendricks for the many hours he spent in proofreading the manuscript. In particular, I wish to thank Lambros Comitas, who was my adviser throughout my graduate study and who encouraged me to rework the dissertation material for publication. It was largely through Professor Comitas that I decided to change careers and enter the field of anthropology—a decision I have not regretted.

The principal acknowledgment of course must go to the people of Constanza with whom I lived. The names of all persons referred to throughout the text are fictitious and it is not possible to name those who became my close informants and provided so much of the material for this book. My debt to them is great indeed.

Politically, the Dominican Republic is not the happiest of countries. Many people live under the shadow of political persecution, many more exist in appalling poverty. Yet, one cannot help but admire the Dominicans for their resilience, their cheerfulness, and their capacity to cope with disaster. I trust that this work will do the people of Constanza and other Dominicans of whom they may be representative no disservice but will result in a better understanding of their way of life and attitudes and of the problems they face.

Finally, I wish to acknowledge the help of my wife, Sheila, for her able assistance in the field and her patience and encouragement under what were often very trying circumstances.

M. T. W.

September 1972

Contents

Editor's Note   vii

Acknowledgments   ix

Introduction   1

CHAPTER 1
The Community and Its Setting   4

CHAPTER 2
A History of Constanza   11

CHAPTER 3
Economic Life in the Countryside   32

CHAPTER 4
Economic Life in the Town   52

CHAPTER 5
Social Activities and Social Groupings   68

CHAPTER 6
The Life Cycle   84

CHAPTER 7
Family Relationships and Interpersonal
Relations   102

CHAPTER 8
Formal Associations   120

CHAPTER 9
Power Structure and Patronage   131

CHAPTER 10
Crisis, Campaign, and the Municipio Elections
of May 1968   145

Conclusions   172

Bibliography   175

Introduction

Constanza, the community with which this study is concerned, is a *municipio* (municipality) in the Central Cordillera of the Dominican Republic, the mountain range sometimes described as the backbone of the country. The *pueblo* of Constanza (the seat of the *municipio*), where I lived with my family from May 1967 until July 1968, lies at the western end of the Constanza Valley, 3,904 feet above sea level.

Constanza is distinctive in the Dominican Republic for several reasons. Economically it is a vegetable-producing area particularly noted for its garlic; it also has something of a tourist trade. Living in Constanza are a number of Spanish and Japanese families who were brought there as colonists by Trujillo during the 1950's. Trujillo himself visited the community frequently and took a great deal of interest in its economic development. In fact, the prosperity Constanza achieved in recent years was, in large measure, due to the Generalísimo's concern.

Constanza is described as a "community"; the justification for considering it to be such is presented in Chapter 1. The community study method was used in field work because the community provided the best setting to examine the power structure and the sources and uses of power, which are the primary concerns of this work. This focus at the community level has not blinded the researcher to the fact that the community is part of a larger whole, nor to the realization that much of the power utilized within the community emanates from sources outside. The extent to which the findings of this study accurately mirror the situation elsewhere in the Dominican Republic raises the problem of whether this particular community or, indeed, any one community in the country may be represented as a microcosm of the whole society. This is another issue altogether, however, quite separate from the community as an object in itself.

To a certain extent, power in Constanza is structured. Those whose status places them at the top of the social structure also have

1

greater access to power, whereas a significant number of *constan-ceros* stand outside the power structure altogether. Because the sources of power are various and power is exercised in a highly personal way, however, it is misleading to consider power in static, structural terms. Throughout field work a principal concern was to determine the informal networks through which decisions affecting the community are made.

In dealing with the aspects of Constanza life that are given the most consideration in this study, an attempt has been made to view these in systemic terms, but it should be stressed that "system" is not conceived as something static. Neither do systems exist independently of one another. It has been expedient to cull out such an area of activities and relationships as the "economic system" and to describe this as a system of dependencies. Essentially the same actors also relate to one another in the "family system" or in the "political system," and the ordering of relations within the one area of activities clearly bears on relationships in the others. This does not mean that those able to initiate within one system can do so in all other relational spheres as well, nor does it mean that the most powerful individual is one who can operate from a position of strength within the maximum number of relational systems, thereby combining his ability to initiate in separate spheres. Strength within the family system, for instance, does not necessarily carry over into the political system, and in the economic system may even work to one's detriment.

Formal interviewing played little part in gathering the data of the study, except for certain historical material. People spoke frankly about very few topics not only because of fear that stemmed from the political situation but also because of suspicion or misunderstanding of the interviewer's purpose. Questions about economic life were rarely answered truthfully. Individuals whose circumstances are favorable grossly underestimated the income that flows into the home because they feared taxation; the poor almost invariably made their circumstances out to be worse than they actually are, even to the point of denying employment, in the hope that they might receive help. Questions about land ownership similarly evoked evasive or untruthful answers.

Most of the data in the study were obtained by prolonged observation of the people interacting in various settings and by questioning close informants who came to understand my interests. Before and during the period of field work the community was subjected to a number of surveys by various agencies. Relevant aspects of this material have been incorporated in the study. As well, the rec-

ords of the *municipio* Civil Office were made available and what
statistical material existed in the capital was also utilized.

Despite the fact that economically and politically Constanza
is closely tied to the country as a whole, it might be argued that
a less atypical location for the study could have been found than
a mountain community inhabited, in part, by foreign colonists, that
relies largely on the production of vegetables and has a tourist
industry.

Climatically and topographically it is not possible to designate
any region as "typical" of the Dominican Republic. Land forms
are complex and consequently there is a very wide range of climatic
patterns and basic economic activities. Sugar is the country's chief
export, but coffee, cocoa, and some rice are also exported and a
number of areas, including Constanza, concentrate on a variety of
vegetable crops for the home market. Apart from these wide regional
variations and the particular socio-cultural forms to which the basic
economic activities are likely to give rise, there are other complicat-
ing factors that tend to make generalizations about the cultural rep-
resentativeness of any locale difficult. Although to some extent the
whole country has been subjected to Haitian influence, the impact
is not at all evenly spread. Further, in some areas there have been
settlers from the British West Indies; scattered throughout the country are agricultural "colonies," some of which are peopled by immigrants from Europe and Asia. Constanza is only one of such centers.

Constanza appeared to offer a number of distinct advantages
for intensive study. Firstly, it was well known (admittedly partly
because of its invigorating climate) and generally considered to be
the center of a distinct region worthy of study because of its economic importance. Secondly, as a valley it is clearly demarcated
and the limits set by nature would largely serve to define the unit
of study. Initially it was thought that the study could be largely
confined to the *pueblo* and the main Valley alone, but because the
boundaries of the community extended beyond these limits this was
not the case. Another reason for choosing Constanza was that there
already exists a considerable body of social science literature dealing
with the effects of plantation economies on various aspects of social
organization, but few, if any studies have been made in areas of
intensive vegetable farming. Constanza is also the seat of a municipality; for the focus of the study, it was necessary that the location
chosen for research be such. Finally, the area is not an old one
and because the study of Constanza could be given an historical
dimension, it offered a distinct advantage.

CHAPTER 1

The Community and Its Setting

From Autopista Duarte, the highway linking the capital (Santo Domingo) with Santiago, the Republic's second largest city, one may reach Constanza either by El Abanico, a small center about four miles north of Bonao, or via Jarabacoa, in which case one leaves the highway just north of La Vega, the provincial capital. Both these routes meet at El Rio, which falls within the *municipio* of Constanza.

The route from the highway to Jarabacoa is paved and in reasonable repair and is less harrowing than the poorly maintained road that begins at El Abanico. In either case the ascent from the rich Cibao plain, through which the highway meanders to the Central Cordillera, is abrupt and not a little frightening. The narrow road winds its way around the mountain sides and ascends over three thousand feet within the first few miles and, with the ascent, there is an equally abrupt change in the countryside. The road skirts precipitous valleys. Occasionally one sees hillside farms of maize and bananas, although there is little real agricultural activity until the road passes through the few wider valleys that precede the Valley of Constanza. This chain of valleys begins at Arroyo Frio, the most eastern section of the *municipio*.

Within the municipal limits there is less climbing and many more signs of agricultural activity. The floors of the valleys are wider and the valley slopes less precipitous. In each valley there is a small settlement stretched out linearly on both sides of the road. These settlements generally comprise a few houses and one or two small stores that serve the *campesino* (peasant) population of the surrounding area. The *pueblecito* (village) of El Rio, the center of the section to the west of Arroyo Frio, is larger than the preceding

4

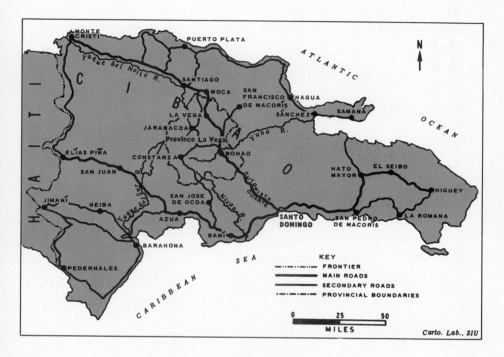

The Dominican Republic.

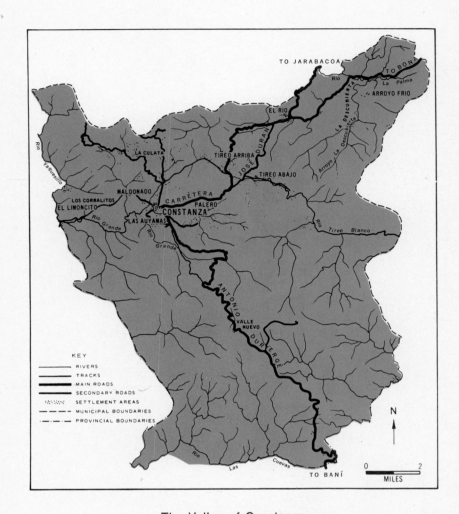

The Valley of Constanza.

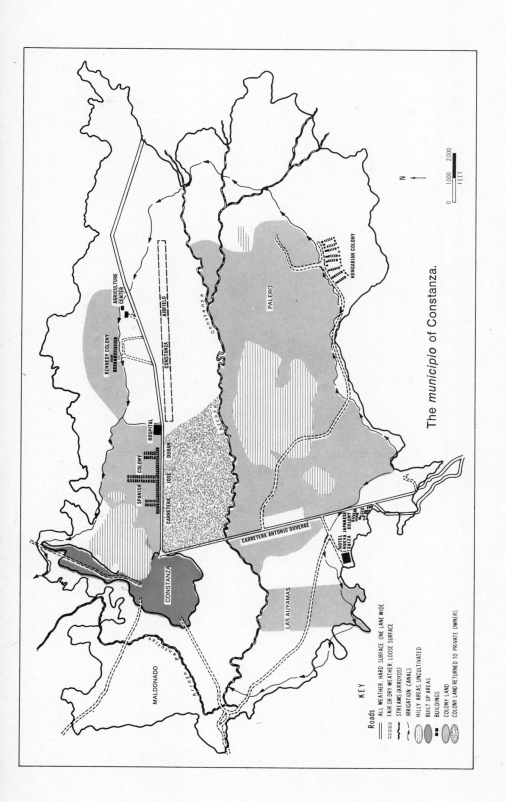

The *municipio* of Constanza.

MALDONADO

CONSTANZA

Arroyo Sabuey

Arroyo

LAS AUYAMAS

SPANISH COLONY

HOSPITAL

CARRETERA JOSE DURAN

KENNEDY COLONY

AGRICULTURE CENTER

CONSTANZA AIRFIELD

Arroyo

Constanza

Constanza

PALERO

CARRETERA ANTONIO DUVERGE

HOTEL JAPANESE NUEVA COLONY

HUNGARIAN COLONY

N

0   1,000   2,000
FEET

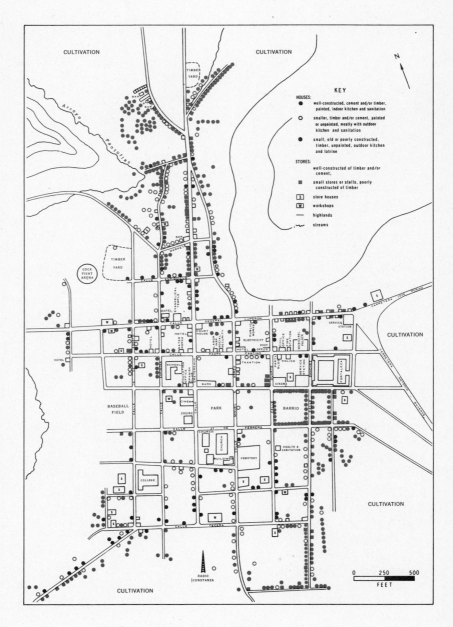

The *pueblo.*

centers; the surrounding population is greater and the El Rio valley is more productive.

A few miles before the Valley of Constanza the road passes two large valleys, both of which support *pueblecitos* about the same size as El Rio; these are centers for the sections Tireo Arriba and Tireo Abajo. Although less developed than the Valley of Constanza, these areas are very rich and, together with a few other smaller valleys where irrigation is practiced, produce much the same range of vegetable crops as the Constanza Valley. Beyond Tireo, the road passes through three other small valleys and then ascends a low range of hills that flank the eastern end of the Valley of Constanza. From the top of these hills one looks down on the Valley stretched out below.

Carretera José Duran leads across the length of the Valley to the *pueblo*, which stands at the western end. On the right and close at hand are the tall hillsides of the northern flank of the Valley, mostly covered with grass but devoid of trees. Stretched out on the left are the rich farm lands; if one should make the journey between late November and March, nearly every area of cultivation appears to be covered with green, for this is the season for garlic.

A short distance before reaching the *pueblo* one passes two impressive cement buildings. These are the office building and living quarters for the staff of the Agricultural Center, which serves the agriculturalists of the community. In times past one of these buildings was the abode of members of the Trujillo family and their friends, who made periodic visits to Constanza. Farther on stands the hospital. Recently renovated and newly painted, it was re-opened in 1968; it had not functioned since 1963, when it was closed down for lack of funds and equipment two years after it was built. Behind the Agricultural Center at the bottom of the foothills is a neat row of painted timber houses. This is the Kennedy Colony, which was built with the assistance of an American Special Forces group to accommodate a number of homeless families. Just beyond the hospital and built almost on the highway is the Spanish Colony, 150 identical houses set closely together and arranged in three blocks. Opposite, and on the far side of the Valley, is the Hungarian Colony (no longer inhabited by Hungarians) and farther to the west the Japanese Colony. The colonies were built to house foreign immigrants brought to the Valley by Trujillo between 1956 and 1958, and many of them still live in the Valley. On the left of the roadway, stretching some 6,600 feet, is a military airstrip and at one point a guard house, where the visitor is required to stop and state his business to the armed guard on duty before proceeding to the *pueblo*.

THE PUEBLO

Carretera José Duran leads into the *pueblo*, at which point it becomes known as Calle General Luperón. Just outside the *pueblo* it intersects with the Valle Nuevo road, which cuts straight across the farm lands of the western end of the Valley. Close by this intersection and dominating the entrance to the *pueblo* there is a large block of stone that serves no apparent purpose. In times past, however, this block supported a huge illuminated monument on which was inscribed:

A Nuestro Ilustre Jefe,
Generalísimo Trujillo
De
Su Pueblo
Constanza

Erected in 1955, the monument was dragged down in 1961 seven months after the dictator's assassination.

Calle General Luperón is the oldest street of the *pueblo*. In the 1880's the first houses and stores were built on this street, the lower end of which is now crowded with small business stores, principally tailors, barbers, shoemakers and repairers, many of which are built of timber and in poor repair. This street runs through to Arroyo Pantuflas, a small river that marks the western boundary of the *pueblo*. In more recent years, settlement has spread north of this street into an area between the river and the hillsides, where the Valley extends for some distance before it rises into the hills. The most northerly section of this area, known to townsfolk only as La Zanja (the gully), is the *pueblo's* main slum area and, technically, is outside the *pueblo* limits. Here nearly all the houses are poor; some are nothing more than shacks and many lack plumbing and electricity. The poorest bars and pool rooms as well as the brothels are located in this area and there is always more activity and noise at night. It is, people say, a bad area and is avoided by respectable citizens.

South of Calle General Luperón and occupying two blocks is the fort, a long, ugly, grey cement structure that houses the garrison. Armed guards lounge in each of the four turrets and at the entrance to the fort, past which runs a short street with a large hump in the middle designed to bring any passing vehicle to a halt. This street is rarely used, even by pedestrians. To the south of the fort is the Barrio de Mejoramiento Social,[1] two blocks of small houses, identical except in color, and originally built in 1951 to accommodate poor families who had erected shacks on the fringes of the town. Most of the *barrio* dwellers work as agricultural laborers or as town workers and, like the people of La Zanja, are looked down upon by other *pueblo* dwellers. Settlement has now extended well beyond the *barrio*, encroaching farther into areas that were previously farm lands. An old picture theater, an extremely decrepit building, is located in the area of the *barrio*.

Calle Padre Fantino, which runs parallel to Luperón and contains the municipal *palacio* (town hall) and most other government offices, is one of the older streets of the *pueblo*, as are the first three streets that intersect it. The park, opposite which stands the Roman Catholic church, is two blocks farther to the south and is thus removed from the main business area of the *pueblo*. The one publicly owned building facing the park is the casino (previously the Club Generalísimo Trujillo), which no longer functions as a club. Also facing the park is a new movie theater, the Spanish Club, two bars, a pool room, and two stores. Settlement extends on all three sides beyond the park, where many of the houses are new and where there is less congestion, although on the fringes of the town where streets are mostly unpaved, houses are often simple structures of timber—very small, badly built, and unpainted.

The better homes and stores tend to be located toward the center of the *pueblo*, although the map following page 4 reveals that good houses are frequently located next door to extremely poor ones. Better houses are well constructed, either of cement or timber, and have indoor sanitation and a kitchen within the house itself. Poorer houses have deep-pit latrines and the kitchen is a separate building placed immediately to the rear of the house; this is also true in the *campo* (countryside), even for new homes built by well-to-do *campesinos*. Placing the kitchen and toilet indoors is a custom strictly confined to a few of the more sophisticated townspeople.

CONSTANZA AND THE OUTSIDE WORLD

Constanza is by no means isolated from the rest of the country or from the outside world. In addition to Carretera José Duran, which links the Valley with Jarabacoa and with Autopista Duarte, there is the Carretera General Antonio Duverge, which links the

---

[1] The *Barrio* (district) of Social Improvement, so named by Trujillo himself.

Valley with San José de Ocoa and, in turn, with Baní and the capital. This road, however, is not overly used. It is a longer route to the capital and is now in very poor repair. The other route is much traveled. In addition to the trucks there are a number of private cars, but more frequently one encounters *carros públicos*,[2] the most common form of public transport in the country. *Constanceros* travel to these other centers a great deal. Movement is not restricted to any one social group, although there is certainly less travel on the part of the poorest *campesinos*.

There is also contact with the rest of the country and, to some extent, with the outside world through the press, radio, and television. Approximately fifty people regularly subscribe to *El Caribe*, the country's main morning newspaper; other papers are sold in the streets. Even among the poor people ownership of radios is not unusual. Since 1964, Constanza has had a privately owned radio station that broadcasts from 6:00 a.m. until 10:00 p.m. daily; most of the programs are of popular tunes, but there is a good deal of commercial advertising and the radio is also used for passing personal messages from individuals in one part of the *municipio* to another. Good reception is also obtained from the capital and other centers and, at times, from Venezuela, Puerto Rico, Cuba, and Radio America. Many people listen to news broadcasts from Santo Domingo but few appear to listen to foreign stations. Contacts with the outside world are made as well through the post office, which also has a telegram service and a radio telephone. The police and the military are in direct contact with the capital and other main centers through radio communication. It is estimated that 87 households own television sets and a considerable portion of the programs are of foreign origin, particularly American.

The influence of the cinema is also important. The two cinemas in Constanza have showings every night and on Sunday afternoons. Programs are generally changed daily. Many of the films are American with sub-titles in Spanish. The preference is clearly for films that deal with sex or violence.

Of more direct impact is the influence of foreign travel, of

---

[2] *Carros públicos* are ordinary passenger cars that generally ply back and forth on set routes, taking paying passengers. Rates are relatively cheap. For example, from Constanza to La Vega the cost is RD $1.50 (U.S. $1.50), from Constanza to Santiago, $2.50, and from Constanza to Santo Domingo, $3.00. Legally, no more than six to eight passengers should be carried, depending on the size of the vehicle, but frequently cars are grossly overloaded. In October 1967, along the El Abanico route to Constanza, I was one of ten adult passengers in an English Austin designed to carry five. In addition, there was one child in the car and another man who traveled for part of the way on the hood.

relatives abroad, and of foreigners who have lived in the town from time to time. A considerable number of families have relatives in the United States and at least thirty persons of the *pueblo* have made trips to Puerto Rico or to the United States. From 1963 until 1965 American Peace Corps volunteers lived in the town but few people remember anything about them or their work. Of greater significance was the presence of a Special Forces group stationed in the *pueblo* after the American intervention in 1965. It is not at all clear why this group was sent to Constanza, but while they were there they built two schools in the *campo*, opened a medical dispensary, and constructed the homes now known as the Kennedy Colony. All remember the presence of these Americans and it seems they made a favorable impression. Some, in fact, express regret that the American soldiers are no longer present.

The Municipio

As a municipality Constanza has a degree of autonomy over its own affairs, although, as will be demonstrated repeatedly in later contexts, politically and economically it is very closely tied to the capital.

The *municipio* is administered by an *ayuntamiento* (council), headed by an unpaid president, a *síndico* (mayor), who is a paid official, and a number of unpaid *regidores* (councilmen), who assist the *síndico*. Once elected, the *síndico* and his councilmen have the right to appoint the *alcaldes*, the local mayors for each administrative section of the *municipio*, who are paid officials, and two or more unpaid assistants for each section, who represent the *alcaldes* in the *parajes*, the subdivisions of the sections.

The *alcaldes* represent the law in their sections and are charged with keeping the peace; they are not permitted to impose fines or otherwise punish lawbreakers and, in theory, are required to bring offenders to the *pueblo*. In practice, however, the *alcaldes* generally deal with all but the more serious matters, which must be brought to the court. In theory, the assistants represent their *parajes* to the local *alcalde* and he, in turn, acts as spokesman for the section interests to the administration located in the town. In practice, this upward channel is sometimes bypassed. On occasions *pueblo* officials meet directly with gatherings of *campesinos*, but they are careful not to undermine the authority of the *alcaldes*.

The members of the *ayuntamiento* are well-known men of the *pueblo* who were either born in Constanza or else have lived there a number of years. Because it is a municipality, Constanza also contains a number of representatives of various government departments who head offices in the *pueblo;*[3] several of these men are outsiders and have little interest in local affairs. As well, there are the police and the military, none of whom have families in the community. The postings of officers and men alike are frequently changed.

The *municipio* of Constanza is a community in terms of sentiment of belonging and, by definition, in terms of Arensberg's criteria as to what constitutes a community.[4] Personnel-wise, there is a full table of organization, containing representatives of all the principal occupations, including functionaries of the government, and, within the limits of the *municipio*, one may observe a full round of life with clear rhythms discernable in terms of the life stages of individuals and in the rounds of social and economic activities as well. There are also occasions when sentiments of community membership are given expression; some of these are recurrent and others are not.

Excluded from the community in its sociological sense are certain of the residents of El Rio, the section lying to the south of the *pueblo*. These people continue to relate to Jarabacoa, to which *municipio* they formerly belonged and where most still have strong family ties. Nevertheless, the fact that the government offices and various other services are located within or near the *pueblo* of Constanza means that on certain occasions people must make visits there. For most, visiting the *pueblo* is not considered a hardship but a pleasurable experience. Politically, socially, and, for some, economically as well, the *pueblo* is the center of community life and it is there that sentiments of community membership are expressed collectively from time to time.

---

[3] These offices include the Electoral Office, Post Office and Telegraph, Public Health, Forestry Department, Social Security, Internal Revenue, Justice of the Peace, Labor Inspectorate, Civil Office, Education, Colonies Office, Public Works, Agriculture, Electricity, Waterworks, Community Development, and Birds and Fisheries.

[4] Conrad M. Arensberg, "The Community as Object and as Sample," *American Anthropologist*, 63 (1961):255–256.

CHAPTER 2

A History of Constanza

Early Settlement

The earliest description of the Constanza Valley appears to be that of Sir Robert H. Schomburgk, who first explored the area on July 21, 1851, and published his report the next year.[1] At that time the Valley was inhabited only intermittently by individuals who made periodic visits to inspect the cattle that grazed in the lush pastures; new beasts were branded and others taken to the market in the plains.

In the years immediately following Schomburgk's visit the Valley began to attract a number of permanent settlers. As far as can be ascertained, all these settlers were extremely poor and, in most cases, illiterate. Generally they were couples or in some cases brothers; family groups were unusual. As some settled in the valley and made a home, they were joined by other members of the family; this pattern continued until recent years. Today, there are fourteen large families in the Valley and all of these trace their beginnings to settlers who arrived in these early years. All have intermarried and all have kinsfolk in other parts of the *municipio* and in other parts of the country, although in many cases these latter links are of little practical importance because of geographical distance and distance in the relationship itself; it appears that for all practical purposes, relationships beyond first cousin are of little account. Of great importance are the ties of ritual kinship (*compadrazgo*) formed between members of different families.

As the Valley filled, settlement overflowed into the surrounding

---

[1] R. H. Schomburgk, "Visit to the Valley of Constanza," *El Alpinismo en la República Dominicana*, edited by Ml. de Js. Tavares, Sucs., C. por A. (Santiago de los Caballeros: Editorial el Diario, 1948), pp. 131–143. Early explorations of the region and other historical sources are dealt with more fully in my dissertation. See Malcolm T. Walker, *Power Structure and Political Behavior in a Community of the Dominican Republic* (Ann Arbor: University Microfilms, 1970).

TABLE 1
Population Figures for the Municipio of Constanza, 1920 to 1966

Year	Municipio population	Males/females	Urban zone population	Urban zone males/females	Rural zone population	Rural zone males/females
1920	3,632	1,860/1,772	N/A[a]	N/A	N/A	N/A
1935	5,910	3,023/2,887	409	209/200	5,501	2,814/2,687
1950	14,737	7,630/7,107	956	460/496	13,781	7,170/6,611
1960	20,920	11,060/9,860	2,920	1,580/1,340	18,000	9,480/8,520
1963	25,484	13,473/12,011	N/A	N/A	N/A	N/A
1966	31,177	16,483/14,649	N/A	N/A	N/A	N/A

Source: Oficina de Estadística, Santo Domingo, República Dominica.
[a] N/A: Figures not available.

territories and individual families laid claims to large areas of land, the boundaries of which were not always clear and, in later years, frequently the cause of disputes. The valleys where there was water were the first to be claimed and the *lomas* (hillsides) were then used for grazing cattle and goats. As population continued to grow, the *lomas* were increasingly utilized for dry cultivation and cattle and goats were relegated to more marginal areas. Today, all land of any worth has been claimed and there is an acute land shortage.

In the Constanza Valley, the bulk of the land fell into the hands of the few founding families, who by no means could be considered gentry. A 1906 description of the Valley states that "Constanza is a town of workers"; and the population is characterized as being "extremely homely and rural."[2] By all accounts there was a great deal of sharing and cooperation during these times and all lived at about the same level. There were no rich and there was plenty of good land for all. This situation was not to endure.

CREATION OF THE MUNICIPIO

Constanza developed very much under the influence of Jarabacoa, of which center it was a municipal section. On May 25, 1900, Constanza became a canton, which gave it an intermediate status between a section and a full municipality. Then, in 1907, by virtue of a law that abolished the status of cantons, it automatically became a *municipio*. This occurred only thirteen years after 1894, when the *pueblo* was supposedly founded.

Originally, the *municipio* consisted of eight sections, all of which were formerly under the jurisdiction of Jarabacoa. In 1953 Jarabacoa lost further territories to the new municipality, including its southernmost section, El Rio. Many of the people of this area today still prefer to consider themselves *jarabacoans* rather than *constanceros*. These additions undoubtably distort the municipal population figures for 1960, but to what extent it is not possible to say (see Table 1). A later law reduced the number of sections throughout the country, although in the case of Constanza it did not affect the overall size of the administrative unit. Today once more the *municipio* is organized into eight sections: Arroyo Frio, El Rio, Tireo Arriba, Tireo Abajo, Palero, Las Auyamas, Maldonado, and El Limoncito. For the most part sections are arbitrarily drawn administrative units; the *parajes*, on the other hand, frequently comprise locality groupings based on close familial ties.

---

[2] Enrique Deschamps, *La República Dominicana, Directorio y Guia General* (Barcelona: Vda. de J. Cunill), Part II, p. 313.

Economic Development

Despite its rapidly growing population, economically the municipality tended to stagnate. Farming practices were primitive and without a road link with Jarabacoa it was difficult and costly to market the beans, yuca, maize, and, later, tobacco, native garlic, and onions, which were the main crops grown in the Valley. Of these, beans were the most important and were carried out by horseback or mule to La Vega, where they were marketed.

After the late 1940's a series of events occurred that were to transform the economic life of the Valley and, to an extent, of the *municipio* as a whole. The construction of roads marked the end of Constanza's semi-isolation and opened up the area to greater exploitation. In 1947 the first of the timber mills was built and, after 1955, the foreign colonists began to arrive. In this period there was also a great deal of building construction in the *pueblo* and, especially after the building of the large tourist hotel on the southern side of the Valley and the construction of a small airstrip, Constanza began to grow as a tourist center. These developments, which in large part may be attributed directly to the personal interest Trujillo took in the area, attracted population and wealth. The Valley and the *pueblo* became prosperous.

Road Construction

Trujillo first visited the Valley in September 1937, arriving on horseback from Jarabacoa. Following this visit a commission was created for the development of Constanza and the construction of the road to Jarabacoa was authorized.[3] This road was not officially opened until March 1947 but was in use some years prior to that date. It profoundly altered the economic life of the Valley. Beans remained the most important single crop but farmers also began to grow other vegetable crops in large quantities to meet the demands of the city markets. In 1951 work commenced on a road to Valle Nuevo, where a large sawmill had begun operations. This road was only one of several that were begun at about this time. Between 1951 and 1957 most of the roads that exist today were built, including the one to San José de Ocoa; it was also during this time that the principal streets of the *pueblo* were paved.

---

[3] An engineer was given charge of the construction; each section of the municipality through which the road passed was required to supply the labor. Road workers were not paid and were supplied only with food. In the Valley, men were obliged to work about one week in every twelve, although apparently this was a somewhat arbitrary arrangement. Those who had the means to do so paid others to work in their stead.

Roads were also constructed to the outlying areas of the *municipio*. This greatly changed the lives of the *campesinos* who lived there. In valleys where water was available it became possible to grow cabbages and other vegetable crops for the city markets rather than to concentrate only on beans and maize and other items that could be carried out by mule or horseback. Road construction also facilitated travel from one part of the *municipio* to the other. Movement to and from the *pueblo* became more frequent.

Timber Industry

Before 1947 there was some lumbering in the area, but in that year the first power mills with circular saws were introduced, and the devastation of the forests began. The first mills were located in the El Rio area and then in the Constanza Valley and in Tireo Arriba; as timber supplies became exhausted, mills were relocated in more remote areas. By 1967 there were some eighteen sawmills in operation employing 436 permanent workers and probably three times that number of temporary workers.[4] Most of the temporary workers and some 40% of the permanent labor were drawn from within the community. Because they could gain more, many *campesinos* went to work in the mills and, in some cases, they sold or deserted their *parcelas* (plots) to do so. In the more remote areas, sawmill owners provided small houses for workers and their families and a store from which they could purchase provisions on credit. Under these circumstances the workers looked to their *patrón* not only for wages and food but also for advice and help in a variety of other matters. Commonly the *patrón* would be *padrino* (godfather) to their children. During 1967 all timber mills were closed on government orders to preserve what was left of the forests; the economic and social effects of this ban have been serious.

The timber industry meant the appearance of owners and managers—a small group of influential men who, for the most part, were not of Constanza but who generally established homes in the *pueblo*, where they were accorded a great deal of prestige. Some of these men yet live in the *pueblo* and, although they are no longer *patrones* as before, their importance is still considerable. The timber

---

[4] It was extremely difficult to gather reliable data on the number of permanent and temporary employees engaged in the timber industry. When it became known that the mills were to be closed and that some form of compensation was to be paid to owners as well as permanent employees, it appears that, in some cases at least, there was misrepresentation of the true numbers employed. The figures above are a conservative estimate.

industry also attracted a number of workers from outside the community and some of these arrived with their wives and families and set up homes in the poorer parts of the *pueblo*.

Growth of the Town

The growth of the *pueblo* very much reflected the economic development of the Valley and *municipio* as a whole. In 1909 there were some fifty houses in the *pueblo;* the number increased very slowly over the years. The dramatic growth did not come until the late 1940's and 1950's, when the economy of the community was transformed.

In 1906 six "businessmen" were listed as living in the *pueblo*.[5] These men belonged to established families of Constanza and were probably small storekeepers and perhaps buyers of Valley produce as well. During the 1920's a Lebanese settled in the Valley and bought up a great deal of land and, in later years, opened a timber mill and a store in the *pueblo*. Today, the descendants of this man, the Arafat family, are the biggest landholders in the Valley. Ten years or so later, a second Lebanese arrived and this man, Sr. Nashash, soon became the biggest businessman in the *pueblo*, owning a large store and other business concerns and much property in the *pueblo* as well. Later, yet another Lebanese appeared who opened a rival store, but by this time, the late 1940's, and during the 1950's, the *pueblo* population had grown considerably with the arrival of many other outsiders and a number of other stores had opened.

The main public buildings of the *pueblo* were erected during the 1950's, including the Palacio Municipal,[6] the building of the Partido Dominicana,[7] the public school, a 24-bed hospital, a new Roman Catholic church dedicated to the "Benefactor of the Country," and the fort. Also erected were the two large houses a few miles to the east of the *pueblo* and another to the south that were intermittently occupied by members of the Trujillo family. The former is now the Agricultural Center and the latter is the home of the local military commander. The Nueva Suiza Hotel,

---

[5] Enrique Deschamps, *La República Dominicana, Directorio Y Guía General*, Part II, p. 313.

[6] The municipal town hall where the *síndico* has his office and where the *regidores* meet from time to time.

[7] The building of Trujillo's Dominican Party, which housed the local party officials. The building now serves as a Roman Catholic primary and intermediate school.

said to have been personally designed by Trujillo's sister, was constructed,[8] as well as a swimming pool with an open-sided bar.[9] Finally, approximately one mile from the *pueblo*, a small airfield was built. Twice-weekly flights from Santo Domingo brought a steady stream of tourists to the Valley. It was this airfield that was put to use late in the afternoon of June 14, 1959, by a group of ill-fated invaders from Cuba who chose Constanza as one of the sites for invasion.

As a consequence of the invasion, Constanza's garrison was increased from thirty or so soldiers to some 400 under the command of a colonel. Mainly to cater to the soldiers, bars, which also served as brothels, opened in the area immediately beyond the northern limits of the *pueblo*—the area known as La Zanja. These businesses were mostly owned by outsiders, and the many prostitutes who came to work there were also not of the community. Small cafes and pool rooms sprang up in the vicinity of the bars; almost every night, it is said, the area was filled with carousing soldiers, who spent their money freely.

The Colonies

In 1955, the population was further added to when the first group of foreign immigrants arrived from Spain; in 1956 and 1957, they were joined by immigrants from Japan and Hungary. The foreigners were settled in "colonies" located in three different parts of the Valley. Less than two years after they arrived, all the Hungarians were deported. Of the 200 or so Spaniards who came, only eighty remain and all but eleven of the original thirty Japanese families have left. Four of these families have moved to Tireo Arriba, still within the *municipio*.

Notwithstanding the many colonists who returned to their homelands or moved elsewhere, the presence of such a large group of foreigners had many repercussions, both social and economic.

---

[8] In John Bartlow Martin's *Overtaken by Events* (New York: Doubleday and Co., Inc., 1966), p. 155, the author states that the hotel is so designed that all the rooms face onto corridors and concrete patios, thus affording no view of the Valley. This is not quite accurate. Of the 59 rooms, eighteen directly face barren hills, 24 look down on an open courtyard, nine have a partly obscured view of the eastern end of the Valley, and eight have an excellent view of the town end of the Valley.

[9] The pool is a dammed-up section of the river and is filthy and rarely used. Some say that it has not been cleaned since Trujillo's death. The bar, which like the hotel is owned by the state, has two full-time employees. During the summer months, in the late afternoons, the place is infested with mosquitoes and sand flies; in the winter months, it is frequently bitter cold.

In the present context, the most immediate impact was on farming practices; it is mainly the Spaniards, the first and largest group to arrive, who are credited with effecting the changes that took place.

To provide the colonists with farms, Trujillo confiscated 7,466 *tarea*s of the best Valley land,[10] which was divided into *parcelas* and placed under the control of a local Colonies Office, the headquarters of which was in the capital. Each family was entitled to one *parcela* and, as well, was provided with a house and various other benefits.[11] It is not at all clear why Trujillo encouraged groups of immigrants to come to the country[12] and why so many were settled in the Valley, where land was already in short supply. It very soon became apparent, however, that the Spaniards and Japanese knew a great deal more about vegetable farming than the Dominicans and, as a result of the example they set, farming practices underwent much change.

Farming in the irrigated valleys really became a business and

---

[10] Families who lost land were paid approximately RD $20 per *tarea* (1 *tarea* = .154 acre), but three families insist they received nothing and are still waiting compensation. In the case of the big landowning Arafat family, which lost more land than anyone else, compensation was said not to have been paid and, in later years, after Trujillo's death, RD $10,000 was paid to the family by the government; some of their land was withdrawn from the colony and restored to them as well. Others say the family did receive payment from Trujillo and that the later transaction was fraudulent.

Families who lost land to the colonies continued to work what land they had left in the Valley or else moved elsewhere in the *municipio*. In some cases, individuals of these families later became colonists when *parcelas* of colony land were made available to Dominicans.

[11] The three groups of immigrants were not accorded the same benefits. All immigrants received rent-free housing and basic furniture and each family was given 60¢ per day for each member until the family was in a position to maintain itself. Colonists were free to leave the colony any time they wished, but theoretically the rights to a *parcela* in the colony could not be sold without state authorization. The Japanese and Spaniards immigrated under separate arrangements made by Trujillo with the governments of their countries and in matters concerning travel costs and posting of bonds, the schemes differed.

[12] Some say the immigrants were brought out to "whiten" the race, yet whole family groups were permitted to immigrate and there was no deliberate attempt to encourage intermarriage with Dominicans. The Hungarians who came were some of those who had fled following the Hungarian revolution in 1956. Apparently Trujillo responded to the appeal to governments to provide homes for the rebels. Others say it was Trujillo's intention to establish a true international colony in the Valley, comprising representatives of many different nationalities who would live together in harmony, side by side with the Dominicans. The most popular explanation, the one invariably believed by the Japanese and the Spaniards, is that they were brought to the Valley to teach the Dominicans about vegetable farming.

there was deliberate planning for the market. The heavy use of fertilizers and insect sprays became accepted practice; there was also greater reliance on machinery. Most of the European vegetable crops that are grown today were introduced at this time, but the most important change was that from beans to garlic as the principal crop. The colonists have influenced farming practices in the other valleys as well; each year fertilizers are more widely used and in a few areas the range of vegetable crops has widened to include lettuce and tomatoes and the larger varieties of garlic.

Employment patterns have changed considerably since the late 1950's and, in large part, this too must be attributed to the impact of the colonists. It had been customary to look to mutual help groups made up of family and friends when much labor was required on a *parcela*, although it appears that from very early days in the Valley wages were at times paid. After the arrival of the colonists, farming became much more intensive and labor requirements grew. At certain times of the year, e.g., in those weeks when garlic are harvested, all growers need large quantities of labor and it is impracticable to rely on mutual help groups. The colonists themselves never were part of these groups but they were largely instrumental in their breakdown, not only in the Valley, but to some extent in other areas as well. When there is much employment available in the Valley *campesinos* arrive from all parts of the *municipio* in search of work; at such times mutual help groups are unable to function. These groups, which make up the *junta* system, still exist in the dry-farming areas and even among some agriculturalists of the Valley, but they do not have their former importance.

Most of the Spanish and Japanese colonists who stayed on prospered; it is said, and it appears to be true, that none of them is really poor. Some of the Spaniards branched out into other businesses but, for the most part, the immigrants concentrated on building up their holdings in a variety of ways and in this, many have been highly successful. They have bought land or rented it from Dominicans and, in some cases, illegally acquired new portions of colony land.[13] The Hungarians' story, on the other hand, is hardly one of success and their deportation was apparently welcomed by most

---

[13] Legally, an individual may not have more than one allocation of colony land and theoretically all applications for colony land that becomes available are treated on their merits. Graft does or did play an important part in obtaining such land, however, and by using Dominicans as "front men" some were able to acquire more colony land. A good deal of colony land is rented, which is also illegal.

of the Dominicans of the *pueblo* and Valley.[14] Most people say that the Hungarians were thieves, were lazy and argumentative, and preferred to steal rather than work. A few deny this and say they were hard-working but knew little about agriculture; it is likely that the Hungarians were former industrial workers from the cities. It is also said by some that they were utterly fearless and had no respect for Trujillo's military and the dictator deported them because he feared them. One story is that they were manufacturing guns in the colony, and some even suggest they were communists.

With the departure of the Hungarians, their land and houses were made available to Dominicans. Most of those who then became "colonists" were people of Constanza. The Hungarian colony is still known by this name but nearly all who live there are Dominicans, as are most who now live in the Japanese and Spanish colonies. Some months after the death of Trujillo there was a series of incidents against the foreign colonists; stones were thrown on their roofs and animals were let loose in their *parcelas* at night. The police and military took no action. The incidents were not repeated but the colonists were frightened and a number of families left and returned to their home countries, thus freeing further land to Dominicans.

The Dominican government, anxious to be relieved of the responsibility for the colonists, offered RD $2,100 to each Spanish colonist as liquidation for his rights to the land.[15] All but twelve of the Spanish colonists have taken this money and vacated the colony land they formerly farmed. Many of them then went home or moved elsewhere in the country but eighty, many of whom have families, stayed on. With the exception of the Spaniards who are still "colonists" because they legally farm colony land, the Spaniards today work land that they have bought or rented or, in some cases, still work land in the colonies illegally rented from the Dominican title-holders.

The fact that Japanese and Spaniards frequently live side by side with Dominicans should not be taken to indicate that a spirit

---

[14] A colony of Hungarians was also established near Jarabacoa and these people were deported at the same time. Most are believed to have gone to the United States. A short time prior to their deportation, a commission is said to have come from Santo Domingo to investigate charges to the effect that the Hungarians were causing disaffection in the community, defying the police and military, and neglecting their land.

[15] This offer was not made to the Japanese colonists, who were bought out under a different system. The seven Japanese families who have remained in the Valley are still waiting for clear titles to their *parcelas*.

of international harmony prevails, if indeed this was ever Trujillo's expectation.[16] There has been some intermarriage,[17] but the foreigners remain essentially groups apart from the Dominicans. There is also little contact between the two groups of foreigners, although possibly there would be more contact were it not for the fact that most of the Japanese still live in the Japanese colony, where there are no Spaniards. The Spaniards have their own club (the only social club now existing in the *pueblo*), where the men gather to drink and talk on Sunday afternoons; no Dominicans are members and none chooses to join. The Japanese have few contacts outside their own group, but, unlike the Spaniards, they are considered "strange," yet honest and hardworking and in no way arrogant. The Spaniards, on the other hand, are contemptuous of the Dominicans and frequently do not hesitate to show their scorn; Dominicans, they say, are irresponsible and immoral. They are equally contemptuous of Dominican institutions, particularly the courts, the military, and the police.

The Dominicans, for their part, resent the aloofness of the foreigners and the success they have achieved, which they believe was at the Dominicans' expense. Trujillo brought the foreigners to the Valley without consulting the local people and the land confiscations dispossessed a number of families. The resentment of these people in particular and of the many others who are now landless has not lessened over the years, and they look with envy on the large *parcelas* of the foreigners. Many of the poor who voted for Juan Bosch in 1962 did so believing that they were going to be given land, including that of the foreigners. The foreigners were particularly fearful during the Bosch period and for the most part welcomed his overthrow.

Politically, the foreigners are considered conservative, although with only one exception they take no part in political affairs. None of the Japanese and only three of the Spaniards have taken citizen-

---

[16] I have dealt with the social consequences of bringing foreign immigrants to the Valley more fully elsewhere; see Malcolm Walker, "Foreign Colonists in a Dominican Rural Community: The Costs of Economic Progress," *Caribbean Studies 11* (1971), pp. 88–98.

[17] Of the several cases of intermarriage between Spanish and Dominicans, there is no instance of a Spanish woman having married a Dominican man. It is true that the Spanish women are greatly outnumbered by their menfolk, but the fact is that the Spanish families do not welcome the idea of a Dominican son-in-law. Even a Spaniard who takes a Dominican wife is criticized by his own people. The prejudice against Dominican husbands is not as strong among the Japanese. Of the five Japanese in the community who have intermarried with Dominicans, three Japanese men have married Dominican women and two Dominican men have married Japanese women.

ship; nearly all of them have the ultimate intention of returning to their countries when they have made sufficient money. For the most part, they regard their sojourn in the Dominican Republic as a trial to be endured for the sake of better days to come. The Dominicans wish only that they were gone. The depth of hostility toward the Spaniards was well summed up by a middle-aged agriculturalist of the Valley who said, "Si America Látina tenga una plaga se llama españoles."[18]

Political Development

Until the construction of the road to Jarabacoa, Constanza remained not only economically backward but to a large extent unaffected by the successive revolutions and wars that shook the rest of the country. No Spanish soldiers were stationed in Constanza in the 1860's during the brief Spanish restoration; American forces that occupied the country from November 29, 1916, until September 18, 1924, administered the province from La Vega and did not enter Constanza. *Constanceros* voted in each election, but from what people remember, early elections never aroused a great deal of excitement.

During the municipal elections held on June 4, 1924, Constanza voted solidly for the Alianza Nacional-Progresista of General Vásquez; the opposition coalition party gained no votes at all. On February 23, 1930, when Vásquez was deposed, Constanza was one of the first territories to support the new provisional government headed by Rafael Estrella Ureña.[19] In that same year Trujillo was elected president for his first term. On September 8, 1936, the council voted to rename the main street of the town Calle Presidente Trujillo (its name has since been changed), and, when one year later Trujillo visited the Valley for the first time, the first visit by a head of state, the leading citizens "took the opportunity to beg him to accept the presidency for the next period."[20]

Over the years Trujillo made many visits to Constanza; a number of these were occasions for huge rallies in the park, at which leading citizens presented eulogies in praise of the dictator and gave pledges of loyalty. On one of his visits Trujillo was rained with

---

[18] "If Latin America has a plague, it is the Spaniards."

[19] J. Augustin Concepción, *Constanza* (Ciudad Trujillo: República Dominicana, 1958), p. 63.

[20] *Ibid.*, p. 73.

flowers by the grateful population because of the many things that had been done for the *pueblo* and Valley. On June 19, 1954, the large bronze monument to Trujillo, erected at the entrance to the *pueblo*, was dedicated; the cost was met by public contribution.[21]

In 1946 and 1947, quantities of blankets, shoes, and children's clothing, as well as evaporated milk, were distributed among the poor. In later years similar distributions took place. During some of his visits Trujillo handed out money to the poor. In 1951 a social service scheme was begun to provide daily help to 300 poor families, but the scheme operated only for a short time. These distributions were handled by certain public officials in the *pueblo* and it is said that their friends and relatives were made the principal recipients of the distributions. It is a common complaint among the Constanza poor that Trujillo's good intentions were constantly frustrated by corrupt officials, who channeled into their own pockets what was intended for the poor. In 1951 the Barrio de Mejoramiento Social was inaugurated; Trujillo had authorized the building of the *barrio* in response to an appeal by a delegation of poor families without homes. In 1961 he "gave" Constanza the hospital where the poor were able to receive free medical care and medicines.

Although relatively few shared in these distributions that took place from time to time, many still speak of Trujillo's generosity and his concern for the poor; this sentiment is particularly strong among the *campesinos*. Many also remember that there was much more work available than today and although wages were lower, costs for many items were less. Even those who are most outspoken in their criticism of the Trujillo regime acknowledge that the progress of the community in these years is to be largely attributed to the interest Trujillo took in the Valley and its affairs.

It would be false to suggest that the Trujillo period was not also a time of fear for many, but people did not live in abject terror. The *campesinos* paid their taxes each year and were left alone; the wealthy paid much more but, by all accounts, they were able to make a great deal of money, too. One individual, the son-in-law of a wealthy businessman in the *pueblo*, warned me not to believe all the bad things I heard about the Trujillo years. "One thing about Trujillo, if you wanted to work, he let you make money." It appears that it was easier to make money during those years

---

[21] Leading citizens who were considered wealthy made contributions that ranged from RD $100 to $3,000, but all heads of families, it is said, were required to contribute something. The *síndico* drew up a list of contributions that would be made and teachers at the school informed each child of the amount his father was to donate.

than today, although there is no evidence that graft and corruption were any less; on the contrary, people say there is now much more.

Trujillo did have secret police in the *pueblo*—there were four of them who drove official black Volkswagens; they went to the bars and apparently lived a fairly full social life and were on personal terms with many. Almost certainly there were a number of paid informers as well (there is at least one in the *pueblo* today), but evidently few felt they had much to fear as long as they had "respect" for those in authority. In all, only three families of Constanza directly suffered loss through Trujillo's secret police. In two cases the individuals concerned were murdered not in Constanza but in a distant *pueblo*.

A number of families suffered economically when they lost land to the colonies and in various ways the poor were exploited by the rich and powerful who had influence with Trujillo. At times, however, it was the rich who suffered. The Arafats, who lost the most land to the colonies, were wealthy and influential in the community. One individual, Martín Espiallat, who became *síndico* and achieved considerable wealth and influence under the patronage of Trujillo, was suddenly deprived of his post and almost reduced to ruin. Trujillo found out, it is said, that Espiallat was directing into his own pockets too large a share of the profits of a Trujillo-owned timber mill. Another incident concerned some brothers, one of whom was married to a relative of Trujillo, who were using Trujillo's name to terrify *campesinos* into selling valuable timber land. When Trujillo learned of this, he confiscated the land and imprisoned the brothers.

During the Trujillo years certain individuals of the *pueblo* who were comparatively wealthy assumed the political direction of the *municipio*. Some of these men were outsiders who had no connection with the founding families of Constanza. If today they are still not considered *constanceros*, however, they are at least well known in all parts of the community. Other than Sr. Nashash and the founder of the Arafat family, who has since died, these men came to the *pueblo* during the 1940's and 1950's. For the most part they were involved in sawmilling or opened businesses in the *pueblo*; some also bought much land, but they did not generally engage directly in agriculture themselves. A few of them were professionals. Others who achieved wealth and prominence in the *pueblo* were members of the founding families. Some of them who owned much Valley land continued to practice agriculture; these men employed large numbers of *peones*.

All these men were considered strong supporters of Trujillo;

most of them at some time or other served on the *ayuntamiento* or on the Constanza directive of Trujillo's Dominican Party. Today it is largely these same men, the *trujillistas*, who dominate in political affairs. All of them sought to identify with the Trujillo regime and were considered to be friends of Trujillo himself or to have some access to his power. Others in the community who wanted favors or merely wished to safeguard their positions sought the friendship and protection of these men and frequently utilized the *compadrazgo* relationship to this end. In the *campo* certain *campesinos* rose to importance during these years. These were bigger landholders and the heads of large families. In Trujillo's time some of them served as rural police; today these same men are sought out to be *alcaldes*, the representatives of law and order in the sections.

One other point should be made concerning political development during the Trujillo years. It has been noted that in at least two instances individuals who became too exploitative were struck down by Trujillo himself. Others, who by all accounts should have been, never were. There are several accounts concerning individuals who were arrested and sometimes savagely beaten after they had been informed against, usually anonymously, but on occasion military interrogators apparently dealt very severely with informers if it were believed that they were wrongfully informing against a person for some private purpose.[22] The point is that there was an element of unpredictability about power that came from outside, and those in the most vulnerable positions sought to protect themselves as best they could. On the community level, the rallies in the park, the eulogies to the dictator, the costly monument, and certain associations that were formed during these years may all be considered as attempts to placate this power and to demonstrate approval and a willingness to cooperate. On the individual level, one tried to make powerful friends. The distrust and suspicion of motives that seem to permeate human relationships in the community today and that doom any voluntary association to impermanence may be a legacy of the Trujillo era. One constantly hears the expression *padre de familia* (head of a family) advanced as a rationale for acting out of self interest and for failing to protest the injustices that others may suffer; as the head of a family, one's

---

[22] There are a number of stories to this effect but few of them concern Constanza people and the veracity of those that do is difficult to establish. The important thing is that people apparently believed that informing against someone could be as dangerous to the informer (if his identity was learned) as to the individual who was denounced.

responsibility is only to the family and each person must look out for himself.

Older residents say that things were not always thus and that in the years before Trujillo everyone lived in harmony without distrust or suspicion. The extent to which Trujillo was responsible for the brittleness and suspicion that today are characteristic of inter-personal relationships among *pueblo* dwellers, and between *pueblo* dwellers and *campesinos*, can probably never be known. But, granted that relationships were not always of this kind, it is not unlikely that the brittleness and suspicion became apparent at the point in time when there developed a clear dichotomy between townsmen and *campesinos*, when there were no longer sufficient resources in the form of land or business opportunities for all, and when economic power became concentrated in the hands of a few. It is possible that these developments would have occurred even in the absence of a Trujillo.

THE CUBAN INVASION

Constanza, the visitor is frequently told, is very tranquil and nothing exciting ever happens. The tranquility was rudely broken, however, on June 14, 1959, when 55 invaders from Cuba landed on the airstrip in a DC-3 aircraft. The object of the Constanza group, it is believed, was to capture the country's main communication center at Alta Bandera, which is located near Valle Nuevo, but evidently the invaders also hoped to rally *campesino* support and wage a guerrilla war that would result in the overthrow of Trujillo. The enterprise was a complete disaster. Within three weeks all of the Constanza group were dead or captured; two other groups of invaders, totalling some 180, who attempted sea landings on the northern coast shared a similar fate.

According to local accounts, the invaders landed at dusk and firing broke out immediately. An alarm sounded and soldiers from the fort began to pursue the invaders, who had divided into two groups and climbed out of the Valley. Many of the townspeople and *campesinos* hurried to the fort when they heard the alarm and the firing; some were given weapons to join in the hunt. The invaders were given no support whatsoever by the local people and they soon became separated into small groups. Some were shot or captured and some surrendered. Most, it seems, were killed by Trujillo's Air Force, which appeared the next day and began an intensive bombing of a very wide area around the Valley and, in the process, destroyed much valuable forest land. After three weeks, the last invader was either dead or captured and Constanza, for a short time, returned to its normal tranquility.

THE DEATH OF TRUJILLO
AND ITS AFTERMATH IN CONSTANZA

Political Developments

News of Trujillo's assassination on the night of May 30, 1961, did not reach Constanza until 4 p.m. the next day, several hours after the news had become public knowledge in the capital. Initially people did not believe the news; there was a great deal of fear and bewilderment. When the dictator's death was confirmed, scores of men from the *pueblo* and *campo* flocked to the Dominican Party building, where they signed their names as volunteers for service against the forces that had overthrown their leader.

Constanza went into mourning; nine days later there was a requiem mass, which nearly all attended. On that day men wore black armbands; during the service many men and women wept openly. The church was full for the mass; crowds stood in the street outside and in the park, where they listened to the service through loud speakers mounted on top of the belfry. After the service, people moved to the monument, which they heaped with flowers, and then listened to eulogies delivered by leading citizens. Many wept and some women became hysterical with grief. Said one man, "Trujillo was our father and always will be," and another, "Do not weep, for Trujillo has not died; he will always live in the hearts of Dominicans." Even those who are now most vocal in their opposition to Trujillo and his regime admit, with some embarrassment, that they, too, attended the mass and placed flowers on the monument and wore black armbands everywhere in public. It was, by all accounts, a time of great uncertainty and fear and no one knew what might transpire.

Not until seven months after the assassination did any real disorder become apparent in Constanza, and this coincided with the breakdown of law and order in the capital. Even so, the disorder was comparatively mild. One morning, toward the end of November 1961, a crowd of young men from the *pueblo* began to gather in the streets in the area around the Dominican Party building. The crowd took up the chant "*libertad*" (liberty) and many then forced their way into the deserted building, where they smashed the windows and doors and did a good deal of damage to the interior of the building. While they were at work, others looted the typewriters and either smashed or stole the office furniture. Still chanting "*lib-*

ertad," the crowd then made its way to the entrance of the *pueblo* and, with little difficulty, toppled the massive Trujillo monument off its stand and crashed it onto the street.[23] This mob, it is said, was led by some of the June 14th men, who were supposedly communists, but others deny this and say the violence was not organized and there were no clearly identifiable leaders. The police and military took no action against the offenders, yet the disorder went little further and things were quiet a few days later. A good deal of economic distress and uncertainty continued until early 1962, when the Council of State assumed power in the capital; the market situation then returned to normal. During this period, agriculturalists had been unable to sell their crops and many of them lost their harvests.

On December 20, 1962, Juan Bosch of the Partido Revolucionario Dominicano (PRD) was elected president by an overwhelming majority. In the *municipio* of Constanza, Bosch gained 5,053 votes out of 6,342, approximately 79.8%.[24] In Constanza, the Union Cívica, the party of the *trujillistas,* was the principal opposition to the PRD, but it was ill-organized and apparently made little serious attempt to attract voters. The PRD in Constanza was formed by political organizers who appeared from outside the community. With the exception of one important family, the Santanas, who owned timber mills and much land in El Rio, where they exercised strong influence, the *constanceros* who became politically active for the PRD and those who were elected to office as *síndico* and *regidores* were largely *pueblo* dwellers of no importance in the community. Shortly prior to the elections, when it became apparent that Bosch was going to win, most of the leading *trujillistas* in Constanza withdrew completely from political activity. They were fearful for their future and at least two of them secretly contributed money to the PRD.

On September 25, 1963, Bosch was overthrown and the violent upheaval that followed in the capital led to American intervention. In Constanza there was no outbreak of fighting, but feelings ran high in the *pueblo* and at times there were confrontations between the supporters of Bosch and those favoring his overthrow. The economic effects of this revolution, however, were considerably more serious for the agriculturalists than those of November 1961, and many were temporarily ruined. In the subsequent elections on June

---

[23] It is said that some of the military later retrieved the bust of Trujillo and took it inside the fort, where it supposedly still stands today.

[24] Source: Junta Central Electoral, Santo Domingo.

1, 1966, Balaguer's Partido Reformista easily gained the victory. In Constanza, where the PRD was largely discredited, the *trujillistas* conducted a vigorous campaign. Balaguer polled 7,642 votes out of a total 8,709 for the *municipio;* the PRD received only 1,004 votes. These totals represent 87.7% of the votes for Balaguer and only 11.5% for Bosch.[25]

In May 1968 municipal elections were held throughout the country. In Constanza there were no opposition candidates to those of the *reformistas;* people who went to the polls had only a choice of voting for these candidates or rendering their votes invalid. 7,160 voted for the *reformista* candidates, seven cast invalid votes.

Economic Developments

After the death of Trujillo, the community suffered an economic decline. The flow of tourists fell off sharply, with a consequent loss of revenue to local merchants and hotel keepers. The tourist industry has not recovered anything like its former importance. The Nueva Suiza hotel is notorious for the poor quality of its service. The air service from Santo Domingo was discontinued, although the Constanza airstrip is still maintained.[26] Roads leading to Constanza received little attention and few tourists were adventurous enough to make the journey by car. Only in the months before the recent *municipio* elections was there a serious attempt to put the roads in order once more.

In 1963, the garrison was reduced to a company of 120, roughly its present strength. Although the community hardly mourned the departure of the soldiers, the girls and small businessmen of La Zanja did. This area is still lively at night, especially on weekends, but not as in former years. Of more serious consequence for the economic life of the community has been growing population pressure, unemployment and underemployment, and acute shortage of land. These problems, of course, have been developing for a number of years and in no way can be attributed to the death of Trujillo.

---

[25] Source: Junta Central Electoral, Santo Domingo.

[26] The airstrip is marked off as a military zone and is heavily guarded. Late each afternoon, the guards roll a number of tires onto the strip with the object of destroying the aircraft of any new invaders who might attempt to land.

During the period of field work, the airstrip was used twice. On the first occasion, four antique fighter planes of the Dominican Air Force landed after performing dangerous aerobatics over the *pueblo.* The planes were seeking shelter from Hurricane Beulah, which was then threatening the coast. The second occasion was when a small trainer plane, piloted by a Dominican Army officer, made a landing after being mistakenly fired upon by soldiers guarding the fort.

It is only in recent times, however, that they have become manifestly serious.

The confiscation of Valley land for the colonies rendered a number of families landless. But well before 1955, when the first of the colonists appeared, many Valley people of old families were already without land; over the years, increasing fragmentation through inheritance had made some *parcelas* so small as to be uneconomic. Today this situation prevails in all sections of the *municipio* where intensive cultivation is possible: those without land considerably outnumber those who have land. It is these people, the landless, who provide the bulk of the daily labor needed on the *parcelas* of others, but such work in quantity is available only at certain times of the year. In the Trujillo years, the great quantity of road work and building construction absorbed much of the labor, but there has been little such work since the dictator's death. In earlier years, it was also easier for *campesinos* in one part of the countryside to move to another area and begin a *parcela* on state land. In recent years, however, the amount of arable land that is still unclaimed is almost nonexistent and the land shortage has become acute. A contributing factor is a law that permits those with the means to fence in land, thereby prohibiting others from entering and making use of land that might otherwise serve as *parcelas* for crops. Most of those who have fenced in large areas make little use of the land agriculturally and simply graze a few cattle, thereby fulfilling the requirements of the law.

With the closing of the timber mills in 1967, some 436 permanent employees were thrown out of work; at least 212 of these are still in Constanza and many have now settled on the outskirts of the *pueblo*. Most of the former employees are without land and must now look for daily agricultural work. The closing of the sawmills has had another effect, because there are now laws that prohibit the clearing of new land; this is designed to protect the new pines that have begun to grow, but *campesinos* who in earlier years were able to make hillside farms on a shifting agricultural basis are now unable to do so.

Lest it be assumed that the picture is one of complete economic decay, it should be pointed out that agriculturally the Constanza Valley and other main vegetable producing areas have made dramatic strides and much of this progress has occurred since the death of Trujillo. Both in quantity and in quality, production of garlic and other vegetable crops has risen as agriculture has become more intensive and more scientific. Good land is not permitted to lie idle and, through the heavy use of fertilizer, yields have steadily increased. One result of this is that labor demands have continued to rise. At some times of the year, work is plentiful; for much of the year, however, this is not the case and there is insufficient work to satisfy the available supply. On all sides one hears two major complaints: lack of work and insufficient land.

POWER RELATIONSHIPS: AN OVERVIEW

Shifting power relationships are consequently to be seen throughout Constanza's history. During the Trujillo years, direction on the community level came to be exercised by a few men who were either outsiders or were men of old Constanza families who had become thoroughly *pueblo* oriented. These people related strongly to Trujillo; with the passing of the years their positions became entrenched, although no one, it appears, could ever be absolutely certain of his position. Favor could always be withdrawn. These men were known throughout the community and were looked to for help. Men who were the heads of large families and, as well, owned much land also rose to positions of influence in the *campo*.

The death of Trujillo drastically disturbed what had become a stable system of relationships, and there was a temporary loss of direction. There were a few random acts of violence as people experimented with their new-found "liberty" and the military failed to act. After the brief presidency of Juan Bosch, the old guard returned to power and, to an extent, the power structure that had previously prevailed was restored. There are, however, some significant differences.

By bringing the foreign colonists to the Constanza Valley, Trujillo himself had caused considerable social disruption and created much bitterness among Dominicans of the Valley and the *pueblo*. The passing of the years has not rendered the presence of the foreigners any less disruptive. There have been other developments too that make the restored equilibrium more tenuous than ever. There is much unemployment, demands for land are becoming louder, and those without work or land can no longer simply move to the *lomas* and carve out a *parcela* on state land. Further, the position of those with power is less secure than before. Those who were owners or managers of timber mills are no longer *patrones* as before and are not in a position to dispense patronage in the form of jobs. At all levels of society there are many indications of restlessness and there is a great deal of uncertainty about the future.

CHAPTER 3

Economic Life in the Countryside

Three ecological settings may be distinguished in the *campo:* the dry farming areas, where little or no irrigation is practiced; the valleys, where irrigation has been sufficiently developed to permit the intensive growing of vegetables; and the Constanza Valley, which is extensively irrigated and where much of the land is in the hands of colonists. In each area there is a greater or lesser dependence on particular individuals for employment, credit, and other forms of help, and the degree of dependence clearly affects the manner in which relations are patterned.

Dry Farming Areas

In those areas where there has been settlement for more than one generation, each valley and the surrounding *lomas* is populated by one or two principal families. All will have intermarried and also have formed *compadrazgo* relationships with one another. Among such people there is a great deal of cooperation and mutual help. Typical of these areas is the *paraje* of Los Corralitos within the section El Limoncito. The description of groupings and relationships that follows is largely based on that area.

Los Corralitos was first settled in 1907 by Sr. Hernandez and his common-law wife. Over the years he formed relationships with four other women by whom he had children; three of these women were established in houses in Los Corralitos; the other lived elsewhere in the *municipio.* In all, Hernandez was survived by some fifty children, 35 of whom were given recognition.[1] All but five of the 42 families that now live in Los Corralitos bear the name

---

[1] Recognition is discussed in Chapter 7, which deals with family relationships.

Hernandez. Those who grew up together as children of the same mother retain a particularly strong bond of affection and cooperate more closely, but all of the adults of Los Corralitos have formed *compadrazgo* ties with one another and address each other as *compadre, comadre, hermano,*[2] or *compañero* (companion). The people of Los Corralitos constantly stress that they are one big family, that they "respect" one another[3] and do not steal from each other's *parcelas*. In all these matters they contrast their behavior with that of the *pueblo* dwellers and many of those who live in the Constanza Valley.

Parcelas in Los Corralitos average forty *tareas* but range from twenty to over 100 *tareas*. The head of each household has clear rights to an area and there is no dispute as to land ownership. Because households range in size from two to eleven members, those with more land are not necessarily better off. Also, without irrigation the more lucrative vegetable crops cannot be grown. In these areas there is a concentration on potatoes, yuca, *guandule* (a hardy type of bean), a poor quality maize, and beans. Beans and maize are the principal cash crops; the other items are grown as much for subsistence as for sale.

In Los Corralitos, with the exception of the local storekeeper, an outsider who married a Hernandez woman, no one family is in a position to help others consistently. A few families in the area clearly have greater resources than others, but the extent of the

---

[2] The term *hermano* (brother), like *compañero*, is used in the *campo* by those who work together or cooperate closely in other ways, whether or not a blood relationship exists. *Compadre* is also frequently used in this way, even though the *compadrazgo* relationship may not have been formally established.

[3] In these areas of the *campo*, forms of address are very formal. The personal *tu* (you) is only employed when addressing children; otherwise the formal *usted* is used, even among close friends and between husband and wife, who will also address each other as *señor* and *señora*, but rarely by their personal names. Children and even grown men, when encountering their *padrino* (godfather), genuflect. In the home, each morning and evening, children genuflect before each parent and receive a murmured blessing.

These usages and customs largely apply among *campesinos* of the irrigated valleys, although in more sophisticated homes there is less formality and children do not genuflect before their parents. Among *pueblo* dwellers there is considerably less formality. *Tu* and personal names are employed between husband and wife and close acquaintances; *usted* is used in addressing women, older persons, and those of higher status. Children do not genuflect before their parents or *padrinos*, although they do address their godparents as *padrino* or *madrina* and show great respect toward them. *Campesinos* find these loose ways of the *pueblo* objectionable and say that their children do not learn "respect." The *pueblo* dwellers consider these customs of the *campo* to be old-fashioned and rather quaint.

cooperation and mutual help that is given is more striking than what evidence there is for the concealing of resources and the with-holding of help.

The most institutionalized expression of the cooperation that prevails in these areas is found in the *junta* system, but the weaken-ing of the system in these areas and its breakdown in others is indicative of the inroads made by changing economic circumstances. The *junta* groups usually comprise one's neighbors, who are all relatives or *compadres;* the groups most frequently form at the time of the bean harvest, when the labor of several men is needed. The group that gathers on the *parcela* of one man is not necessarily identical to the one that gathers on the *parcela* of his neighbor; each man simply calls upon a few of his kinsmen and *compadres* to help him and thereby incurs the obligation to help them at a later date. No strict accounting is kept of who is owed work; when questioned, people are unable to say what is done to the man who does not fulfill his obligations because this, they say, has never hap-pened. Yet it is evident that even in areas like Los Corralitos, where the *junta* system still has great economic importance, the numbers of those who cooperate in this way have decreased. It appears that the loosely organized groups of the past are giving way to smaller groups of two to five men who cooperate closely together.

People explain that the *junta* system is not as strong as in earlier years because wages are now expected and, in any case, there is "less cooperation." A more likely explanation for the decline of the system here and elsewhere is that there are now many more without land or with insufficient land and thus are dependent on wage labor. In all areas of the *campo* many of the households are now too large to be supported by the *parcela* alone; many of those with only a few dependents still find it necessary to seek paid work to supplement the income that comes from the sale of crops.

It is mainly in the months of May, June, and July that these *campesinos* seek employment outside their areas. By May their beans and corn have been planted and there are no constant demands on their time until July and August, when beans are harvested and the soil prepared for a second crop. For the most part, employment is sought in the Constanza Valley, where, during these months, a variety of vegetable crops are grown. In the Valley, the *campesinos* have no particular *patrones* but interestingly enough many say they prefer to work for the Spaniards because they pay more and are more dependable than the Dominicans when it comes to payment. While working in the Valley they stay with friends or relatives who live in the *pueblo* or elsewhere in the Valley and repay this hospitality with gifts of produce from their *parcelas*. This contact that many of the *pueblo* dwellers maintain with *campesino* relatives is not only mutually advantageous, but is of particular economic importance to *pueblo families* who are poor.

In both *pueblo* and *campo* storekeepers are men of importance because they are in a position to withhold or grant credit. With the exception of the school teacher, who has a regular salary, and a few other families, most of the people of Los Corralitos and other such areas are to an extent dependent on storekeepers for credit. In the first six months of the year there are no bean or corn harvests and, especially in March and April, life is extremely difficult for the *campesinos* and credit not easy to obtain locally, as the small *campo* store is fully extended in credit. Under these circumstances, *campesinos* will frequently shop around for credit to see if they cannot obtain it from stores in the *pueblo* or in the *pueblecitos*. For most *campesinos* of the dry farming areas, life is very much a struggle and they are unable to break free from the constant cycle of debt and repayment. In this, they are no different from the small growers of the irrigated valleys, except that the cycles of those in the dry farming areas are of longer duration.

No one in Los Corralitos is able to offer more than an occasional day of paid work but El Limoncito does have its *patrón*, to whom those in Los Corralitos and all others in the section relate. This is Ramón Ornes, who owns much land, is the head of a very large family to which many in the section are related, and is also the *alcalde*, a position he first assumed during the time of Trujillo. Known as "Uncle Ramón" in his area and somewhat patronizingly referred to as "the chief of Limoncito" by some in the *pueblo*, Ramón's leadership of the section is unchallenged. He is recognized in the section as the authority, but he is respected for this rather than feared. He is the man to whom one must go for help if things become desperate or if something is needed from those who represent authority in the *pueblo*. Within the *pueblo*, Ramón is regarded as the spokesman for El Limoncito and publicly is treated with a good deal of flattery, although privately he is held in contempt by those of more influence because he is considered to be an ignorant *campesino*, despite his influence in the section.

Ramón Ornes is comparatively wealthy. He owns a considerable number of cattle and goats, which wander over the *lomas*, and also has property elsewhere in Constanza. There is nothing in his manner of living, however, that would suggest he is better off than his neighbors and he may be distinguished from others in El Limoncito only by the fact that he dresses a little better, rides a very fine mule, and is never without his revolver, which is worn at the waist in a leather holster.[4]

For the *campesinos* of El Limoncito, there is no escaping the influence of Ramón. He is their spokesman, protector, helper, and arbitrator, and although he is envied by many for the wealth and influence he commands, there is generally acquiescence to his judgments. Further, this dependence is encouraged by Ramón himself, who readily forms *compadrazgo* relationships with those in the area and likes to boast that he is *padrino* "to hundreds." Wherever he goes in the section, Ramón is greeted with respect and no one passes his house without at least shouting a greeting. Particularly in the evening, neighbors gather in the kitchen of his house, where they drink coffee and talk; when Ramón talks, which he does frequently, others listen with respect. His opinions, which are dogmatic, are never openly contested.

It is a common custom in the *campo* for an individual to stage an annual *fiesta*, to which relatives and friends will be invited. Frequently, such *fiestas* are provided to fulfill a promise made to a saint and the *fiesta* therefore will be held on the day of the saint concerned.[5] In other cases, *fiestas* are held on a particular saint's day but no promises are involved. Some of these *fiestas* are quite small affairs and may involve no more than thirty or so people; others draw very large crowds.

Each year on January 20, the *fiesta* of the Virgin of Altagracia is celebrated at the home of Ramón Ornes. Some 400 people from all parts of El Limoncito and many from other areas and a few from the *pueblo* gather to pass the entire day and night gambling and taking part in the prayers. Ramón says that he has no particular reason for providing the *fiesta* other than that it has now been held for several years and people like to come. No promise to the saint was ever involved. Ramón likes to boast of the numbers who come

---

[4] To be well-mounted and to possess a revolver bestows great prestige among *campesinos*. Mules are more valuable than horses and a very good mule in Constanza may cost as much as RD $200. *Alcaldes* have the right to carry a revolver, but some individuals, like Ramón Ornes, who are considered to be good supporters of the government, have also been granted private licences. The possession of a revolver, then, indicates that the owner is a man of some account. Many of those who own revolvers are rarely seen without them and in the *pueblo* they may be worn even on social occasions such as to the dances in the bars.

[5] A promise is made "in the heart" and generally is offered at a time of crisis, such as a serious illness within the family. The priests in Constanza disapprove of these promises and *fiestas* and also of the women (*rezadores*) who are paid to lead the prayers on these occasions and during the nine days of mourning that follow a death.

and is particularly proud of the fact that "they come from all parts, even the *pueblo*." He also speaks expansively of the many things he provides and of the cost to himself, although in actual fact little more than coffee and a sweet dish made from corn is provided. Even so, the cost is considerable and no one else in the section could afford to stage such a *fiesta*.

At the *fiesta* in January 1968, some important visitors from the *pueblo* appeared: the judge, the new chief of police, and Mario Rosario, the former *síndico* with many friends among the *campesinos*. The judge introduced the chief of police to Ramón and then took the opportunity to make a short speech to the crowd that had gathered around. Ramón Ornes, they were told, was well known throughout the entire community and the new chief of police had been brought here so that he might meet Ramón and witness the grand *fiesta* at the same time. He went on to say how fortunate they were in El Limoncito to have a man like Ramón as *alcalde*, for he understood their needs. He added that Ramón was a strong supporter of President Balaguer; all were urged to vote for the Reformista candidates in the forthcoming municipal elections.

There are other men in local areas of El Limoncito, as in all areas of the *campo*, whose opinions are respected and who exercise some influence. In Los Corralitos, for instance, the school teacher, who is of the area himself and related to nearly everyone there, has more influence than others and is turned to for advice on some matters. In dealings with outsiders, he tends to speak for the area and it is he and the assistant *alcalde* of the area who are asked by the political organizers from the town to form a local party committee in the *paraje*. It should be stressed, however, that the influence of these men is locally defined; they have no strong contacts with influential people in the *pueblo* and do not really seek to establish any. Rather, they and all others of the section look to Ramón Ornes, their chief. It is significant that during the brief presidency of Juan Bosch, when the PRD organizers in the town appointed such a local figure as *alcalde* (Ramón Ornes apparently had declined to accept the post under the PRD), the people continued to relate to Ramón and to take their troubles to him, believing him to be the only man with real influence with those outside the section.

IRRIGATED VALLEY AREAS

In addition to the Constanza Valley, the only important irrigation areas are the valleys of Tireo Arriba, Tireo Abajo, some parts of El Rio, and a few other smaller valleys, of which La Descubierta and La Culatta are the most important. In all these valleys, however, the canals are of earth and not concrete and the irrigation system is primitive compared with that of the Constanza Valley. Whenever irrigation is practiced, however, vegetable growing is intensive; crops are grown in rotation and some use is made of fertilizers and insecticides. In the main Valley, reliance on these is heavy.

Most of the land in the irrigated valleys is privately owned. Over the years there has been much fragmentation through inheritance and, although there are a number of *parcelas* with over 200 *tareas*, the average is about twenty *tareas;* anything over seventy *tareas* is considered large. Further, few of the larger *parcelas* that do exist are fully irrigated and consequently are not farmed as intensively as they would otherwise be; they are usually given over to the cultivation of beans and corn, which can be grown with limited water and require less constant labor than do most vegetable crops.

In the valleys, neighborhood groupings can nearly always be defined. These groupings are based on kinship; one's neighbors, more often than not, are close relatives, and there is constant visiting and borrowing and a great deal of cooperation. The fact that some have a great deal of land and others have virtually none at all, however, is important for an understanding of family relationships and why and in what manner certain families relate to others.

As in the dry farming areas, the *junta* groups still exist, but they operate only among small growers and generally only when beans are harvested. Many individuals also rely on occasional work as agricultural laborers and frequently obtain this work on the *parcelas* of others in the area. This means that a man is working for people he knows intimately and to whom he is probably related. A man wanting work will go to any individual in need of laborers, however, and, if continuous work is available in the Valley of Constanza, he will prefer to go there because daily pay tends to be higher. On large *parcelas*, a very few permanent agricultural workers may be retained; only then does one observe an enduring relationship of dependence. Those employed as permanent workers are close relatives or *compadres* and the relationship between employer and employee is thus always close and personal.

In the dry farming areas previously described, all live at about the same level; what inequalities of income do exist are not readily apparent. In such areas, which are characteristically egalitarian, there is necessarily a close reliance upon one another in everyday matters, and, in the case of El Limoncito, also a dependence upon "the chief," Ramón Ornes, who, at times, is able to do favors for others and who consistently represents El Limoncito to those in the *pueblo*. By contrast, in the irrigated valleys and in the Constanza Valley there is a considerable range in wealth; inequalities are revealed in housing, in household possessions,[6] and in the ownership of small or large trucks and agricultural equipment. Among families that live at about the same level there is much sharing and mutual help, but poor branches of a family are unable to depend upon better-off kinsmen in any permanent way; relationships of permanent dependence are discouraged. A poor relative may be lent a piece of land and, at times, offered paid work or given food, but beyond this, little help is given. A person who repeatedly seeks help from others is said to be *sin vergüenza* (without shame) and is made to feel dependent.

In the valleys, the system of dependencies is less clear than in such areas as El Limoncito. According to the economic circumstances of any individual, he will be, to a greater or lesser extent, dependent upon *pueblecito* stores for credit, his neighbors for various forms of assistance, and bigger growers of the area, who offer occasional employment. A number of these people will be relatives or *compadres,* and there is a strong tendency to exploit these familial relationships to one's material advantage, a tendency frequently resisted by those whose help is wanted. Nevertheless, provided that an individual has a good reputation and does not repeatedly seek help, assistance is rarely refused. Most credit needs are met locally and, although many purchases are made in the *pueblo,* credit is not generally sought from *pueblo* stores. Small growers are able to rely upon one another a great deal. Equipment is readily lent; a man with insufficient resources to pay for the insecticides and fertilizers he needs will generally be able to obtain these on credit from one of the *pueblecito* stores or will combine resources with another agriculturalist and manage to get a crop planted. Arrangements by which labor, costs, and profits are shared are common in all parts of the *municipio,* but in the dry farming regions and in the irrigated valleys most partnerships involve men who are *compadres* or close kinsmen. Frequently, these partnerships, known as *a media* schemes, become fairly permanent working arrangements.

For many, there is also a reliance upon growers in the Constanza Valley for employment, particularly during October and No-

---

[6] Housing and household possessions are not always an accurate reflection of wealth. Some *campesinos* of means continue to live in very poor houses that are crudely furnished. Even the superior houses in these areas are only equivalent to average houses in the *pueblo*. In the Constanza Valley, a few agriculturalists who themselves live in very poor houses on their *parcelas* own good houses in the *pueblo*, which they rent to others.

vember, and March and April, when garlic are planted and harvested. Unlike those of the dry farming areas who have no particular
patrones in the Valley, some men from these irrigated areas make
up groups that grow garlic by contract, an arrangement often favored by the Spaniards. These groups resemble the *junta* groups
only to the extent that they comprise close relatives and *compadres*.
They are organized by one man, the contractor, who deals with
the agriculturalist concerned and pays those who work with him
in the group. If a contract has been successfully fulfilled, a relationship of trust may be built up between the contractor and the agriculturalist and the contract is regularly offered to the same man to
grow the crop. In turn, men who secure such contracts are sought
out by others who wish to work in the group.

In these areas, "chiefs" like Ramón Ornes do not exist. Populations are considerably larger and there is not one important man
but several. There may be rivalry between some of these individuals,
although this is not usually expressed openly.[7] *Alcaldes* are always
men of importance, but in El Rio and in Tireo Arriba and Tireo
Abajo there are others of equal or greater influence, such as prominent storekeepers, who may also own trucks and more land than
most, as well as others who own much land and occasionally offer
employment. Their resources are always greater than those of others
and, although they hold no *fiestas* on the scale of that held in the
home of Ramón Ornes, they mark occasions like baptisms and the
marriage of a daughter with large *fiestas* that many attend. These are
men of old families who have extensive kinship links with many
in the area. As well, they are sought out as *compadres* and the
initiators of these relationships are then in a favored position when
seeking their help.

These men are also well known in the *pueblo*, where they are
greeted with some respect and recognized as individuals of importance in their sections. At the time of elections, they are approached
by political organizers from the *pueblo* and asked to form committees
in their areas. The standing they enjoy in the *pueblo* places them
in a strong position in the sections, and they frequently act as intermediaries between their fellows and the police and various public
officials of the *pueblo*. This role is not to be over-emphasized, however. The *campesinos* of the valleys are considerably more sophisticated than their brethren in the dry farming areas and are less

---

[7] This rivalry is more apparent in El Rio, where certain families relate more
to Jarabacoa than to Constanza and where there are still some strong supporters
of Juan Bosch.

reluctant to approach influential townsmen on their own behalf.

Within the sections, these men enjoy a reputation for generosity and understanding and are approached for help and advice of various kinds and, although help may not always be given, they are never unresponsive. Their judgment is also respected because they are considered fair and it is generally men of this calibre who are called upon to resolve conflicts. An incident witnessed in Tireo Abajo illustrates this.

Two young boys had been involved in a fight and one of them, the younger and smaller of the two, had taken a beating and had then thrown a stone, which cut the older boy's head. A crowd gathered and there was much argument as to what should be done. Some wanted to go to the *alcalde;* one man insisted that they should all go to the *pueblo* to see the police. A certain Sr. Castro walked up to the group and listened as a number of the men and each of the boys gave his version of what had happened and what should be done. As it turned out, the older boy had started the trouble by insulting the younger. Sr. Castro examined the cut and declared that it was not serious. He then berated first the older boy for having insulted the other and then the younger for having thrown the stone, and told him that for injuring a person in this way he could be sent to prison. He advised the men that it was wiser not to involve the police and that the matter was best forgotten. A few did not appear to be pleased with this decision but there was no more argument and the crowd dispersed. Sr. Castro is of an old family in the area, his *parcela* is 72 *tareas,* which is larger than most, and he is a former *alcalde.* He is well-known in the section and it seems that when his judgment is appealed to, his decisions are accepted.

Notwithstanding the differences in resources that are apparent among the *campesinos* of the valleys and the resistance of those who are better off toward poorer kinsmen seeking help, in all areas of the *campo* there is a great deal of cooperation and mutual help. There is constant visiting, lending, and borrowing, and little permanent factionalism or long-standing family feuds. Quarrels are frequent but they tend to be quickly forgotten. There are, in fact, strong feelings of commonality among all the *campesinos* that are occasionally expressed in sentiments concerning "We, the *campesinos,*" and revealed in a resentment toward those of the *pueblo* and the government, whom, it is believed, seek to exploit them. All this is in clear contrast to the situation one finds among the agriculturalists and agricultural laborers of the Constanza Valley.

THE CONSTANZA VALLEY

In this section, the discussion will be concerned largely with four groupings: the *peones*, the small agriculturalists, most of whom work colony land, the well-off agriculturalists, and the Spaniards. The *peones* considered here are those who live more or less permanently in the *pueblo* or in one of the colonies and who rely upon day labor in Valley *parcelas*. As such, their numbers make up the bulk of those who are described in the next chapter as *los pobres* of the *pueblo*.

Of the 17,000 *tareas* under irrigation in the Constanza Valley, 7,446 are owned by the state. This is the colony land, which stretches in a broad belt across the floor of the Valley and, unlike the privately owned areas, is devoid of houses. Those who farm colony land live in the *pueblo* or in one of the colonies, although many of those who now occupy colony housing are without land, the houses no longer being associated with particular *parcelas* in the colonies as was the case in earlier years. *Parcelas* in the colony average 26 *tareas*, but some are as few as five *tareas* and a few are over 100. In some cases, several members of the same family have colony land and thus have been able to augment their holdings. The irrigated, privately owned land surrounding the colony land is either rented out to others (this applies also to much of the colony land), or worked by the owners. Some of these privately owned *parcelas* are relatively large.

What makes the Valley situation distinctive today is the intensity of the agriculture, the employment of large numbers of *peones*, who have no personal ties with their employers, and the fact that the bulk of the day labor is supplied by men who live in the colonies or on the fringes of the *pueblo*, where they have no familial ties with their neighbors. This is true of most of the Valley agriculturalists themselves who, whether they be colonists, renters, or owners, live in no set neighborhoods either in the *pueblo* or in the Valley.

In all the valley areas where vegetable crops are grown intensively, labor requirements at certain times are high. Many farmers make use of tractors and animal-drawn plows when preparing the soil, but most other tasks such as seeding, transplanting, fertilizing, and harvesting are done by hand. Labor requirements for each vegetable crop differ, but because cycles of land preparation, planting, and harvesting tend to be similar, labor needs are intense at some times and slight at others. This has a marked effect on the way of life and attitude of the *peones*. The fact that an agriculturalist will one day need the labor of eighty or more *peones* and the following day the services of only half or less that number works against the development of a firm *patron* system.

Most agriculturalists have no permanent workers and employ day labor as the need arises. In a very few cases they tend to draw their labor from the same area each time; the *peones* then come to look upon their employer as their particular benefactor and will go to him when necessary with requests for help. Generally speaking, this relationship only clearly pertains on a few larger *parcelas* owned by Dominicans who have a permanent group of workers. One such agriculturalist, Sr. Baez, who has eight permanent workers living in quarters on his property, explained that he is like a father to his *peones*. He gives them medicine and other help and feeds them in his own kitchen. There he sits down with them, explains things to them, and "tells them what to think about everything." Another agriculturalist, Sr. Antonio Torres, has fewer permanent workers but, at times, employs up to eighty, largely recruiting from the Kennedy Colony and the Spanish Colony. In discussing their employer with me, the *peones* from one of these areas were loud in their praises. He is a good man, very *simpático* (sympathetic), who gives them food and medicine when they need it and who also explains things to them and speaks on their behalf to others.

For the most part, employer-employee relations on Valley *parcelas* show few signs of paternalism. No particular effort is made to draw labor from one location and generally the agriculturalist simply makes it known to one *peón* that he needs laborers the next day and will leave it to him to find other workers. Some agriculturalists who need a very large group of workers will advertise on the radio and will give work to those who turn up first. Even then, the selection of workers is not entirely arbitrary. Being known to the agriculturalist and having the reputation for hard work greatly assist one in procuring work. The stranger is always at a disadvantage. The foreigners, for their part, deliberately discourage patronship; many decline to be *padrino* to the children of their employees and have no other relations with them than that of temporary employer.

In view of this impersonality and the general uncertainty of their economic position, it is not surprising that those who must depend primarily on agricultural labor are the most insecure of all groups in the community. People of this level constantly seek to form relationships with persons of some influence who they believe may be of use to them, but for the most part they are frustrated in these endeavors. It is extremely difficult to obtain permanent work with any agriculturalist and finding jobs in the *pueblo*, which is what most desire, is also difficult. To obtain road work or other government employment, one must have friends. Other than such work, the only other opportunity lies in the land.

Some *peones* do become involved in *a media* schemes but, for the most part, this possibility is only open to those who already have some land or have sufficient money to finance a crop on some- one else's land. Some become temporary or permanent squatters on state land in more distant parts of the *campo*, but as was men- tioned earlier, there is little land left of any worth that has not already been fenced and thus precluded from use, and the ban on clearing new land on which pines have begun to grow has made it impossible to open new areas of state land. The land shortage is now acute and this situation, coupled with the tremendous popula- tion increase, is likely to produce an explosive situation in the near future.

Another possibility is to obtain colony land either in Constanza or elsewhere, but such land is very difficult to obtain, notwithstand- ing the much vaunted agrarian reform program of the Dominican government. Colony land in Constanza only occasionally falls avail- able and it then seems to go to those who are friends of the local head of colonies or else have influence at a higher level. In any case, a prospective colonist must have some money to put up initially and few of the *peones* have any reserve money at all.

The lot of the *peones*, particularly those without any land, is hardly a happy one. For much of the year, work is extremely difficult to obtain and the competition is fierce. To obtain any other kind of work one has to compete also, but here the competition is one for favors and in no way is based on merit; the best man does not get the job and no one expects that he should do so. Further, it is the *peones* who can least rely upon kinsmen for help and, unlike those of the irrigated valleys and the dry-farming areas who, at times, obtain work in the Constanza Valley, they are almost en- tirely dependent upon the wages they earn. There are frequent occa- sions throughout the year when even the hardest working *peones* are without employment. To make matters worse, few are paid the wage to which they are entitled.

The legal minimum wage is RD $2 for an eight-hour day, but few receive this or work only these hours. Most *peones* work an eight- to ten-hour day and earn between RD $1.50 and RD $1.75, with a mid-day meal of rice and beans provided. Many of the for- eigners pay RD $2, but it appears that few Dominicans do so. *Peones* say they have no recourse but to accept whatever they are paid; that if they complain to the labor inspector, whose responsibility it is to see that the legal minimum is paid, nothing will be gained and they will only lose their jobs.[8]

As a group, the *peones* are considered a poor lot. Storekeepers condemn them because they do not pay their debts and therefore, unless a man is well known or has some personal relationship with the store owner, he will not, as a rule, be granted credit. The agriculturalists who employ *peones* say they are often lazy, they must be supervised closely, and they are also unreliable: they promise to return to work the next day and then do not do so. The Spaniards and Japanese, in particular, condemn them for this last reason. It is also said of the *peones* that they spend much of their wages on rum and in gambling and are always in debt.

The *peones* are not lazy, although possibly they would be if they had the chance. Work is supervised very closely; the employer stands over the men, who in many tasks work in a line, each man keeping pace with the other. Many tasks, like planting garlic, for instance, are extremely arduous and there is little letup throughout the day.

Many *peones* are unreliable; they will work for a few successive days and then not appear the next, after having promised to do so. It is also true that much of their wages are spent on rum and in gambling. It is difficult to obtain reliable data on the extent of such spending but, in several cases, it appeared that men earning in the vicinity of RD $8 a week were spending RD $3 or more on rum and the lottery or in other forms of gambling. These were men with families to support. It is a common occurence for a *peón* to gamble his entire wages for the day or to spend it on rum, and frequently *peones* owe the employer work because they have drawn a portion of their wages in advance. Often this money is needed to buy food for the family because the money earned the first day was spent immediately on rum or was gambled. It is often the women of these households who are more consistent bread winners than the men.

The *peones*, it should be added, are not alone in being heavy

---

[8] Felipe Arafat, the man who was the Inspector of Labor in Constanza throughout most of the period of field work, insisted that all were being paid the correct wage and that employers who did not pay this were prosecuted. There were no such prosecutions during his time in office. Felipe's brother is the head of the local Colonies Office and the Arafats are the biggest land-owning family in the Valley. A new Labor Inspector who took over the office in March 1968 admitted that the legal wage was not generally being paid, but said that most agriculturalists could not afford the wage and prosecutions would be to no one's advantage. Then he added that some of the Spaniards were underpaying and that these cases would definitely be investigated.

drinkers or big spenders in the lottery. A number of the young men of the *pueblo* who have more money drink a great deal and many *constanceros* invest heavily in the lottery. In fact, the success of a significant number of business enterprizes in the town is attributed to wins in the lottery and stories of wins, often quite exaggerated, are widely circulated.

For the *peón*, getting drunk with his friends is a pleasurable escape from the monotony and drudgery of life; the lottery is the one chance of changing that life. Even if the *peón* were thoroughly imbued with the Protestant Ethic and worked on every occasion he was able and tried to save, the possibility of improving his status is remote. The daily wage he earns is insufficient to feed and clothe a family adequately, and certainly not enough on which to save. Even if he did save a little, it would be a considerable time before sufficient money could be accumulated to rent a *parcela* or open a small store, which are the only investment possibilities the *peón* perceives. It may be argued then that in spending much of his meager earnings in gambling, the *peón* is not necessarily squandering his money, but is utilizing the one real avenue for changing his status.

For the small agriculturalists of the Valley, many of whom utilize colony land, life is also precarious. These people live in the town or in the colonies and in neither case compose neighborhoods definable in terms of kinship. Unlike the situation in other parts of the countryside where intensive vegetable farming is practiced, the colonists, although almost all are of Constanza, come from widely differing parts. In the three colonies, there are no predominant families, there is no clear leadership, and there is no real sense of communal identity. The turnover in colony housing is high. It is not surprising then, in view of these factors alone, that one finds little cooperation among the colonists in agriculture. This lack of cooperation is in part explained by the peculiar demands of vegetable farming. This explanation is borne out by the fact that in an area like Tireo Arriba, where a colony situation does not exist and where one's neighbors are generally kinsmen or at least close friends, cooperation in agricultural activities is less than one might expect; it is certainly considerably less than what still persists among the *campesinos* who farm the *lomas*.

On the group level there is little cooperation in work activities; what cooperation does occur usually takes place between individuals who come to some business arrangement. The colonists in particular frequently work on one another's land, but when they do so it is generally as hired labor. The Valley agriculturalists say of themselves that they "lack cooperation," and this is very evident. It is also evident that there is a lack of trust. Partnerships that do spring up between particular pairs of individuals show little permanency. Two men may work an *a media* scheme to plant and harvest a crop but not infrequently the partnership then breaks down amid charges that the one did not do his share, or was dishonest.

Thefts from Valley *parcelas* are also very common, but the most continuing source of friction is over water. The flow of water through the canals of the Valley is regulated by a series of locks, which are operated by employees of the Riego (Irrigation) Office, located in the *pueblo*. In theory, each area of the Valley receives an equitable amount of water, but the Riego employees are open to bribery, and it is the bigger agriculturalists who, because they are in a position to give constant bribes, are best supplied with water. Disputes over water are particularly common between men who work neighboring *parcelas;* one will accuse the other of taking more than his share; not infrequently fights occur and the police become involved.

The men who farm the irrigated land of the Constanza Valley rely on bank credit more than do the *campesinos* of the valleys. The bigger agriculturalists often do not need credit, but nevertheless have little trouble obtaining it from the Banco Agrícola, the Agricultural Bank, which advances money to growers at 8% interest. Growers outside the Valley make less use of this credit both because of their distrust of government agencies and because they have less need of it. Here, the man without resources to buy the seeds, fertilizers, and insecticides he needs will, in all probability, borrow these from neighbors or obtain them on credit from a *pueblecito* store. The small holder of colony land or the small renter is generally unable to obtain such help or credit, and, unless he is in a good standing with the bank, no money will be lent. Without credit, the small agriculturalist of the Valley has little recourse but to rent his land to another individual or come to some sharing arrangement. Businessmen in the *pueblo* do not, as a rule, advance money to agriculturalists against the profits of a future crop.

Many agriculturalists in this category do manage to get a crop planted (good, irrigated land, in fact, is never allowed to lie idle) and then sell the seedlings themselves or the future crop to a bigger agriculturalist. They will sell under these circumstances either because they do not have the capital to buy insecticides and fertilizers or to pay for the labor necessary to bring the crop to fruition, or because they fear the future market will be poor. The bigger man can afford to take this risk. Forced selling of this kind does not generally occur among growers in the other areas described. It seems that a happier arrangement can usually be worked out with a better-off neighbor or kinsman.

Many of those who own or rent large *parcelas* in the Valley are Spaniards. Many people blame the Spaniards for the lack of cooperation in the Valley and also for the land shortage, but this is not altogether justified. In fact, the Spaniards are blamed for a multitude of sins, but this undoubtedly stems from the fact that unlike others in the Valley and *pueblo*, they are largely independent of townsmen of importance. The Spaniards do not seek credit from *pueblo* stores and need rely on no Dominicans for favors; for many of their needs they go outside the community altogether. A number of them have cars and trucks; when they wish to purchase major items, they deal with the stores in Santo Domingo, where prices are lower.

With good reason, the foreigners have little confidence in the local doctors and generally deal with doctors and dentists in the capital. When the Spaniards travel to Santo Domingo, they go either in their own vehicles or with Gregorio, a Spaniard who owns a *público* and makes daily trips to the capital. Those Spaniards who live in the Spanish colony make purchases of minor food items from one of their countrymen who has a small store in the colony, and in the town most such purchases are made from a new store recently opened by a Spaniard. Agricultural needs such as seeds, insecticides, and the like are supplied either by an agricultural store in the *pueblo* owned by a Spaniard, or else from a traveling salesman who regularly visits Constanza and is also a Spaniard. The biggest vegetable grower in the Valley, who is a Spaniard, has a truck and handles his own marketing, and many of the Spaniards who are unable to handle their own marketing sell to Sr. Peralta, a Spaniard who is one of the principal buyers in the Valley. This man, because he is considered fair and honest, also has the business of many of the Dominican growers.

Local businessmen complain that much of the wealth that is produced in the Valley (and the foreigners account for a large portion of this) bypasses the *pueblo* altogether. In their business dealings, the Spaniards tend, where possible, to deal with one another and not with Dominicans, in whom they have little confidence. Some of the Spaniards also capture a good deal of the business of Dominicans. Even the bars lose the business of the Spaniards, who do virtually all of their drinking in their own club. The foreigners are also to a great extent independent of the system of political control as it is exercised in the community and when they are singled out for attack in any way, they are able to refer matters to their consulates in the capital. The problems are then settled at a higher level. For the most part, the foreigners are left alone and most *constanceros* seem to realize that little is to be gained by antagonizing them.

THE AGRICULTURAL COOPERATIVE

All agriculturalists of the Valley rely heavily on the garlic crop for their main profits, but the smaller agriculturalist in particular suffers because of the extreme variation in the price obtained.

In 1963, following the visit of some agricultural officials from the capital, Valley agriculturalists were persuaded that many of their problems would be overcome if they were to market their garlic through a cooperative. At a public meeting held at the Agricultural Center, the decision to form a cooperative was made and a directive was elected, which contained representatives of the small and large Dominican growers and of the Spaniards. It was intended that growers would market their garlic through the cooperative at a set price, and the cooperative alone would deal with buyers.

Evidently the cooperative did not function very well; there was much bickering among the elected directors and some accusations of dishonesty. Smaller agriculturalists complained that the cooperative was too slow in making payments and was only working for the benefit of the big growers. The President of the cooperative, Sr. Antonio Torres, accused some of the Spaniards of marketing their garlic outside the cooperative; they in turn claimed that the President was dishonest and was using his position to build up a political following among the small agriculturalists and the landless *peones* of the Valley.

With the outbreak of the revolution in December 1963, the market collapsed and large quantities of the cooperative's garlic stored in the capital were looted. The cooperative broke up amidst charges of dishonesty and political subversion, but it is evident that behind these charges there was, and still is, strong antipathy between the Spaniards and the Dominicans, and between the big growers and the small. After the collapse of the cooperative, a number of events occurred that illustrate these antipathies, and also demonstrate how leadership may be exercised by those who wish to exploit their positions as *patrones*.

Sr. Antonio Torres has a large *parcela* of colony land and has also married into the big landowning Arafat family. He is an extreme rightist and claims to be a personal friend of Generals Perez y Perez and Wessin y Wessin, who are *padrinos* to some of his children. Torres has a particularly strong following among the *peones* of the Kennedy and Spanish colonies, to whom he frequently offers employment; he is *padrino* to many of their children. As well, he and his close friend Sr. Baez are admired by many of those in the Valley who have little or no land because they have voiced the demand that the Spaniards be expelled and their land divided among the landless.

From the time of Trujillo's death, Torres had tried to stir up trouble against the Spaniards. He claimed that the Agricultural Center was serving only the Spanish colonists and ought to be closed and its land given to the landless. This complaint resulted in an inquiry in which the center was exonerated. The same year, he and Sr. Baez took some 150 landless *peones* of the Valley to the capital with the intention of confronting the President and demanding that the *peones* be given the land held by the Spaniards. They did not see the President and both men were arrested, but later released. Soon after this incident, Torres wrote a letter to one of the papers in which he accused the Spaniards of taking all the colony land, with the implication that they were getting more land by using graft. As a result of this letter another commission arrived, this time to look into the colony land situation. A public meeting of all interested groups was held at the Nueva Suiza hotel.

According to the Spaniards, Antonio did not come to this meeting because he was frightened, realizing that he had gone too far. Instead, he sent a large group of his *peones*, telling them that at this meeting the land of the Spaniards would be distributed among them. The Spaniards were there *en masse* and so also were many of the small agriculturalists; most of the bigger agriculturalists stayed away. The commission then sent for Torres and when he appeared, the story goes, he was unable (or unwilling) to name any Spaniard who had dishonestly acquired more land. Rather, some of the Spaniards pointed out, he himself was actually farming more Valley land than anyone present at the meeting. No one sided with Antonio Torres and he was reprimanded by the commission for stirring up trouble and spreading untruths. Antonio's version of the story is rather different; he claims that the *síndico* and some of the big agriculturalists who promised him support backed down at the last moment, deciding that it was more prudent to side with the Spaniards.

The *peones* who frequently obtain work from Antonio Torres consider him to be a fine fellow who is doing his best to get the land back from the Spaniards; a number of the smaller agriculturalists who are envious of the large *parcelas* of the Spaniards admire him for the same reason. Most of the better-off agriculturalists and a number of those of importance in the *pueblo* consider that he is an opportunist who is trying to build up a following.

During 1968, a new attempt was made to form a cooperative among growers in the Valley. This was initiated by a young agronomist who was the head of the Agricultural Center, and it was his hope that all the agriculturalists of the Valley would join. Numerous meetings were held to get the organization started, but only the Spaniards and a few of the bigger Dominican growers showed any interest. Sr. Torres was opposed to the new organization and none of the smaller growers sought to become members. In May, the agronomist left Constanza and it was apparent that the organization would come to nothing, notwithstanding the clear need for such a cooperative. Scheduled meetings did not take place and there was some dissention among the Spaniards, who largely formed the directive. Small agriculturalists considered the group to be an organization of the Spaniards and likely to benefit them and a few of the other bigger growers alone.

CHAPTER 4

Economic Life in the Town

The social and economic links between town and country are reinforced by the presence within the *pueblo* of a large number of agriculturalists. For the most part, these agriculturalists farm Valley land and travel to their *parcelas* each day to supervise work.

A number of businessmen in the *pueblo* have extensive land interests in addition to their normal business pursuits. This land may be rented to others or they may work it themselves but, in terms of interest, agriculture tends to be secondary to these people. Again, there are others of the *pueblo* representing a wide range of occupations who rent a *parcela* on a short-term basis and plant a crop in the hope of making a profit. Frequently, some form of *a media* scheme will be entered into in these cases. Those who engage in these temporary agricultural enterprises have no long-term interest in agriculture and frequently have little experience; not unexpectedly, they often lose money. Individuals who become temporary agriculturalists in this way include professional men such as doctors and dentists, as well as school teachers, other government employees (in some cases including the heads of offices), storekeepers, and even soldiers and policemen. To enter such an enterprise involves no loss of face and it is not considered to be in any way strange. In fact, I was frequently urged to rent a *parcela* myself and many were convinced that the numerous questions I asked concerning agriculture were preparatory to my commencing operations as an agriculturalist.

For agriculturalists of the Valley, the distinction between *pueblo* dweller and *campo* dweller is not a very meaningful one. The agriculturalists of the Valley who do not live in the *pueblo* might just as well do so; they are in no way to be differentiated from the agriculturalists who do. This does not hold true for most of the other *pueblo* dwellers who follow a variety of pursuits, and it is those others who are now discussed in terms of occupation and economic life, and in terms of dependency relationships. One significant

Pueblo women winnowing dried beans. Such work is often undertaken by groups of women who are relatives.

Peones planting garlic in the Valley of Constanza.

group, namely the Spaniards, who, for the most part, are to be numbered among the better-off agriculturalists, has already been dealt with. Many of these people live in the *pueblo*, but they are largely independent of those who dominate economic and political life.

The principal occupational groups that will be described are storekeepers, other business people, the professions, civil servants, the military and police, and *peones* and town workers, who together make up *los pobres*. Reference also will be made to another group, *la gente mas importante* (the most important people), who are drawn from a wider group, *la gente importante* (the important people). The important people and those of most importance are not found among any one occupational group, but all of them are in a position to offer help to others.

OCCUPATIONAL GROUPINGS OF THE PUEBLO DWELLERS

Storekeepers

Economically, those owning various businesses are the most significant of the *pueblo* dwellers, but there is a wide range in the types of business enterprises and in the returns they bring. Within the main business section of the *pueblo*, there are a number of large stores that employ up to three assistants, usually members of the owner's family. In most cases, the owners of these businesses are relatively wealthy and have other interests as well. Sr. Nashash, for instance, owns some nineteen houses and other buildings and businesses in the *pueblo*, as well as a good deal of land on the *lomas*.

Many of the stores located in various parts of the *pueblo* are extremely small and struggling. Most deal primarily in foodstuffs and draw their customers from the few houses around. If the store has a good location, however, it is possible to build up a fairly profitable business. One such business is that of Juan Conde, whose general store is well located on a corner toward one extremity of the *pueblo*. The store carries a fairly wide range of perishable foodstuffs and vegetables, as well as some canned foods and a number of general items such as soap, nails, and batteries. Most purchases are in very small quantities and profits on each item are small. The storekeeper himself buys his stock from larger stores in the *pueblo* at a slight discount, but must keep his prices down to attract business. People who have the money to do so buy certain items in bulk from these same larger stores, obtaining the same discount, and thus one group of potential customers for such items is lost to storekeepers like Juan. For the poor who lack money to buy in bulk, costs of many items are always higher.

The more prosperous stores that sell to the smaller stores do so at a profit. The small storekeepers then must try to compete for customers with their suppliers in these same items, and they can only do this if their prices are more or less the same. One way for the small storekeepers to compete is to offer credit, although they are reluctant to offer credit to customers other than those who are known to be reliable, or who can offer some security, such as a pig or a potential harvest. Extending credit is a risky business; the larger stores rarely grant it because, people say, they do not need to do so. Juan claims to have lost over RD $2,000 in the last four years in bad debts.

In the case of relatives and friends, it is difficult to refuse credit, although this frequently occurs, particularly in *pueblo* stores, and much bitterness results. It is not uncommon, however, for small storekeepers, both in the *pueblo* and *campo*, to be ruined by overextending credit. It will be recalled that the people of Los Corralitos relied heavily on the store located within the *paraje* for credit. The owner of this store, who had married into the large family that virtually comprised the local population of the small valley, was so harried by his affines into giving credit that he later left the area and opened a store in a new area altogether. The Los Corralitos store was put in the hands of a young man (a stranger to the area) on a share basis, and he was instructed to give credit to no one.

Two of Juan Conde's brothers live with their families in section Palero, within the Valley of Constanza to the east of the colony lands. There were already some small stores in Palero, but Juan and one of his brothers decided to open another. Juan discussed the project with Sr. Pedro Espiallat, the owner of a large *pueblo* store from which he purchases most of his supplies, and persuaded him to grant extra credit to permit him to stock the new store, which actually was nothing more than an extension built onto his brother's house. The new store failed miserably. It appears that Juan's brother, from the start, showed little business acumen, but the main reason for failure was overextension of credit, and the principal recipients of this were Juan's kinsmen and friends who lived in the area of the new store. In an effort to keep the store going, Juan continually restocked it from his own supplies but, unable to obtain more credit himself, and not wishing to risk losing his own trade through being out of stock, he was forced to close the Palero store. A great deal of money was lost in the venture, and the chances of ever recovering the money owed are remote.

It is common to shop around for credit, and a household may have credit in several stores at the same time. Storekeepers are aware that this goes on, but information concerning particular customers is not circulated among the storekeepers themselves. There is keen competition among the stores, particularly those in close proximity to one another, and owners are considered not merely business rivals but frequently "enemies." So great is this bitterness that it can seriously disrupt inter-family relations, as in a case when close relatives own rival businesses.

For the larger and well-established stores, most of which are near the center of the *pueblo*, economic life is not quite so precarious. The general provision stores that supply smaller stores like those of Juan's are themselves supplied by various concerns in Santo Domingo. They buy their goods on a thirty-day credit system and this is all the credit they will generally extend to the small dependent stores; in some cases, they will not grant this if the small storekeeper has a poor reputation. Generally, these bigger stores have particular clients among the smaller stores; if there is sufficient trust, and if the smaller storekeeper consistently makes most of his purchases from one larger store, the normal credit period may, at times, be extended, as occurred when Juan Conde was granted extra credit by Pedro Espiallat.

What have been called the bigger provisions stores in the *pueblo* number only eight; of these, only four are regular suppliers of a number of smaller stores. The owners of these stores are men of great importance; insofar as the smaller stores are tied to them, their economic importance is not restricted to the *pueblo*, but reaches into the *campo* as well. The larger *pueblo* stores supply a number of smaller stores in the *campo*, and these *pueblo* storekeepers also have direct contacts with many *campesinos* of the dry farming areas, from whom they buy corn and beans. The names of these townsmen are known to all in the community and they are highly respected.

For the small storekeeper, existence is somewhat precarious. The large number of customers may give the appearance of a prosperous business, but quantities sold are small and the margin of profit is slight. Indeed, were it not for two other enterprises centered in such stores, a business like Juan's would hardly appear worthwhile. These enterprises, however, make a great deal of difference. Juan's store, and a number of others like it, also functions as a bar; the sale of liquor and soft drinks, which are frequently consumed on the premises, accounts for a major part of the business. Because it is a bar, men frequently gather there in the evenings to talk and drink and operate the juke box, although it is the owner himself who usually puts coins in the juke box. The other activity is an illegal lottery that operates from the store and brings in an average profit of RD $1,300 per annum. A few other persons are involved in selling tickets in some areas of the Valley, and tickets are sold from the store itself. Certain other stores in the *pueblo* also run such lotteries; one in particular, which has a very large clientele, is said to bring in a considerable profit.

The police generally do not interfere with these lottery activities provided that they are paid off; this is done not in money but in liquor. A policeman may ask the storekeeper from time to time to "lend" him a bottle of rum, and this will be handed over. Of course, it is recognized by each that money will never be forthcoming and will not be asked for. Soldiers, particularly officers, more so than police, are frequently given free drinks in the town bars, especially the bars associated with the brothels; more commonly, they will be granted credit in the bars (something that is rarely granted to others) and their bills may never be paid in full.

There are many general stores similar to that of Juan Conde but whose trade is much smaller and, without a bar trade or illegal lottery, profits are much less. One storekeeper in the section of Maldonado on the outskirts of the *pueblo*, who has no resources other than his tiny store, declares he only makes RD $480 a year. There are also many stalls located in the *pueblo* and in the *pueblecitos;* these are generally very humble and do little trade. Most stalls are operated by women and concentrate on just a few lines such as fruit and vegetables, bread, or cigarettes and candy. Opening a store or a stall is one of the very few ways of investing capital that may have accrued; there is the added advantage that the running of the concern can be left to one's wife or a relative. Small stores and stalls are frequently opened but, more often than not, they fail and money is lost. Only the well-established stores in good locations show clear stability, although all storekeepers complain that times are hard and that profits were greater in the Trujillo era.

In the weeks before harvesting any crop, the smaller agriculturalists try to obtain credit at the stores; they repay this when crops are harvested. In the Constanza Valley, the main demand for credit falls during the garlic growing season; money is particularly tight in February and March, immediately before the garlic are drawn. In the weeks following the garlic harvest, there is more money but, as was noted earlier, much of the money earned by the bigger growers of garlic is spent not in the *pueblo* but in Santo Domingo. The cycle of credit extension and repayment for the *cam-*

pesinos of the dry farming areas differs and, because fewer crops are harvested during the year, the cycles are of longer duration. Bean and corn harvests take place between July and December and the heaviest spending occurs in the *pueblo* in July and August, and in December and January. It is particularly in March and April, when credit is difficult to obtain locally, that these *campesinos* look to town stores for their credit needs.

The general provisions stores in the *pueblo* and *campo* have been presented in a hierarchical arrangement: the larger stores extend credit to the smaller and they, in turn, extend credit to the people around. The cycles of credit extension and repayment, which differ somewhat in the *lomas* and valley areas, are clearly geared to the seasons, which, in turn, dictate the planting and harvesting of crops. It is tempting to go one step further and represent the system of stores and credit extension as completely exploitative: the bigger stores exploit the smaller and all of them exploit the public. This, however, would be a misrepresentation for a number of reasons.

In the first place, competition among the stores for customers is intense; if prices for items in one store are too high, people will simply go elsewhere. Storekeepers like to claim that their permanent clientele shop there out of loyalty, but this is only partly true; one tends to shop where it is most convenient, where prices are lower, and, for those who need it, where credit is available. Even having obtained credit at a particular store, people are still free to shop elsewhere; this is a choice they frequently exercise, although once credit is obtained at a store, people will do most of their shopping there, and the storekeeper is then in a better position to overcharge.

Even when credit is granted by one store to another or by a store to certain customers, no interest is charged; in the case of credit granted to customers, no absolute date is set by which the bill must be paid. To a limited extent, extending credit gives the storekeeper a hold over his customer, but it is a risky business and not infrequently the storekeeper suffers by the credit system. Credit is only extended with great reluctance; the smaller storekeepers would not grant it at all were it not necessary to do so.

Even in the *pueblecitos*, where people are more firmly tied to the larger stores, the system is only mildly exploitative. These larger stores supply seeds and fertilizers on credit to many small growers and to *campesinos* who grow on the *lomas;* at harvest time, they wipe out the debt by buying the crop. There is no obligation on the part of the debtor, however, to sell his crop to the storekeeper;

there are always other buyers and if he can obtain a better price elsewhere, he is free to do so.

All storekeepers, but particularly those of the *campo* and of the smaller stores of the *pueblo*, have a reputation for being dishonest because they frequently overcharge and give short measure to their customers, most of whom buy in extremely small quantities. It is relatively easy to cheat a customer, for instance, who is buying ten *centavos* worth of rice or five *centavos* of oil. But there are obvious limits to dishonesty of this kind. If the storekeeper is flagrantly dishonest, he will be talked about and will begin to lose his trade.

To sum up, the storekeepers who grant credit are themselves more the exploited than the exploiters. The most common complaint one hears about storekeepers is that they will not grant credit, not that through credit one is held in permanent debt to the store. Nor can a case be made to the effect that the bigger storekeepers are in league in any way to exploit smaller stores or the community at large; business rivalry among these men is fierce and between some of them there is real enmity.

Finally, not all sections of the community are equally dependent upon stores for credit. The better-off agriculturalists do not need credit; many in the *pueblo* can also do without it and hence can afford to be more discriminating in the stores they patronize. One group, significant in terms of its numbers, namely *los pobres*, which includes the landless *peones* of the *pueblo* and colonies, is also largely precluded from the system. Because they can offer no security, these people are rarely granted credit.

Those most involved, then, in the store credit system are the *campesinos* of the dry farming areas and the small growers in the irrigated valleys. The economic life of these groups, in particular, follows a regular cycle, and their economic needs at particular times are clear and predictable. Leaving aside the small agriculturalists who are colonists and those who have settled in the *pueblo*, it is also these two groups that show greater reliance on kinsmen for help in one form or another and among whom leadership patterns are clearest.

Other Business Groups

In addition to the general provisions stores, there is a store that supplies agricultural needs and a large store that deals almost exclusively in dress materials and shoes. The business of the latter appears poor and the owner has other interests, one of which is acting as Constanza's banker. He is also involved in usury. This store is owned by a Lebanese who is considered an "enemy" of Sr. Nashash because they are business rivals. There are also two chemist shops, two hardware stores, and a store selling radios and electrical goods. These stores are well located and all of them are reasonably prosperous.

In addition to the stores, there are barbers, shoe repairers, bakers, tailors, watch and radio repairers, etc., all of whom have places of business. These range from small but prosperous looking to miserable, ramshackle structures that give the impression of extreme poverty. There are also the bars, pool rooms, boarding houses, and hotels, which exhibit a similar range in quality. Generally speaking, the businesses closer to the center of the *pueblo* tend to be more prosperous looking; those located in the *barrio* and in La Zanja are particularly poor.

Other business people who live within the *pueblo* include middlemen who buy up vegetables from growers and truck them to the cities, carpenters and furniture makers, *carro público* owners and drivers, mechanics, lottery ticket sellers, and at least two individuals who make money by buying government pay checks from public employees at 12% or more below their value, in advance of receipt of the check by employees. There are also street hawkers, carbon sellers, prostitutes, women who take in washing and ironing, dressmakers, a few beggars, and some twenty or so shoeshine boys. All the above, in a sense, might be said to be in business for themselves, although not all of these represent full-time occupations.

In general, the larger and more prosperous businesses of the *pueblo* are owned by individuals who are *constanceros* by birth or at least have lived in the community for many years. The smaller concerns are frequently owned by relative newcomers to Constanza who were already accustomed to town life. Businesses in the *pueblo* are generally opened by townsfolk or by individuals who have come to Constanza from other *pueblos*. *Campesinos*, who, at times, may open stores, generally do so in their own areas and not in the *pueblo*.

The Professions

In Constanza the professions are represented by five doctors, three of whom are university graduates, two dentists, a lawyer, an architect, agronomists working at the Agricultural Center, and public school teachers. There are also two priests and five nuns who serve as teachers in the Roman Catholic *colegio* (college). Of the school teachers, only the school inspector and those who teach in the *pueblo* are counted among the professions by *constanceros*. Teachers and agronomists are state employees and as such are considered in the next section; they are not included in the present discussion.

Of the professionals, only one dentist and the lawyer are natives of Constanza, but the school inspector (who has married a Constanza woman) and two of the doctors have lived in the community sufficiently long to be considered *constanceros*. With the exception of the lawyer, who was a supporter of Juan Bosch and has now lost much of his influence, these five men, who are numbered among the *trujillistas*, continue to take a strong interest in political affairs. They are widely known and respected throughout the community. Both the doctors have very large practices; one of them also receives a government salary as the head of the Public Health Service. The dentist and the school inspector both spend much time in the *campo*, where they are well-known figures. The school inspector makes periodic visits to *campo* schools and the dentist travels to various locations in the *campo* giving dental care.[1]

Other than those just mentioned, the professional people take no particular interest in community affairs and are accorded no special status as a group. Further, with the exception of the nuns and priests, the professionals may be considered a group only in a categorical sense. They have few dealings with one another and, in the case of the doctors, actually tend to avoid each other. What status does accrue to those men is more a matter of the wealth and influence they have rather than a consequence of their superior education.

Civil Servants

By far the biggest single employer in Constanza is the state. The various *municipio* and government offices located within the *pueblo* account for approximately 133 full-time employees and a number of others who work in different parts of the *municipio*. In addition, there is the Agricultural Center with ten full-time employees; stationed within the *pueblo* are twenty police and 120 sol-

---

[1] Dental care is generally in the form of extractions; there is little concern on the part of most *constanceros* with saving their teeth. Presumably because of the excessive amount of sugar in the diet, the people of Constanza have very poor teeth. In the *campo*, payments to the dentist are generally made in pigs, goats, or chickens, and, in the later months of the year, in corn or beans. The dentist sells these items in the *pueblo*. None of the doctors travels to the *campo* in this way and medical care is available only in the *pueblo*. The other dentist also confines his practice to the *pueblo*.

diers, although this last figure is uncertain. From time to time, certain of the offices also employ casual labor. In the few weeks preceding the *municipio* elections, for instance, the *ayuntamiento* employed nineteen temporary workers and the irrigation authority had 87 employed on canal work in the Valley. At about the same time, Public Works also had a large number of men repairing the main road leading to Constanza.

The heads of most government offices are generally outsiders and their stay in the community is for an indefinite length of time. Frequently, these people have nothing more to do with *constanceros* than is required of them, and their loyalties are in no way local. During most of the period of field work, however, the heads of seven government offices were either *constanceros* or men who had married into Constanza families and become closely involved in community affairs.

Other than the military, teachers form the biggest single group of civil servants; nearly all of them are from Constanza or have lived within the community for many years. With the exception of two or three larger schools in the *pueblecitos*, where the principals are paid more, appointments to the *pueblo* schools are generally preferred and are considered more prestigeous.

Teachers do hold an official monthly meeting in the *pueblo*, but there appears to be no shared sentiment of belonging to a professional group, and teachers make no collective impact on the community. The qualifications of Constanza's teachers are extremely low; most, in fact, have received little or no real training for their work. It is not surprising then that the schools could scarcely be worse. Individually, a few of the teachers are active politically, particularly in the *campo*, where the teacher is a person of some importance. Here, the teacher will often be approached by his neighbors with requests for help in writing letters or asked to explain things that are not understood; near election time, he will frequently be approached by some in the *pueblo* and asked to become a member of a local party committee in that area of the *campo*.

The system of patronage in obtaining jobs in government offices is discussed in a later chapter, but it may be stated at this point that to obtain such positions one generally needs influential connections within or outside the community. Moreover, having obtained such a position through patronage, it behooves one to maintain these connections and perhaps seek to form others, either to advance oneself or merely to safeguard the position presently held. It is not surprising then that those who owe their appointments to certain *constanceros* relate to these people; all civil servants are careful not to offend those who exercise the greatest influence in community affairs.

Military and Police

The soldiers and police are outsiders, and periodically the postings of both officers and men are changed. This is not to say, however, that they fail to make contacts of a purely social nature with the local people or that they deliberately hold themselves aloof. The *commandante* and his officers and the police chief are on friendly terms with the more important men of the *pueblo*, although they do not, as a rule, visit these men socially.

The military and the police represent an authority that emanates from outside the *municipio* and, to a large extent, is independent of the local power structure. This is more true of the military than of the police, who at times intervene directly in local affairs and are very much a power unto themselves. In the *pueblo* and *campo* people will greet police and soldiers, sometimes going out of their way to do so, but it is evident that the military, much more so than the police, represents an ever-present threat and an authority over which people feel they have no control but are unwise to ignore. Particularly in the bars, officers are greeted with an elaborate courtesy that verges on fawning; they will respond with much backslapping and joking behavior that is patronizing in the extreme.

Men of importance have an easy relationship with the police and at times are able to influence their actions. The military, on the other hand, with some notable exceptions, is feared by all sections of the community, although greatly respected by the *campesinos*. The exceptions are primarily members of the Arafat family, who have close ties of ritual kinship with important military figures outside the community. These ties place them in a special relationship with the local military.

In 1967 the military was given the task of patrolling certain forest areas to ensure that no trees were being cut; consequently, the *campo* is now being patrolled more frequently than previously. The army also has the task of finding volunteers to fight fires that occasionally break out in forest areas; this is done by literally grabbing citizens from the streets and placing them in the back of a truck under armed guard. The "volunteer" fire fighters are not paid and more than a full day or night may elapse before they are returned to the *pueblo*. Generally, the fire fighters are taken from the streets in the *barrio* or in La Zanja. Citizens of any prominence are never recruited for this task.

The *pueblo* folk, particularly the younger people of some education, both fear and detest the military; the ordinary soldier, slovenly dressed and most unmilitary in his bearing, is privately a figure of contempt and is considered nothing better than an ignorant *campesino*. Publicly, of course, the military is never ridiculed.

Los Pobres: Peones and Town Workers

The *peones*, who make up a large number of *los pobres*, were considered in the previous chapter, where it was noted that a number of the *peones* maintain strong ties with families in the *campo* and at times are able to obtain land and gifts of food from these relatives. The majority of *los pobres* of the town, however, are more recent comers to Constanza and have no extensive family connections with people of the *pueblo* or *campo*. Their numbers have been added to substantially by the former mill workers, most of whom have settled in the greater *pueblo* area. Others of *los pobres* are *constanceros* who have lived in the *pueblo* for many years and, like those who have arrived more recently from other centers, are well accustomed to town life. For all practical purposes, many of these have ceased to maintain their ties with relatives in the *campo*, but if they have better-off kinsmen in the *pueblo*, they will relate strongly to these people and seek to exploit the relationships.

Although the majority of *los pobres* work as day laborers on the *parcelas*, they prefer another form of work if it can possibly be obtained. The work of a *peón* is hard and is considered degrading; to earn a living in this way is to invite contempt.[2] A few obtain work on the council truck and occasionally, when funds become available, road work or work on canal construction is available. To those seeking such work, the *síndico* and others whose prerogative it is to hand out employment are men of immense importance. It is necessary to win the favor of these men (or of others who can who are largely unknown have little hope of securing this kind speak to them on one's behalf) if work is to be obtained. Those of employment.

A number of *los pobres* have permanent jobs as laborers on vegetable trucks, but this does not mean that work will be available every day. Others work as laborers for furniture makers or builders; since the timber industry closed down, however, there are fewer furniture makers and less building because of higher timber costs.

---

[2] Any form of unskilled manual work is deprecated, but *peones* in particular are held in contempt because of the nature of their work and because of the manner in which many of them live. With few exceptions, most *peones* who live in the *pueblo* are numbered among the people *sin vergüenza*. The use of this term is described below.

In short, the greater majority of these *pueblo* dwellers have no permanent work and most of them are unable to do anything about acquiring land. Unlike the *campesinos*, they are less able to look to their kinsmen for help, although among neighbors there is a good deal of cooperation. Further, although a few vegetables may be grown around the house, most of the daily food needs must be bought at the stores; this group, it will be remembered, is not generally granted credit. For people in this category, life is very much a struggle. The main burden of keeping the home going not infrequently falls upon the woman. Family life shows little permanence, and it is often the mother who is the more consistent breadwinner and gives home life what little stability it has.

Those of *los pobres* who frequent the brothels or who gamble and drink heavily and show no concern for their reputations are said to be *sin vergüenza*. In terms of residence, all those who live in the La Zanja area are said to be *sin vergüenza* and so, too, are many of the *barrio* dwellers and others who live on the fringes of the *pueblo*. Occupationally, only prostitution, begging, carbon selling, and a very few other tasks (primarily reserved for women) are clearly said to bring shame, but it is evident from the undisguised contempt in which many *constanceros* hold the *peones* and poorest *campesinos* that to belong to these groupings is to be considered *sin vergüenza*.

The women of *los pobres*, more so than their menfolk, have a variety of ways of making a little money. A number take in washing and ironing and some do sewing; there are also many dressmakers in the *pueblo* but, for the most part, these women are not of the poorest class. Some women grind coffee and a few earn a living washing pig's intestines, from which *longanesa* is made. At least one woman in the *pueblo* regularly buys such articles as lengths of material or cheap shoes and then raffles them; others also run such raffles from time to time. In a few cases, women are reduced to begging, but this is more often on behalf of a sick child for whom medicine or clothes must be bought. A number of women are employed as domestic servants in homes or in hotels, but generally only girls or young women are thus employed, and the pay is very low.

There are several tasks concerned with vegetable farming that are open to women. It is to these tasks that women who must work frequently look for employment. A considerable number find employment husking garlic in preparation for planting and, later in the season, stringing them together in readiness for sale. Others, after the dried beans have been separated from the bushes and pods, winnow the beans by hand. Such work is often undertaken by small groups of women who are neighbors; some may be relatives. A number of these groups regularly work for the same agriculturalist, but when this occurs, the employer is generally a relative. Providing such work (which is always paid) is one way of helping poorer kinsmen who live in the *pueblo*. Women are also sometimes employed to pick potatoes, tomatoes, or corn. Opportunities here, however, are fewer and, unlike garlic work, these tasks are considered demeaning for women of the *pueblo*.[3]

Women who look to these agricultural tasks for employment are, like the *peones*, subject to seasonal unemployment. Only when the garlic are being drawn is there sufficient work for all, each day of the week. When there is no agricultural work available and no work to be had in the *pueblo, los pobres* pass the days in idleness.

THE IMPORTANT PEOPLE

Constanceros employ a variety of terms to refer to certain individuals whose wealth, influence, or position clearly marks them off from others, but some of these terms are deceptive.[4] For the purpose of this study, the most significant individuals are those referred to as *la gente importante* (the important people) and, in particular, a few among these who are *la gente mas importante* (the most important people).

Constanceros judge a person's importance according to the amount of patronage he has to dispense, whether this be in the form of credit, gifts, temporary employment, or government positions. It follows then that the degree of importance tends to be a

---

[3] A young woman of an extremely poor *pueblo* family who worked as our maid boasted of her skill in platting garlic. She considered other forms of agricultural tasks shameful for women because they were dirty and involved working in the sun like a *peón*.

[4] Terms commonly used include *los líderes* (the leaders), *gente de influencia* (influential people), *los jefes* (the chiefs), and *los ricos* (the rich).

A popular question in various surveys that have been conducted from time to time in Constanza is to name *los líderes*. In answer to this question, *constanceros* usually give the names of the *síndico* and the *regidores,* ignoring others who exercise leadership but do not hold public office. Likewise, when identifying *la gente de influencia,* people think in terms of political influence but, again, generally name only those individuals who hold political office or make no secret of their political aspirations. *Los jefes* is another term popularly used, but usually it is applied only to those who are in charge of a government office or an organization such as the party committee. Not all of *los ricos* exercise leadership, but most of *la gente importante* and all of *la gente mas importante* are numbered among *los ricos*.

relative matter: depending upon the situation and present needs of any individual, certain ones will be important or not to him. There are some, however, whose importance is clearly recognized by all; these are *la gente mas importante*, and it is these men who today manage community affairs. There is not always agreement on how many should be numbered among *la gente mas importante*, but all are agreed on a few names. These are men who are *constanceros* or have lived sufficiently long in the community to be considered as such. All of them live in the *pueblo* but are widely known throughout the *municipio* and have been influential in political affairs from the time of Trujillo. All of them are wealthy.

Three of the four principal storekeepers who extend credit to smaller stores are numbered among the most important. One of these is Raóul Espiallat, who was elected *síndico* in May 1968, a position he previously held during the time of Trujillo. The position was also held for a number of years by his uncle, Martín, who now has an important political post in the capital. Pedro Espiallat, a half-brother of Raóul, also owns one of the four principal stores, but does not share his half-brother's importance. Between these two men, there is much enmity. The Espiallat family is one of the oldest and largest families in Constanza. Another of the three is Sr. Nashash, the former Lebanese with extensive property holdings in the *pueblo*. This man acquired most of his wealth during the Trujillo years and, although he has few kinship ties with other Constanza families, the economic importance of this family is great. Sr. Nashash and his sons own the radio station, one of the cinemas, the main bakery, which supplies most of the *campo* stores with bread, and one of the two bars opposite the park; their store is the biggest in the *pueblo*.

The fourth store is owned by Rafael Arafat. The Arafat family, it will be recalled, owns much Valley land and thus is in a position to offer a good deal of employment. Two of the brothers head important government offices and the family also has powerful connections with the military. Only Rafael Arafat, who is acknowledged as the head of this family, is numbered among *la gente mas importante*.

In Chapter 2, it was mentioned that some of the former sawmill owners or managers still live in the *pueblo*, where they are accorded high status. Until very recently, when all sawmills were closed, these men were able to offer employment to considerable numbers, and it appears that they related to their employees in a highly paternalistic way. When the sawmills closed, the dependency that had been built up over the years was abruptly terminated. One ex-sawmill owner described how, for some time, his former employees repeatedly called at his house with requests for money and food and pleaded that he use his influence to secure them work or colony land. When it became clear that he was unable to help, they eventually ceased to call.

Today, there are ten former sawmill owners or managers in Constanza; although none of them is able to offer employment as before, all have retained importance in community affairs. One of these men, don Alejandro Gonzales, is clearly numbered among *la gente mas importante.*[5] Don Alejandro is not connected to any Constanza family, but is widely known and respected for his wealth and the influence he commands within and outside the community. He holds no political office but is very close to President Balaguer and is in a position to play the role of broker in the community.

The four professional men referred to earlier are also included among *la gente mas importante*, for, like those just described, they have maintained a position of influence in the community over a number of years. Each has a wide range of acquaintances and a significant number of individuals have consistently looked to these men in the past for various kinds of favors.

---

[5] Don Alejandro is the only man in Constanza who is consistently called *don*, which indicates the respect in which he is held. A number of highly respected women in the *pueblo*, including don Alejandro's wife, are always addressed as *doña*, but this term is also commonly used in addressing any woman who would normally be addressed as *señora*. *Campesinos* tend to use *doña* more frequently than *señora* and explain that this is because they have more "respect" for women than those who live in the *pueblo*. The Spaniards attribute this loose use of *doña* to ignorance on the part of the Dominicans.

CHAPTER 5

Social Activities and Social Groupings

This chapter will show how relationships are structured in the community. This is attempted through a delineation of various informal groupings and a description of the manner in which certain ones customarily relate to others. Particularly significant for this study are the use of space and the ordering of relationships on those occasions when large numbers of *constanceros* are drawn together in the *pueblo*. This chapter also considers the points of assembly where groups regularly tend to gather and describes the cycle of activities of diurnal, weekly, and longer duration. The extent to which these activities differ for various groupings in the community is also indicated.

Most of the groups referred to are relational, and many of the activities described occur outside the formal institutional systems and are engaged in by small informal groupings. Here, informal groups will be considered to be "those whose structure has not been consciously or deliberately created and whose organization, while bearing on the attainment of goals, is not deliberately formed for specific ends."[1] These same authors define formal groups in opposite terms, but add that the distinction between the two forms of groupings is relative and not absolute. Formal groups are "formed with a specific purpose in mind and their structure is instrumentally organized to attain the purpose."[2] This definition will be adopted, but the term "formal association" will be used rather than "formal group." Only a few references will be made to formal associations or groups in this chapter; a fuller discussion of these is contained in Chapter 8.

---

[1] Harry C. Bredemeier and Richard M. Stephenson, *The Analysis of Social Systems* (New York: Holt, Rinehart and Winston, Inc., 1962), p. 33.

[2] *Ibid.*

The Rhythm of Activities

Daily and Weekly Cycle

Within the *pueblo*, the main center of informal social activity is the park. In the late afternoon and early evening, groups of young people stroll arm-in-arm around the park, eyeing each other and occasionally stopping to converse. Couples also stroll in the park, but in the streets, one sees groups rather than couples. The bars, a few stores that also serve as bars, the pool rooms, and some street corners are gathering places, as are the cinemas, the churches, the cockfight arena, the baseball field, and the casino. In the *campo*, in those areas where they exist, the stores and the pool rooms provide assembly places for informal groups of old and young men in the late afternoon and evening. In both town and country there is a tremendous amount of visiting, particularly during the evening, when families and friends will gather together in one another's homes. In the *campo*, guests are usually entertained in the kitchen; in the *pueblo*, entertainment more generally takes place in the living room.

Daily and weekly life in the *pueblo* follows a fairly regular pattern. People stir early, but in most households breakfast is of little account and the family generally does not sit at the table together. For the agriculturalist and *peón*, work begins at 7:00 a.m.; most shops are open by that hour. Women are generally up earlier than the menfolk and set about the household tasks early. Children must be sent to school, which begins at 8:00 or 8:30 a.m.; most women then do the daily shopping. Because the majority of homes are without refrigerators, meat and milk must be bought daily. Butcher shops are particularly busy in the early morning; more so than other shop-keepers, butchers are the target for a great deal of good-natured abuse from the women who crowd around the openings of their tiny shops. Cleaning and washing are generally done in the morning. Women of the *barrio* and other poorer parts of the *pueblo*, whose homes lack laundry facilities, will often do their washing in the river, where they will gossip in groups as they work. In the *campo*, washing is also done in the river, but in the Valley many use the irrigation canals for this purpose. Mondays and Thursdays seem to be the preferred days for washing.

After these tasks, the mid-day meal, the main meal of the day, is prepared;[3] after eating, many people take a *siesta*. Most of the

---

[3] Rice and red beans are staple items for all *constanceros*. There is no basic difference in the diet of wealthier families, but more meat, poultry, and fruit are eaten and there are heavier expenditures on canned foods, much of which comes from abroad.

shops and all the government offices close and the town is very quiet. Those who are able to do so return home to eat and then rest; *peones* generally eat a hot meal of rice and beans on the *parcela* of the agriculturalist for whom they are working, but the agriculturalists themselves will return home for their meal unless the distance is too great.

Siesta time ends about 2:00 p.m., when the shops re-open and work is generally resumed, although many government offices do not re-open until later. In the *pueblo* there is much visiting by those women who have free time, but for the majority of women there is little time for leisure. There is always housework or mending to do and, in the late afternoon, the evening meal to prepare.

Most government offices close at 5:00 p.m.; the men employed in these offices may wander into the bars or chat on street corners or in the park before returning home. *Peones* are generally required to work later; they can be seen each evening, machetes strapped to their sides, making their way home to the *barrio* and to the fringes of the *pueblo*, where most of them live. Frequently small groups of *peones* and town workers gather in stores near their homes, where they may drink rum, make small purchases, or merely pass the time conversing together. They are not, as a rule, seen in the park except on special occasions. Artisans, *público* drivers, and the like, and young agriculturalists who live in the *pueblo*, frequently gather in the park or in the bars or pool rooms in the late afternoon; *peones* also patronize the pool rooms and bars, although they are never seen in the bars opposite the park. Important people at times go to the bars opposite the park but never enter the pool rooms.

In the late afternoon and early evening, there are more people strolling in the park. A few groups of boys gather in open spaces on the outskirts of the town to play baseball, and the pool rooms begin to fill. The bars then open and the juke boxes blare, but on most week nights there is little activity late at night. At 9:00 p.m., the high school students emerge; about two hours later the cinemas empty. Generally, those who have been visiting will have taken their leave before this hour (people who have television sets always seem to have visitors), and Radio Constanza, which has been fully audible all day in nearly every street of the *pueblo*, mercifully goes off the air until 6:00 a.m. the next day. There is always more noise in and around the bars and pool rooms in La Zanja but, as a rule, everything closes before midnight and the only people one generally encounters on the streets are the heavily armed, mixed patrols of police and soldiers, who guard the peace of this extremely tranquil *pueblo*.

Saturday is a work day much like any other but there are more people in the streets, particularly in the afternoon. Lottery ticket sellers are more active and, in the evening, bars do a brisker trade and stay open later. When dances are held in the bars or in the Nueva Suiza hotel, which is very rarely, they generally fall on Saturday night. Sunday is the real day of relaxation, although for shop people it is business as usual during the morning. Only the most dedicated agriculturalist or *campesino*, however, works on Sunday. From early morning, large numbers of the *campesinos* come into the *pueblo* on foot, in vehicles, or mounted on horseback, mule, or burro. They may go to mass[4] and then return home, visit friends, or stand in groups conversing outside some of the bigger stores.

Those from the irrigated valleys and the dry farming areas that surround these valleys do not visit the *pueblo* with the same regularity as those from El Limoncito, for instance, and other such areas that have no nearby *pueblecito*. Instead, they visit friends in their own areas or rest at home, and a number of the men pass much of the day in and around the *pueblecito* stores and pool rooms. There are also small chruches in Tireo, El Rio, and La Descubierta, and services are held there on most Sundays. Considerable numbers from these areas do appear in the *pueblo* on Sunday, however. Men like to attend the cock fights, and many families use Sunday to go shopping because *pueblo* prices are lower and many items available in the *pueblo* are not on sale in the *campo*.

The poorest *campesino*, often barefooted, filthy, and ill-clad, mounted on his half-starved burro or mule, is readily identifiable; a pathetic figure, he is held in contempt by *pueblo* folk. There is, however, nothing pathetic about the relatively well-to-do *campesino* when he rides into town. He is neatly dressed and well mounted, his bearing is proud, and he frequently carries a pistol in a leather holster or a long-bladed knife tucked into his belt. The poorest *campesino*, like the *peón*, is rarely seen without his machete.

Campesinos frequently enter the *pueblo* as a family but then generally disband and return to their homes individually. A family that enters the church together may sit as a group, but more fre-

---

[4] Constanza, the visitor is repeatedly assured, is a very religious center and Catholicism is strong, but the fact is that religion is a preoccupation of women and children, and there are considerable numbers in the *pueblo* and *campo* who have no regular contact with the church. The *campesinos* are generally considered to be more concerned with religion than are the townspeople. In many of their homes, there is a whole array of pictures and images of saints, in front of which the women will place flowers in small glasses or light candles. In almost every Constanza home there are pictures of the Heart of Jesus and the Virgin of Altagracia.

quently it will separate, the women and children sitting to one side
and the men to the other; frequently the men prefer to stand at
the back of the church. In the evangelical temple, which draws
only fourteen to twenty people for its Sunday services, there is also
a clear separation of the sexes; the men sit on one side and the
women on the other. Those who attend the temple are mostly small
business people or artisans from the *pueblo*. None of those of importance in Constanza is Protestant. People are defensive about the
presence of the Protestants and there is some animosity toward them.

After church, women and young children, boys and girls, and
the menfolk all tend to go their separate ways. The mothers generally return home with the children to prepare dinner, and the young
people and the elderly meet with friends and wander about or stand
gossiping in groups. It is unusual, in fact, to see a whole family
together in Constanza, except for the few who own cars and who
sometimes set off together. For many of the men, the most important
morning activity is the lottery. Early Sunday morning, a large group
of *campesino* men and many from the *pueblo's* lower ranks begin
to gather in front of one of the stores in Calle Luperón, where
lottery ticket sellers set up their stands. There is much last-minute
buying of tickets and a good deal of loud talk and excitement. Shortly
before midday, the group disbands and almost every radio appears
to tune in to the broadcast of the results: two hours of monotonous
reading of numbers.

Sunday dinner is eaten later than usual and tends to be more
elaborate: it is the one day of the week when many prepare chicken
and rice, a luxury dish to most households because of the high cost
of poultry. More frequently on Sunday than at any other time,
cooked food is sent to friends and relatives living nearby; this is
more common in the *campo* than elsewhere. This is also the meal
at which families are likely to have guests, whether invited or not,
and, in many households, women prepare more food than the family
needs in case someone should arrive and expect to be fed. Any
visitor who arrives at mealtime will be invited to eat, although if
his status is decidedly lower, as in the case of an employee or a
very poor relative, he may be fed in the kitchen and not at the
table with the adult males of the family. Only among a very few
of the more sophisticated families of the *pueblo* do the women eat
at the table with the men; generally the women wait on the men
and then eat apart with the youngest children.

In the afternoon there may be a cockfight or baseball game
to watch; some will go to the bars. A number of the Spanish men
regularly repair to their club; on occasional Sundays, functions are

held there that involve their families as well. On the one official occasion when prominent *constanceros* were invited to the club, none attended except the *commandante* and the *síndico*. The latter appeared only briefly when the function was all but over.

Large numbers go to the cinemas, which charge only ten cents for the Sunday afternoon performances. *Campesinos* and many of *los pobres* attend the older cinema near the *barrio*, which generally shows a Western or some film dealing with violence; the newer cinema shows a film supposedly intended for children, although, more often than not, it is anything but suitable.[5] For the majority, Sunday afternoon is the principal time for visiting. Those with cars usually choose this day for pleasure drives to picnic spots in the countryside; occasionally a whole group of picnickers will set off in the back of a truck. For *campesinos* and many of *los pobres*, Sunday is also bath day,[6] and the one time in the week when they dress up. Even the poorest, in fact, make an effort to be clean and well dressed on Sunday afternoon.

Early on Sunday evening a large group, primarily young people of the *pueblo*, assembles in the park to listen to the discordant efforts of the Constanza town band. The concert begins and ends with the playing of the national anthem, which happens to be exceedingly long, during which people stand respectfully at attention. When the concert is over, there is nothing else but the bars, the cinemas, and the pool rooms, all of which do a brisker trade than on weeknights, although less than on Saturday evening. Generally, by midnight, the town is asleep and the silence is broken only by the occasional barking of dogs and braying of donkeys in the *campo*.

Seasonal and Yearly Cycle

There is a seasonal rhythm to Constanza life that affects both social and economic activities. In the colder months between January and April there are few tourists, no band performances in the park, and no cockfights or baseball in the *pueblo*; in February and March particularly, fewer people go out at night and there is less visiting

---

[5] This cinema has a small gallery; soon after these matinee performances were commenced, early in 1968, it was decided that girls only would be permitted to sit upstairs. This restriction was imposed to protect young girls, who were frequently knocked over in the wild scramble for seats that sometimes ensues when the doors of the cinema are opened.

[6] People bathe in the river or in streams. Poorer houses in the *pueblo* are not supplied with running water and, like the *campesinos* of the dry farming areas, these *pueblo* dwellers must carry their water each day from the river or streams. Many of the better houses in the irrigated valleys have tanks that catch water from the roof.

and no *fiestas*. For the poor of the *pueblo* and *campo* who lack warm clothing, the cold is difficult to endure. At night the family huddles around the small cooking fire on the kitchen floor and goes to bed early. Colds and influenza are common during these months; many complain that medicines are not free and that there are no distributions of clothing or blankets as in the days of Trujillo.

As was pointed out in the previous chapter, the early months of the year, particularly February and March, are the times of greatest economic hardship for all who directly or indirectly rely upon agriculture. After these months, particularly from July until the end of the year, there is more money in the *pueblo* and much more activity. The period of most intense activity falls between July and September. In these months, a number of tourists appear in Constanza, the bars do most of their trade, and spending in the *pueblo* is heavy. This activity climaxes on September 24, when the *día de la Mercedes* (Day of Mercedes) is celebrated to honor the patron saint of Constanza.

The church calendar also defines a festive cycle. There is much activity during Easter and the Christmas season, which includes Three Kings' Day. As well, *constanceros* celebrate the *día de los defunctos* (Day of the Dead), when masses are held for the dead and flowers are placed on graves. Throughout the year there are a large number of saints' days, some of which involve religious processions. Only the *día de la Mercedes* has real community importance, however. It is the one recurring event that draws large numbers of *constanceros* together in the *pueblo*.

INFORMAL GROUPS IN CONSTANZA

Informal Groups in the Town

Most of the groups beyond the pair level that one observes from day to day in the *pueblo* show little permanence in their composition. Small groups of young people meet casually in the park or in the streets; they may stand talking together or wander into one of the bars. When baseball games are being played against visiting teams, older men and young people of both sexes gather to watch. Here girls stand in small groups, often holding hands and carrying on secretive conversations with much giggling, and throwing sly glances at the boys. On some afternoons and most weekends, a number of older boys and girls from the secondary school play volleyball on a court located to one side of the school, but the games are not organized on any regular basis and it is not always the same ones who play together.

By far the most popular recreational activity involving both sexes is dancing to *merengue* music; this generally occurs in the bars to music provided by the juke boxes. In the bars, whether the principal activity is drinking or dancing, one nearly always sees groups; it is rare to see a couple or an individual sitting alone unless they are strangers in the community. More commonly, two couples will enter the bar together or a group will form inside the bar. These mixed groups are stable, however, only in the case of young people who are courting or are engaged and who are regularly chaperoned by a married couple, and this stability, of course, is not to endure. There are no mixed groups of young people who associate together sufficiently often to be described as cliques.

The bars in La Zanja are the haunts of prostitutes. Young men of respectable families[7] occasionally visit these bars, but always with one or two male friends. To frequent these places too often is to gain a reputation for being irresponsible; married men who value their reputations are never seen there, although some of them secretly maintain mistresses. For the most part, those who regularly go to the bars and pool room in La Zanja are men who live in that area or who come from the *barrio* or other poor parts of the *pueblo,* and soldiers. *Constanceros* condemn these people because they are *sin vergüenza.* They are drunkards who gamble and fight among themselves and, except for the soldiers, have no steady work. The people without shame are mostly drawn from among the *peones* and town workers. With the exception of officers of the garrison and NCO's, they tend not to visit the bars opposite the park or to be seen often in the company of the young people who do so. There is a tendency on the part of the military to stay apart in all social situations, and when they are seen drinking or conversing socially with civilians in the bars, it is generally the civilians who invite them to join the group.

Dress tends to be an indication of social status, but, although it is always possible to distinguish the poorest *campesinos* and *peones* by the poverty of their dress, young women of poor *pueblo* families cannot always be distinguished from those who are well-to-do. Nowadays, many of the *señoritas* wear tight sweaters and slacks. All wear makeup, although if a girl is too heavily made up, she is considered cheap. Hair curlers, at times covered by a light scarf, are worn almost incessantly and only on very special occasions will a girl literally let her hair down. Some women have dyed hair

---

[7] What constitutes respectability and responsibility in Constanza family life and the importance of reputation are discussed below in Chapter 7.

(blond seems to be the preferred color), but this is considered very daring. Many women with darkish skin liberally apply face powder to lighten their complexions.[8]

The dress of men in the *pueblo* is not particularly distinctive except in their liking for large, buckled leather belts and a variety of head gear. The slim, raised-heel, black ankle boot is popular among teenage youths of the *pueblo;* otherwise men generally wear sharp, pointed, black shoes that are always highly polished. *Campesinos* wear boots, but the poorest *campesinos* and *peones* wear thongs made from old car tires. A black sombrero is particularly smart, but many wear blue felt caps or straw boaters, and a few young men wear plastic helmets such as are worn by American construction workers. The Spaniards, in particular, favor cork pithies while supervising labor on their *parcelas*. *Campesinos* and some agriculturalists who live in the *pueblo* wear straw caps.

Don Alejandro Gonzales invariably wears a suit. Those who have them always wear dark suits when attending any important social function, such as the annual graduation day of the *colegio* or of the high school and dances that are held in the bars opposite the park, in the casino, or at the Nueva Suiza Hotel. On such occasions as political rallies, when large numbers of *constanceros* come together, and for the procession held on the *día de la Mercedes,* only a few of those who own suits will wear them. These are *la gente importante* and, on such occasions, they are clearly distinguishable by their dress. Ownership of a suit is clearly a mark of social status; those who own them include professional men, owners of larger stores, the bigger agriculturalists who live in the *pueblo,* including a number of the foreigners, and virtually all of those who work in government offices. Even among well-off *campesinos* the ownership of a suit is rare. Most of those who own suits go hatless or wear felt hats or boaters. They are rarely seen in caps.

What has been said so far about informal groups in the *pueblo* is not to suggest that *los pobres* have little to do with other townsfolk or that they confine their social activities exclusively to the areas in which they live, although there is a clear tendency in this direction. The bars opposite the park are frequented more by the bet-

---

[8] There is an acute consciousness of skin color and other racial characteristics, principally hair form and the shape of the lips and nose, and there are a number of terms in popular use to describe gradations in each of these characteristics. *Constanceros* insist that they are not conscious of color, but it is clear that very dark skin and negroid features are considered ugly. None of those in Constanza's upper class has a particularly negroid appearance, although a few are very dark; negroid types are found primarily among *peones* and poor *campesinos,* but it should be added that *blancos* (whites) can be found among these people also.

ter-off young people of the *pueblo,* who do not, as a rule, go to
the cinema near the *barrio* on Sunday afternoon, although there
would be no question of criticism if they did so. The people of
La Zanja, in particular, all of whom are considered to be *sin vergüenza,* largely confine their social activities to their own area; this
is true of many *barrio* dwellers and of others who live on the *pueblo*
fringes. Well-dressed young people from the *barrio* and *pueblo*
fringes frequently gather in the park on Sunday afternoons and
occasionally are seen in the bars opposite the park. Those of their
number who can afford the admission may also attend dances held
there and in the casino. Their elders rarely enter these bars and,
as a rule, are only seen in the park on special occasions.

Most of the groups in the *pueblo* show little permanence in
their composition. There is one group of young men of some significance, however, although its members cannot always be identified
clearly. This is a group of five or six that centers around two individuals, both of whom are connected with the Arafat family. These
young men, who have been involved in occasional unpublicized acts
of violence directed against particular individuals, are extreme rightists and, at heart, like the fathers of the two ring leaders, are Wessin
supporters. They are often seen drinking together in the bars opposite the park. There are others in the *pueblo* referred to variously
as "leftists," "communists," or "louts," and some of these are often
seen drinking together in the La Zanja area and in the bars opposite
the park. These young men are malcontents; although they have
some education, most of them have no steady work. Some have
been in trouble with the police. Politically, they have no
commitments.

Certain individuals are often the center of a small number of
followers, although they do not make up groups of individuals who
consistently associate together. The *síndico* is frequently in the bar
drinking with three or four others, who form a group of admirers.
These are generally men who owe their jobs to him. Others in the
pueblo who also are in positions to distribute patronage are often
seen in the bars or on street corners, where they are the center
of such groups. Some of these men act in what appears to be an
extremely imperious manner, although no one considers it to be
such. Two, in particular, don Alejandro and Raóul Espiallat, pass
much of their time driving around the streets of the *pueblo* in their
expensive cars, sounding the horn to get attention and then waving
or calling greetings. If they wish to speak to someone, they sound
the horn several times and then beckon the individual concerned to
come.

These men, more so than others who are counted among *la*

gente mas importante, are constantly seen relating to others. But although some of these men are close friends and visit each other a great deal, they do not themselves regularly associate together as a group either in the bars or anywhere else, except when there are matters of common concern to discuss. Once the business has been settled, the group disbands. *La gente mas importante* also tend to dominate the committee membership of certain organizations that are formed from time to time, but organizations in Constanza show little permanence.[9] Among *la gente importante,* only some married brothers of the Arafat family and certain others related to them by marriage form a clique. These men visit each other a great deal and, in particular, relate strongly to Rafael Arafat, who is clearly the most influential member of this group and is also numbered among *la gente mas importante.*

On set occasions during the year, certain persons in the *pueblo,* as individuals, may be seen to relate to the many and they do so in an intensely personal way. On Three Kings' Day, Raóul Espiallat and two other men who are among *la gente importante* drive to various poor parts of the *pueblo* and to the colonies and throw candy and trinkets to the children of *los pobres* who crowd around the car. What follows is near pandamonium as boys and girls of all ages scramble on the street for the gifts. The older or more robust children generally gain the most items and there are pleas for more gifts. A few more items are flung to the waving hands and then, protesting that there is nothing more to give, *los ricos* drive on to the next spot to distribute more largess. People thoroughly approve of this distribution and speak well of the men involved. People also speak well of Sr. Edmundo Ríos, a close friend of Rafael Arafat, who each year, from his home, distributes parcels of food to *los pobres* who assemble there to receive it at his hands. This act of generosity stems from a vow Sr. Ríos made to a saint many years before. Edmundo Ríos is a former timber mill owner. He is well known throughout the community and is highly thought of; in particular, he is respected by *los pobres.*

Informal Groups in the Country

Young men in the *campo* complain that life is monotonous and that there is little to do. For them, what diversions life has to offer are mainly located in the *pueblo,* and, indeed, there is little

---

[9] Formal associations are considered below in Chapter 8, where it is shown that many associations come into being only in response to pressure exerted from outside the community. Once pressure is removed, such associations cease to function.

in the way of organized recreational life in the countryside. There
is the occasional dance held in someone's home, with music provided
by a small band comprising an accordion player, a drummer, and
a scraper, whose instrument is a long cylinder perforated like a
grater and is rhythmically scraped with a stick. Such dances, which
draw groups of relatives and friends together, are very popular;
they are attended by young and old, who dance the *merengue* and
drink rum, if they have it, into the early hours of the morning.
There are also large *fiestas* that are occasionally held in some of
the dry farming areas of the *campo*, such as the one staged by
Ramón Ornes in El Limoncito. In the irrigated valleys, there are
no regular occasions when all of the people of the area are drawn
together.

At times, boys and young men gather together to play baseball
but, like the volleyball games in the *pueblo*, these games are not
organized on any regular basis. There are also unofficial cockfights,
but for the most part these are not regularly organized and generally
take place when the owners of two cocks having a training fight become excited, a crowd gathers, and the cocks are permitted to fight
on. In the *pueblecitos* there are large stores, some of which serve
as bars, and there are pool rooms. These are assembly points for
the men of a number of adjoining localities, who gather together
and talk. As well, men, more so than women, spend an inordinate
amount of time within or in front of one another's houses, gossiping.

In Chapter 8, reference will be made to 5-D clubs, which have
recently been formed in some of the *pueblecitos*. Other than these,
there are no formal associations in the *campo* that regularly draw
set groups together, except prior to elections, when local political
committees are activated in the *pueblo*. Men on these committees
meet in the house of one of their members and, individually or
as a group, visit the homes of others in the area to persuade them
how to vote. When political rallies are called in various areas of
the *campo*, it is always on the initiative of the *síndico* or other
individuals in the *pueblo*. *Pueblo* men of importance are always
the .chief speakers at such meetings and clearly take precedence
over local leaders.

Those in any one area of the *campo* who have importance and
have built up a position of leadership, like their counterparts in
the *pueblo*, tend not to associate together as a group unless there
are matters of common interest to discuss. In both town and country,
between men seeking popularity with the same individuals, there
is a certain amount of rivalry.

Earlier in this chapter, it was stated that the poorest *campesino* is a figure of contempt among *pueblo* dwellers. To a lesser extent, this contempt is shared by *campesinos* of the irrigated valleys and by many in the older dry farming areas as well. These poor *campesinos* are considered to be brutish and stupid people who live little better than animals. Generally, they live in huts on steep *lomas* areas throughout the *campo*, and some of them live more or less in isolation. For the most part, they are recent settlers who have few kin ties with other *constanceros*. When they appear in the *pueblecitos* or in the *pueblo* stores to sell their harvests, or merely to visit, they stand on the fringes of the groups that regularly gather in these places.

COMMUNITY GATHERINGS

On a very few occasions throughout the year, large numbers from all parts of the community assemble in the *pueblo*. Some of these occasions are recurrent and, particularly in the case of the *día de la Mercedes*, are expressive of communal sentiment. All of these gatherings may be considered "rites of intensification," in Chapple's and Coon's terms,[10] because they are occasions when habitual relationships among various groupings are dramatically presented. Chapple and Coon further state: "This acting out of the ordered interaction of the members [of various groups] has the effect of reinforcing or intensifying their habitual relations, and thus serves to maintain their conditioned responses.[11]

The *día de la Mercedes*, in honor of the patron saint of Constanza, was celebrated on Sunday, September 24. On the preceding night, there was a dance in the Nueva Suiza Hotel, the main dance of the year, that was attended by some 150 men and women from the *pueblo* and a number of visitors from other centers, most of whom were relatives or friends of *constanceros*. All those who attended the dance were well dressed. None of them came from the *campo*. Within the ballroom, groups of friends and relatives sat around tables. The few Spaniards who attended made up their own groups; there was also a table of army personnel.

On the Sunday, preceded by the town band, the image of the Virgin de la Mercedes was carried through the *barrio* and the main streets of the *pueblo*, a procession in which hundreds took part. Until early evening, the park and the streets were filled with people from all parts of the *municipio* and many from other centers. The

---

[10] Eliot Dismore Chapple and Carleton Stevens Coon, *Principles of Anthropology* (New York: Henry Holt and Co., 1942), Chapter 21.

[11] *Ibid.*, p. 507.

mood was one of festivity; the vendors of ices, religious pictures, and candy, not to mention the bars and pool rooms, all did a brisk trade. Throughout much of the afternoon, two *campesino* bands played in different parts of the park, and a number of *campesinos* and some tourists gathered to listen to these impromptu performances; *constanceros* from the *pueblo* showed little interest. By dusk, most of the *campesinos* had returned to their homes and the streets once more were left to the *pueblo* dwellers.

There are other traditional days, including Christmas Day, Three Kings' Day, Good Friday, and Good Sunday,[12] when many come to the *pueblo* to attend religious services or merely to visit relatives or friends, but none of these occasions draws as many people as does the festival of Mercedes. There are also a number of religious processions held during Holy Week and on a few other occasions throughout the year, but although some of these may involve large numbers of people, particularly the one held early in the evening of Good Friday, none of these days or processions invokes or expresses community sentiment in the same way. *Constanceros* consider the *día de la Mercedes* to be their day and a time of celebration for the entire community.

Religious processions are generally led by the town band, which also leads the funeral processions of better known citizens. Invariably the band outdistances those behind and periodically will wait for the processors to catch up. In religious processions, one of the priests and a group of men bearing the image will be in the front when the procession first gets under way, but thereafter there is likely to be a good deal of confusion and the processions appear almost formless. There are no clear positions assigned, nor is there any spontaneous grouping of personnel in terms of status. Men dressed in suits may be seen scattered throughout the procession; they do not segregate themselves in any way; this also holds true of funeral processions. Only when groups of particular religious orders[13] are processing does it become possible to discern fairly clear groups, but even then these tend to break down as the procession advances.

---

[12] Carnival is also a traditional celebration, but in Constanza it is celebrated only by a few of the young people of the *pueblo*. These are the *máscaras* (the masked ones) who, on a few successive weekends preceding Lent, dress in costumes and masks and attack people in the park and nearby streets with small sand bags and portions of inflated bicycle tire tubes. Their principal targets are groups of girls.

[13] Religious orders are referred to in the chapter on associational life (Chapter 8). When the *cruzadas*, a religious order for children, are processing, they are generally placed in front of the procession.

In the procession of the Virgin de la Mercedes there was one individual who stood out. Immediately behind the priest and those bearing the image of the Virgin walked the *commandante*. As always he was in uniform and on this occasion he walked alone, separating the priest and the men around him from those who followed behind. The *commandante* does not appear in any other public religious procession, although he generally appears in the funeral processions of better known persons. On these occasions, he assigns himself no special place.

It was noted above that the visits of Trujillo were occasions for large rallies and pledges of support. During the field work for the present volume, President Balaguer twice officially visited Constanza; on each occasion, large numbers of people from the countryside congregated in the *pueblo*, although it was said by many that the visits drew far fewer people than had those of Trujillo. The first visit was on Sunday, June 25, 1967, when truckloads of *campesinos* from all sections of the *municipio* were brought to the park, where they stood listening to speeches while waiting for the arrival of the President. On this occasion, there were only two groups clearly discernible: the well-dressed *gente importante*, for whom chairs had been provided behind the President's dais, and the rest, who stood in a hollow square held in line by large numbers of armed police and soldiers. Many of those standing to the sides on the President's left and right were townspeople, however; those at the far end facing the dais were mostly *campesinos*, a number of whom bore signs welcoming President Balaguer in the name of their particular sections. A second visit in April 1968, when the President opened the newly renovated hospital and a new market, drew a smaller number of people, the same types of groupings were discernible and it was largely the same individuals who were in the place of honor. On this occasion, the *pueblo* dwellers crowded closest to the dais and the *campesinos* stood behind, again a number of them bearing signs of welcome.

On both of these visits, the form of the speeches and the reactions of the crowd were much the same. On neither occasion did the President himself speak; others, most of whom were local party officials, stood before him and spoke of the accomplishments of the government and the benefits Constanza was deriving and would enjoy in the future. During and at the conclusion of each speech, "vivas" were called for in the name of the President, and sometimes for the Vice-President and for the Reformista Party as well. Each time the crowd responded enthusiastically by shouting "Viva!" and then applauding.

After both of these visits, the President and his party had lunch; a number of those who had been seated on or behind the dais were part of this group. On the second visit, the lunch was held at the home of Sr. Raóul Espiallat. While the President was inside the house, a large crowd of *campesinos* and *pueblo* dwellers assembled outside. Most of them were extremely poor and were waiting there in the hope of meeting the President and making requests of him. Pieces of paper on which to write petitions were distributed among the crowd; these were then handed to the armed guards on duty outside the door of the house. This was of little help to the many who could not write, and there was some bitterness after the President had departed. One illiterate *campesino* woman believed that the whole thing were merely a trick to prevent them from reaching the President. It is not known whether any of these petitions were responded to or whether they even reached the President.

Earlier in the chapter, a description was given of Three Kings' Day, when *los ricos* distributed gifts to the poor children of the *pueblo*. Behavior not unlike this was also observed at a large *fiesta* when the Spanish Club was officially opened. On this occasion, the roadway across from the Spanish Club had been blocked off with intertwined palm leaves to enlarge the facilities; the Spaniards sat at tables in the club and in the enclosed area. Many children of *los pobres* gathered outside and peered through the leaves to watch the Spaniards making merry; a number thrust their hands through the leaves, begging food from the tables. Some food was given; more and more hands appeared, and as those outside became more excited, the noise grew. Finally, they were chased away.

At every *fiesta* that is held in one of the bars or in the casino, many children and young people who are of *los pobres* assemble outside to watch, and at times people have to push through the crowd of spectators to enter. But not infrequently some who stand outside are asked in by someone able to pay their admission; a number of the girls who go as spectators wear their best clothes and wait in this hope.

Any *fiesta* in the pueblo reveals two broad groups: (1) those who regularly attend; most of the men wear suits or at least are well dressed; and (2) a much larger group of those who do not attend and either stay at home or merely come to watch. Among young men, the line between attenders and nonattenders is more clearly drawn than it is among the girls. *Peones* and town workers are always among the non-attenders. As a rule, they do not come as spectators, although some of their children may do so.

CHAPTER 6

The Life Cycle

Redfield has suggested that one way in which the community may be conceived as a whole is in terms of a typical or generalized biography: ". . . the human career characteristic of the community."[1] Such a generalized biography ". . . would tell something of what people think ought to happen, of what they expect to happen and of what actually happens."[2]

This chapter presents a generalized account of the life cycle but, as will be pointed out, the experiences considered normal or typical by some are not shared by significant numbers of *constanceros*. In fact, the incidence of departures from the normal that create differing expectations for different people provides one index for the broad social groupings that have been delineated.

CHILDHOOD

The life stages of most individuals are clearly demarcated by the ceremonial events one traditionally finds in a culture with a strong Spanish background. Within a year of a child's birth, following a religious ceremony, the *bautismo* (baptism) is celebrated in the parents' home. The baby is dressed in good clothes and is brought out to be admired. At this celebration, friends and relatives will usually sit down at the table and consume an enormous quantity of food. Before and after the meal, a good deal of rum is drunk, and there is also dancing—principally the *merengue*, which is extremely popular in all circles.

After the *bautismo*, children may have birthday parties to which others are invited, but the celebration of each successive birthday is more common among *los ricos* of the *pueblo* and is comparatively rare among *campesinos*. Birthday parties are also occasionally cele-

---

[1] Robert Redfield, *The Little Community* (Chicago: The University of Chicago Press, 1955), p. 53.

[2] *Ibid.*, p. 59.

The mother of a poor *campesino* family preparing a meal in the kitchen. Cooking is done on the floor.

Campesinos gambling during a *fiesta* in the *campo.*

Buying meat in the *pueblo*.

brated by teenagers, rich and poor alike, although this is more usual for girls than for boys. A girl's fifteenth birthday is considered particularly significant and generally will be marked in some way.[3]

A birthday party for a young child appears to be organized as much for the benefit of adults as for the child. The more lavish the party and, in particular, the more expensive the cake, the more favorable will be the comments.

At one typical birthday party held in the home of a moderately-well-off agriculturalist, the three-year-old child had a few brief moments of glory when she was stood on a table to be better seen by the large crowd of guests. The child's new dress was greatly admired, as was a tall pink party hat the little girl was made to wear. There was one short party game organized for the little children; the afternoon was then taken over by teenagers, who danced the *merengue* to recorded music. Generally at birthday parties for young children, there are no organized activities of any kind except a lucky number prize (tickets bearing numbers are distributed among the guests) and a game in which a heavily wrapped parcel is passed from hand to hand; the child who removes the last piece of wrapping gains the present it contains. Balloons and small toys are distributed among the children but almost invariably there are not enough to go around and it is the youngest children who are more likely to miss out.

Children of all ages attend birthday parties. Mothers who come frequently sit with their children; the men of the house and their friends sit on the front porch and drink rum. Usually there are also a number of uninvited poor children who stand outside the doors and watch the proceedings within. Frequently these children are given food; some may be lucky enough to be given balloons or some of the toys.

When it is time to leave, the cake is cut and pieces distributed among the guests to be taken home. The cake is not eaten at the party. At the party mentioned above, the cake was an elaborately decorated affair made in the shape of a violin; at another party the cake was in the form of a sailing ship, and on another occasion, at a party held in one of the bars for a fifteen-year-old girl, it was an enormous three-tiered structure like a wedding cake. These cakes are generally purchased in the capital and cost anything up

---

[3] A girl who lived with her elderly mother in a hovel on the outskirts of the *pueblo* very much wanted to celebrate her fifteenth birthday by holding a party. When arrangements to hold the party in the home of one of her friends broke down, the celebration took the form of distributing pieces of birthday cake among her friends.

TABLE 2
ENROLLMENTS AND PUPILS WHO PASSED IN PRIMARY RURAL SCHOOLS, 1965–66 AND 1966–67

Grade	I Boys	I Girls	II Boys	II Girls	III Boys	III Girls	IV Boys	IV Girls	V Boys	V Girls	VI Boys	VI Girls
1965–66												
Enrolled	617	547	301	294	158	145	99	64	20	11	12	5
Passed	356	302	192	190	111	103	72	60	15	5	11	5
1966–67												
Enrolled	829	658	363	309	148	170	96	68	20	18	8	4
Passed	451	419	213	205	119	121	73	55	14	12	9	2

Source: District Inspectorate of Education, Constanza.

Note: In Tables 2, 3, and 4, enrollment figures are those recorded for each grade at the beginning of the school year. The numbers of those who passed are taken at the end of the school year and these pupils are eligible for promotion to the next grade. Pupils who do not pass either repeat the grade or leave school.

TABLE 3
ENROLLMENTS AND PUPILS WHO PASSED IN THE URBAN PRIMARY SCHOOL AND COLEGIO, 1966–67

Grade	I Boys	I Girls	II Boys	II Girls	III Boys	III Girls	IV Boys	IV Girls	V Boys	V Girls	VI Boys	VI Girls
Urban primary												
Enrolled	124	106	50	43	22	40	38	38	43	28	30	12
Passed	61	54	47	42	16	36	26	29	35	21	19	9
Colegio												
Enrolled	33	59	12	37	4	19	5	18	7	9	8	16
Passed	17	29	10	31	3	13	4	14	0	0	5	9
Total												
Enrolled	157	165	62	80	26	59	43	56	50	37	38	28
Passed	78	83	57	73	19	49	30	43	35	21	24	18

Source: District Inspectorate of Education, Constanza. Figures for 1965–66 were not available for these schools.

to RD $80. At birthday parties and weddings the cake is the object of much admiration; its cost is always known to the company and is a topic of conversation. There is also much interest in the presents that are brought on these occasions; although they are generally not opened until after the guests have departed, it is always carefully noted who brought what and comparisons are made.

Children may commence school when they are six. If the parents live in or near the *pueblo* and are able to afford the cost, the child is enrolled at the Roman Catholic *colegio* rather than in the public schools, which are considered extremely poor.[4] Having one's children attend the *colegio* clearly confers status, but at the seventh and eighth grade level this is only so in the case of girls. After sixth grade, boys generally transfer to the public intermediate school, where discipline is extremely lax and there is little pressure to study.

Those wishing to pursue schooling beyond eighth grade enroll in the *pueblo* high school, which has classes in the evenings. After four years of high school, students who graduate may apply for university entrance. Very few indeed carry their education to this level, and there is little incentive to do so.[5] Education beyond the primary level does not ensure a job, although to obtain a post as a clerk in certain government offices or to become a primary school teacher, an eighth grade education is supposedly required. Those who continue their education beyond sixth grade will usually try to obtain an eighth grade certificate. For the most part, these are the children of businessmen, professionals, or bigger agriculturalists who live in the *pueblo*.

Education is not highly valued by most *constanceros;* as Tables 2, 3, and 4 reveal, relatively few spend more than a few years in school. The effect of what little schooling these children have is to make them barely literate. Even those of greatest wealth and importance in the town see little point in carrying education beyond the eighth grade. Other than the few professionals, none of these

---

[4] Fees at the *colegio* are only RD $2 per month but, unlike the public schools, all books and stationary must be purchased and parents must also provide a school uniform. A number of the children have scholarships and pay no fees; at the intermediate level (grades seven and eight), fees for these children are paid by the state. Books and uniforms must still be provided by parents, however.

[5] The high school in Constanza only began graduating students in 1964; prior to that date, it was necessary for students to travel to La Vega for further schooling. In 1967, six students graduated from the high school. One of these has secured a position as a teacher, but the other five are still unemployed and are living in the *pueblo*. Thus far, Constanza has produced two university graduates; five are currently attending university.

TABLE 4

ENROLLMENTS AND PUPILS WHO PASSED IN THE PUBLIC
INTERMEDIATE AND COLEGIO INTERMEDIATE
GRADES, 1966–67

Grade	VII		VIII	
	Boys	Girls	Boys	Girls
Public Intermediate				
Enrolled	18	17	22	18
Passed	18	16	13	16
Colegio				
Enrolled	1	13	3	12
Passed	1	9	3	12
Total				
Enrolled	19	30	25	30
Passed	19	25	16	28

Source: District Inspectorate of Education, Constanza.
Figures for 1935–66 were not available for these schools.

men has any great pretension to education. They made their way
in the world through business acumen and influential contacts, and
the future of their own children is more or less assured. Most of
the foreigners, it should be added, are concerned about education.
Generally, their children are sent to the *colegio*.

Both the *colegio* and the *pueblo* public school have an annual
graduation day, when the pupils graduating from sixth and eighth
grades are presented with certificates. The *colegio* also includes the
second graders in this ceremony. The graduations for each school are
held on different days; it is very clear that only that of the *colegio*
ranks as an important event in the community.

The *colegio* graduation is held in the evening and involves a
procession of the graduates, led by the town band, from the school
to the *palacio*. Many stand in the street to watch the procession
and then crowd to the *palacio* to see the certificates being presented.[6]

This function draws together most of the important people of
the town as well as a large crowd of spectators, who are also from

---

[6] The girls of each grade dress distinctively. The sixth grade girls wear blue,
and the eighth grade girls wear white dresses and mortarboards; each girl carries
a posy of red roses. Boys dress in dark blue trousers and white shirts, and
all wear neckties.

Each boy is accompanied by his *madrina* and each girl by her *padrino*; it
is the duty of these people to present the certificate to the graduate when
called upon to do so. Many of the *madrinas* and *padrinos* of the sixth and
eighth grade pupils are adult freinds or close acquaintances of the family who
were chosen for this occasion only. Older children serve as *madrinas* or *padrinos*
for the second grade children

the *pueblo*. The public school function, on the other hand, is considerably less formal and arouses little interest. Other than certain public officials who are directly concerned in the proceedings, few individuals of importance bother to attend.

COURTSHIP AND MARRIAGE

Courtship for the female may begin at a very young age; some girls of respectable families have married at fifteen, although this is considered very young. Boys and girls become attracted to each other through casual encounters in the park or in the bars and then make arrangements to meet primarily by means of letters or messages sent through friends. Meetings generally occur in the company of others or at least under the watchful eye of a third party, who is not necessarily within earshot. The formal announcement of the *compromiso* (engagement) is usually made at a party. A ring is given and the date of the wedding is decided. Prior to the wedding, the *novia* (fiancee) may have a kitchen tea and the *novio* (fiance) a bachelor's party.

The wedding is supposedly a solemn affair involving a procession down the aisle, with the chief actors taking up clearly defined positions.[7] After the ceremony, there is a feast, which is usually held in the home of the *novia*. A wedding cake is provided and there is much eating and drinking. The couple then leaves for the honeymoon, if they can afford one and, in due course, takes up residence in their new home.

All this represents the ideal; for many, the reality bears little resemblance. It is every girl's ambition to be married in the church, for such a wedding will give her not only a greater degree of legal protection, but will also confer status.[8] Many, however, must be

---

[7] The wedding of one young informant was anything but a solemn occasion, although it was clearly so to the young couple concerned. No one seemed very clear as to where they were to stand. Throughout the service, guests and many others who had entered the church merely to watch crowded around the bridal party, making a good deal of noise. Once the priest called for silence, and later interrupted the service a second time to order mothers with crying babies to leave.

[8] A church wedding indicates that the young man is "serious" and a good Catholic. The couple thus begins married life with some status in the community and with the thorough approval of the girl's family. Because they fear the marriage may prove unsatisfactory, however, many young men even of respectable families prefer a civil ceremony only. For those with few resources, the cost of a church wedding is also a deterrent, for in addition to the fee for the priest, a wedding feast be provided. If the religious ceremony is deferred until some time after the couple has been living together (whether legally as man and wife or in a concubinage relationship), no wedding feast is held and the fee charged by the priest is less, or there may be no fee at all.

satisfied with a civil ceremony only, in which case divorce is a relatively simple matter for the man and not at all uncommon. For the majority, there is no marriage but only a concubinage relationship to look forward to, and the likely prospect of eventual desertion when the man finds someone more attractive or when the responsibilities of maintaining the woman and children become too burdensome. Many women whose marriages survive without divorce also must face the likelihood that their husbands will drift into semi-permanent relationships with other women and father a number of illegitimate children.

Divorce laws heavily favor men and there is little open criticism of men who father illegitimate children. No girl, however, can afford the suggestion of scandal without her chances for matrimony being seriously ruined.[9] The unwed mother has the legal right to sue for maintenance of the children until they are eighteen and many do receive some degree of support without going to court, but the children have no claim on the estate of their father and may not bear his name unless he bestows legal recognition on them.[10] The women in these cases have no rights whatsoever. There is no legal status for a common-law wife; such a woman may be thrust aside at any stage of her life and left to fend for herself. This appears to be a fairly common occurrence and, in particular, is characteristic of the people *sin vergüenza*.

The men of this grouping are condemned not because they have illegitimate children and do not marry but because they generally fail to establish permanent families and therefore do not enjoy the status of *padre de familia*, father or head of a family. This status only accrues to the man who resides more or less permanently

---

[9] It is not considered scandalous to live with a man in a state of concubinage (although the daughter of a respectable family would not do so), for this is a recognized and frequently enduring relationship, and one that often leads to marriage. It is particularly common in the *campo* for couples who have been living together for many years and who may even have grown children to decide to marry; at times, when the priests visit particular areas of the *campo*, they encourage such couples to marry in a common ceremony.

Even if the couple part company, the fact that the woman has lived with a man does not spoil her chances of finding someone else or even of marrying, provided she is still attractive and is not burdened with many children. A girl who is often seen in the bar or who goes out unchaperoned with a succession of boys, however, easily acquires a reputation and consequently has little chance of marrying.

[10] This is carried out in the Civil Office for a fee of RD $1.50 for each child to whom recognition is granted. A child who is not recognized takes the surname of the mother, but in some cases the father's name may be placed after that of the mother.

in the household, who is acknowledged as its head, and who takes responsibility for the welfare of its members. Among those *sin vergüenza*, serial polygyny is the norm; throughout his life, the male will live with a succession of women and may father a number of children without taking clear responsibility for any of these. The attitude of the male toward the relationship is similar to that of Trinidadian negroes described by Freilich; it is a "now-for-now affair" and considered temporary and not for life.[11] Also, as was noted in an earlier context, these men frequently get drunk and quarrel among themselves and openly consort with the prostitutes who live in the town. Some of them live with these women and share their earnings. Nevertheless, these unions cannot be considered as "casual mating" in the sense of ". . . a sexual congress without co-habitation or any intention for forming a permanent relationship."[12] Co-habitation is involved and although such unions tend to be of a transitory nature, some of them do endure for a number of years.

At the other extreme are the respectable people who are legally married and may also have married in the church. Among these people, reputation is important and, although the men may maintain mistresses[13] within or outside the community and have illegitimate children, they are circumspect in their behavior and never openly live in concubinage. Don Alejandro, for example, has six children by his present wife, to whom he is legally married. By his first wife, from whom he is divorced, he has several others. This woman, who is not of Constanza, lives elsewhere and is supported by one of her married sons, not by don Alejandro. In turn, this married

---

[11] Morris Freilich, "Serial Polygyny, Negro Peasants, and Model Analyses," *American Anthropologist, 63* (1961):961.

[12] Edith Clarke, *My Mother Who Fathered Me* (London: George Allen and Unwin Ltd., 1957), p. 30.

[13] Whitten, in discussing polygyny among Negroes of San Lorenzo in northwest Ecuador, uses the term "wife" rather than "mistress" for secondary unions. He states: ". . . a man is considered to have two wives when (1) both women share his life chances and style of life; (2) both unions have semi-permanent status in the eyes of the parties concerned and of the community; and (3) others in the community, as well as the man and his wives, regard both relationships as marriage." Norman E. Whitten, Jr., *Class, Kinship, and Power in an Ecuadorian Town* (Stanford: Stanford University Press, 1965), pp. 126–127, footnote.

In Constanza, for the relationship being described, although the second condition may be said to apply, the first and third do not. In the dry farming areas, however, where instances of multiple concubinage are found, all three conditions apply; here one may well legitimately refer to these women as wives and not as mistresses.

son has a child in the *pueblo* by another woman. Neither she nor the child is supported by this man, but she does receive periodic gifts of food, money, and clothing from don Alejandro's present wife. Don Alejandro is said to have a mistress in the *pueblo* and probably has other women in the capital, which he visits a great deal. He is discreet about his affairs, however, and, like others in the *pueblo* who are counted among the respectable, does not publicly flout conventions.

Juan Conde, on the other hand, the owner of a medium-sized store, who was mentioned in Chapter 4, is not counted among the respectable, but neither does he belong to the people *sin vergüenza*. Juan has eleven children by three women, none of whom he has married, although one of the women has since married another man. He has been living with Elena, his present *mujer*,[14] who is also his parallel cousin,[15] for eleven years, and at one time confided to me that he thought he might marry her because she managed the household very efficiently and was also a considerable help in his business. Subsequently, strains in the relationship became evident and it is not at all unlikely that Juan may drift into a semi-permanent relationship with another woman. He has already given recognition to the six children he has had by Elena, however. Even if he were to have further children by another woman, it is the children of Elena whom he would be bound to support and who would have first claim on his loyalty.

The fact that their children are illegitimate is of little concern to Juan Conde and his *mujer*, or, indeed, to the children themselves. Among the majority of *constanceros* of both town and country, living in concubinage and having illegitimate children is not immoral, notwithstanding the exhortations of the priests to marry. Rather,

---

[14] The term *mujer* (woman or wife), like *señora*, is commonly used by all *constanceros* when referring to their women, whether they be married or not. The terms *esposo* (husband) and *esposa* (wife) are used only by those who are actually married.

[15] Civil marriages and concubinage relationships between cousins are common, although more so in the *campo*, where children of related families grow up together, than in the *pueblo*, where relatives have less contact. Such marriages and relationships also meet with less approval in the *pueblo* than among *campesinos*. The attitude toward cousin marriage in Constanza appears to be similar to that described by Eric Wolf for San José, in Puerto Rico. Eric R. Wolf, "Subcultures of a Traditional Coffee Municipality," in Julian H. Steward, ed., *The People of Puerto Rico* (Urbana: The University of Illinois Press, 1956), p. 221.

The priests in Constanza say that they do not perform marriages between cousins because permission must be sought from Rome, and this is rarely given. Others say that the priests will perform such a marriage but for a price that is beyond the reach of most.

as suggested by Mintz in discussing the persistence of such unions among the lower classes of Cañamelar, it is a form of behavior that to the participants is no more immoral than butchering animals without a licence or taking part in the illegal lotteries.[16] In engaging in such behavior, questions of morality do not arise.

Juan takes no responsibility for the other children he has fathered and contributes nothing to their support. This, in fact, is the norm for most *constanceros* of the *pueblo*. Once a man ceases to maintain a relationship with a women, there is no clearly felt obligation to provide for her support or for that of the children, unless they are legitimately born or have been granted recognition. The women in these cases more often than not are left with the children and generally must rely upon their own resources or look to their families for support. It is customary, however, that the man leave the woman the house in which they lived together.

In the irrigated valleys, wealthier families who exercise influence are generally married. Among others in the *campo*, concubinage is clearly perferred by men, and, in some cases, is defended by women, who point out the advantage of a relationship that can be broken off with relative ease should serious differences arise. It is significant, however, that when a daughter of those who themselves are living in concubinage elopes and begins to live with a young man, there is great distress on the part of the parents and bitter denunciations of the girl, the young man, and his family. Pressure is placed on the man to force him to marry the girl but, should it become clear that the couple is determined to stay together without marrying, the relationship is generally accepted.

The form of concubinage of which Juan Conde and Elena are representative is perhaps best described as "purposive," ". . . a result of a free and deliberate selective process, a man and woman decide to test their compatibility with a view to spending the rest of their lives together."[17] Should the relationship break down, however, it is easier for a woman in the *campo* to rely on her kin for support than it is for most of those in the *pueblo*. Further, many *campesino* women have land or will someday inherit land, small though the quantity may be, and therefore enjoy a certain degree of economic independence. Under these circumstances it is not uncommon for the woman to expel the man should he prove unfaithful or fail to contribute adequately to the upkeep of the household.

---

[16] Sidney W. Mintz, "Cañamelar: The Subculture of a Rural Sugar Plantation Proletariat," in Julian H. Steward, ed., *The People of Puerto Rico*, p. 377.

[17] Edith Clarke, *My Mother Who Fathered Me*, p. 10.

Such a thing rarely occurs in the *pueblo* except among the *barrio* and fringe dwellers, where the woman may, at times, be contributing more to the upkeep of the household than the man is.

In the dry farming areas, it is common for some of the better-off *campesinos* to maintain several households at the same time, and recognition may be granted to the children of more than one woman. Ramón Ornes in El Limoncito, for instance, has four women living in small houses in the surrounding area, in addition to the woman he clearly recognizes as his wife and with whom he has lived for many years. His children by this woman have been granted recognition, as have those of one of the other women. Ramón, who is a man in his early sixties, visits all of these women as well as one other woman in the *pueblo* and another woman outside Constanza. In all, he appears to have some 28 children (he is uncertain of the exact number) and thus far has recognized twelve of these. As mentioned above, most of the residents of Los Corralitos are descendents of the original settler in the area, who had some thirty children and granted recognition to fifteen of these. Those who gained recognition were the children of mothers who lived in the area and had regular contact. There are stories concerning *campesinos* who have more than one woman within the same house,[18] but this is considered highly aberrant and there is probably little truth in most of these accounts.

It appears that multiple concubinage, which is now largely confined to a number of the better-off *campesinos* in the dry farming areas, is less general than in previous years. Whether or not recognition is granted to the children of more than one *mujer*, it is expected that the father will provide for these women and their children by leaving a house and a *parcela* of land to each one. Today, unlike earlier years when there was a greater abundance of land, relatively few *campesinos* are in a position to provide for their women in this way. It is this factor, in particular, that would seem to account for the decline in the numbers practicing this form of concubinage.

Ramón Ornes and many others attribute their interest in having a number of women to "the blood," and say it is because the French influence in them is strong. This, in fact, is popularly believed.

---

[18] Don Alejandro and some other *pueblo* men told of a certain *campesino* who at one time supposedly had three women living permanently in his home and he customarily slept with all three in the same bed. This, they thought, was bad enough; to make it worse, the women were black!

These men were unable (or unwilling) to name anyone in the community at the present time who kept more than one mistress in a single house.

Others attribute it to the influence of the Spanish *conquistadores* and their casual ways with women. Juan Conde also attributes it to "the blood" but, in his own case, believes he has the vigorousness of his father, who was Lebanese and had fifty children by six different women. His own large family is a source of pride and he boasts that he expects to have several more children before he loses "his strength." Elena is less than enthusiastic.

ESTABLISHING A HOME

Whether a couple is married or living in concubinage, they prefer to rent or build a house rather than live with relatives. Couples in the *campo* who have land or who are lent land by the man's father or by his father-in-law usually build a house on this land close to the home of the parents concerned. It is considered desirable that married children should live nearby in this way; only when there is insufficient land will they move elsewhere. Friction between the husband's mother and the daughter-in-law is very common; if the couple has a choice, matrilocality is preferred. In the *pueblo*, too, it is preferred that the married sons and daughters live close to the parents, and this is sometimes the situation.

Those without land who rely entirely on day labor generally rent or build a shack on the fringes of the *pueblo*. Such a dwelling can be built for as little as RD $100 or rented for RD $5 or so a month. Others who have regular employment, as well as many agriculturalists, rent or buy houses in the town. Rents range from RD $10 per month for an unpainted timber house of two rooms with a cement floor, to RD $40 for a modern, five-room cement house with indoor kitchen and sanitation. Costs of building such houses range from RD $200 to RD $6,000 or more.

If there has been a church wedding, the average couple will begin life saddled with a heavy debt. The parents of the *novia* customarily bear the main cost of the wedding but the young man will have heavy costs. When Tulio Moya, a government clerk earning RD $80 a month, became married, his new suit cost RD $50, the fee for the priest was RD $15, and furnishing the house cost RD $120. Tulio pays RD $15 a month rent and claims to spend RD $56.90 a month on food, clothing, and other essential items. He hopes one day to own a house and a television set and to send his children to the *colegio*. His wife is now expecting a baby; if she goes to the clinic for attention and the delivery, as she intends to do, the cost will be RD $50. Tulio and his wife hope to limit

TABLE 5

BIRTHS AND DEATHS IN CONSTANZA, 1963

Stillborn	Live births	Total number of deaths	Deaths under age of 1 year	Deaths between ages 1 and 4 years
34	1,101	214	69	75

Source: Oficina Nacional de Estadisticaș, Santo Domingo, República Dominicana.

the size of their family and are interested in contraception, but have little understanding of what is involved.[19]

Many people are less fortunately placed than Tulio and his wife, as has been indicated in the section on economic life. There is frequently insufficient food to eat and there is much undernourishment and sickness; infant mortality is extremely high, as the figures in Table 5 indicate.

For the poor, the death of a baby is sometimes a blessing and not at all unexpected. Some of the poor with very large families even have difficulty recalling how many of their children died in infancy. All the doctors live in the *pueblo;* although free care is available at the hospital and doctors will generally treat a sick child who is brought to them without charge, most medicines must be bought at the pharmacy and paid for immediately. In the poorest of homes, a sick baby will be treated with various herbal remedies or by a curer who often relies on recited charms; there will also be prayers and vows made to the saints. If none of these proves

---

[19] Many Constanza women are interested in contraception, but there is little understanding of the means available and there is confusion over the Church stand on the matter. Shortly before he married, Tulio spoke to one of the priests about contraception and was told that artificial means may be used by couples who are unable to provide for children, but that the pills were damaging to the health of the woman, and could cause permanent harm to the child. A woman, the mother of five children, claimed to have been given permission to use contraception; others say that contraceptives may be used only for three years following the birth of each child. There is, in fact, a good deal of uncertainty as to what is and what is not permitted by the Church, but it is evident that irrespective of the Church's views, many women use a variety of means to prevent conception.

The pill is available in chemist shops but is expensive (RD $2 for a month's supply) and also popularly believed to cause sickness. Many women take a herbal tea two times daily; this, it is said, will prevent conception. Others only take the tea following intercourse to clean out the uterus. A variety of means are used to induce abortion.

to be effective, the baby will be taken to the doctor.[20] It is said that parents generally make every endeavor to save the life of a child, but doctors complain that frequently a sick child is not brought for attention until it is on the point of death.

The death of a baptized child under seven years of age is not considered a tragedy because the child goes straight to heaven, where it becomes an angel. If the child was not baptized, it stays forever in limbo, but when an unbaptized child becomes sick, parents will try to have the rite performed in case the child should die. For the child older than seven, some people are in doubt as to whether it goes straight to heaven. For those of thirteen years and above, the cycle of mourning is the same as that for an adult. The death of a young child is a cause for grief, but the grief is clearly mitigated by the firmness of the belief in the assured fate of the child's soul.

Rich or poor, all parents will seek out godparents for their children and, in some cases, will endeavor to form this relationship with a person of higher standing than themselves. All *constanceros* insist that the relationship has little importance, and it is true that the formal duties of the *padrino* are few.[21] The relationship created among the *compadres*, however, is of considerable importance, as will be shown in Chapter 7.

If a couple is living in concubinage, the birth of the first child

---

[20] Reliance upon herbal remedies and recited cures and various charms that are worn is greater in the *campo* than in the *pueblo;* this is also true of beliefs in witchcraft and magic.

Constanceros in both town and country who are more sophisticated belittle these beliefs and practices, but all *constanceros*, it seems, are highly superstitious and believe in lucky and unlucky numbers and omens. It should be added also that many appear to have an almost magical belief in the curative value of any medicine purchased at the pharmacy, and there is particular faith in injections, which are commonly given in the home by a neighbor, and in vitamin pills. One mother, whose child was dying of what appeared to be malnutrition and jaundice, came to my house begging money to buy vitamin pills for the child. She firmly believed that if these were given to the child, it would live. The pills were given but the child died a few days later.

[21] *Padrinos* are chosen before or after the birth of a child and are then expected to sponsor the child when he is baptized in the church. This involves payment of a fee to the priest (RD $1.50); it is customary that a small gift be given to the child on this occasion and thereafter on each Three Kings' Day. Should the child die before his second birthday, the *padrino* will provide the coffin and pay the cost of burial and also provide coffee for the mourners. Apart from this, there are few other duties of any importance for the *padrino* to perform in relation to the child.

Different persons may be chosen as *padrinos* at the time of confirmation and graduation, but this is more common among the upper class of the *pueblo*. *Padrinos* chosen for these special occasions incur no lasting obligations to the child or to the parents.

is considered to formalize the arrangement and, to an extent, this is so for married couples as well. It is considered strange, in fact, if a baby does not arrive within a year or so; even couples like Tulio Moya and his wife, who hope to plan their family, do not seek to delay the arrival of the first child.[22] Couples prefer that the first child be a son, but thereafter daughters are equally desired. Having many sons is considered to reflect favorably on the father's virility; among *campesinos* and agriculturalists, sons are desired for the contribution they make to the work force. Today, however, with smaller holdings, this is less a factor than previously; only on large *parcelas* could it be said that having many sons continues to be a worthwhile economic investment. In those cases in the *campo* where multiple households are maintained, the fact that the labor of all one's sons may be utilized no doubt partly explains the greater willingness to extend recognition to children of women other than one's principal *mujer*.

OLD AGE

The aged are treated with respect and courtesy but, if they are dependent upon others for their support, they are expected to contribute as best they can. Idleness is not considered to be the natural prerogative of the old.

Responsibility for the care of the aged is taken as a matter of course, and it is probably true to say that an elderly relative is never abandoned. Nevertheless, caring for an aged relative is a duty that many will seek to avoid and one frequently hears complaints from people who are so burdened because others of the family have not done their part. An elderly relative who can do little to earn his keep will be treated with a good deal of tolerance but,

---

[22] Even though the arrival of the first child is looked forward to, all but the most sophisticated women of the *pueblo* seek to disguise pregnancy as long as possible and tell only the husband and perhaps a few close friends. In particular, the woman seeks to hide the knowledge from her own mother.

Following childbirth, which takes place either in the clinic, for those who can afford the cost, or in the home, in which case the woman is attended by an untrained midwife, the mother passes forty days of virtual inactivity. During this time, relatives or friends take charge of the house and attend to most of the housework. The husband may not resume sexual relations until after the passing of this period; the woman observes a number of prohibitions, such as not washing the body and avoiding contact with cold air and certain foods. These prohibitions are more carefully observed by *campesino* women and those of the *pueblo* with little education. All Constanza women observe the forty days of inactivity as far as is possible, however.

in some households at least, in various ways that are not always subtle, he will be reminded of his dependent status.

Children are expected to "respect" their parents and care for them in their old age, but the keenness with which this obligation is felt depends very much upon the situation of the children when parents reach old age, and the form of the household in which the children grew up. Many adults, for instance, speak reverently of their mother and contemptuously of the man who is their father but who abandoned their mother in favor of another, leaving her largely to fend for herself. The father, in such cases, by ceasing to be primarily responsible for his own children, generally loses their affection and forfeits any claim he would otherwise have had for support in his old age.

The support of the mother, on the other hand, is almost a sacred duty and there is always a certainty that at least one of the children will take responsibility for her care. Generally this is the lot of an unmarried daughter, who may herself have children; the sons, if need be, will contribute money or food to her support.

DEATH AND MOURNING

When an elderly person is seriously ill and believed to be dying, relatives and friends are notified and the house is prepared for mourning. Much of the furniture is removed and chairs are placed in the largest room, where the main mourners are accommodated. A small altar with candles is built in the bedroom where the dying person lies; after death the corpse is placed in an open coffin in this room. The sons assemble around the bedside to hear the last advice;[23] a watch is maintained day and night to wait for the moment of death. It is most important that others be present when the moment of death arrives, for no one, it is believed, should die alone.

An individual's death brings together a wide circle of family and friends from the entire community. If the person was well known, many who have only a slight acquaintance with the deceased

---

[23] It is believed that a dying person speaks with special insight and advice given at such a time is ignored at one's peril.

The advice given to his sons by an elderly man who was dying was that those of them living in concubinage should marry and that they should confess their sins to the priest. The sons solemnly promised to heed his advice; shortly after, the old man died. It is not known whether any of the sons confessed his sins, but none of them took the step of marrying his *mujer*.

attend the funeral and probably put in at least one appearance at the home during the nine-day period of mourning.

Mourning behavior follows a clearly defined cycle. Burial usually takes place the day following death; the coffin is borne to the church[24] in a procession that is led by the town band if the family has some importance in the community. During the *misa del cuerpo presente*, the mass for the body, the band, which waits outside the church, is usually joined by a large crowd of spectators, who chatter noisily while waiting for the mourners to reappear. After the service, the band takes up its position once again and the procession moves to the cemetery, where the burial takes place.[25] More often than not, there is no graveside service, because this requires a further payment to the priest.

To an extent, the display of grief appears to be highly formalized. The last sight of the body before it is encased within the concrete tomb or covered with earth is invariably the occasion for an outburst of grief on the part of the women of the family, who are then led away by other mourners. The burial is followed by nine days of mourning; each evening during this period, friends and relatives gather at the home of the deceased to comfort the family and join in the prayers that are recited by the *rezador religioso*.[26] It is primarily the women who gather inside the house for the prayers; each new visitor is generally greeted with an outburst of weeping. For the most part, however, the women who were not closely related or intimate friends of the deceased show no particular grief or reverence during the prayers. Some carry on private con-

---

[24] At times, the procession moves directly to the cemetery for the burial; in this case, there is a requiem mass nine days later. If there has been a *misa del cuerpo presente*, the requiem mass generally does not take place.

[25] There are two main cemeteries, both owned by the municipality; one cemetery is opposite the Roman Catholic Church, where most burials are above the ground in concrete tombs; and another is outside the *pueblo* limits, where bodies are interred in graves. Rich and poor are buried in the town cemetery but only babies, very young children, and extremely poor persons who have few kin ties with other families are buried in the other. Protestants may be buried in either cemetery; there is no special section set aside for their use. A few areas of the *campo* have their own cemeteries but funerals held there are rarely attended by townspeople unless there is a clear family connection. Large numbers of *campesinos* will attend the funeral of any well-known town resident, however.

[26] These are women who are considered very religious and who specialize in saying prayers in return for payment. The priests say they disapprove of these women and have spoken against them because they have no religious training for their work and the prayers they recite are frequently erroneous. Nevertheless, they are employed on these occasions by all *constanceros* who are Roman Catholic.

A mother and child of La Zanja (the *pueblo's* main slum area).

Some impoverished *campesinos* live in distant parts of the *municipio* in comparative isolation.

Infant mortality among the poor is very high. Baptized children under seven years of age are believed to go straight to heaven, where they become little angels.

This elderly *pueblo* woman, abandoned by her husband and sons, is
dependent upon her daughter for support.

versations and at times others yawn and give every appearance of boredom.

On the night of the ninth day, a particularly large crowd gathers within and around the house. Prayers go on all night, but again it is primarily women who take part in these. The men gather in groups drinking coffee, which is always provided; some may drink rum. The mood of the crowd is not festive but neither is it particularly reverent. Conversation is general and people who have not met for a long time greet each other warmly. At one such gathering, there were also three venders of cigarettes and candy present; one group of men disappeared behind the house with a radio to listen to a baseball broadcast. No one seemed to think this was an unnatural way to behave.

For some members of the family and close friends, the main activity of this night is the preparation of a large wreath, a task that takes many hours. Early the next morning, the wreath is carried at the head of a procession to the church, where the requiem mass is held, and then to the cemetery, where it is placed on the grave. The mourners then return to the home, where they are fed and given coffee; later during the day, the front door of the house, which has remained closed since the time of death, is opened. This ends the nine-day period of mourning and the household resumes its normal activities. The women of the family, however, will wear black for periods varying from one to three years. On subsequent occasions, the family may pay for masses for the soul of the deceased; even poor families will try to have at least one mass said a year. On November 2, *el día de los defunctos*, masses are held throughout the day for the dead; large numbers of people go to the cemeteries, where they place flowers on the graves or tombs.

CHAPTER 7

Family Relationships and Interpersonal Relations

In describing concubinage, it was pointed out that except in the dry farming areas, where several households are sometimes openly maintained, most *constanceros* cohabit with only one woman at a time.

Among those *sin vergüenza*, serial polygyny is the norm, but of those of whom Juan Conde is representative, concubinage is "purposive" and typically, after what may be considered trial marriage with one or more successive women, leads to a permanent union with the male attaining the status of *padre de familia*. Recognition is granted to the children and, if either party has children by a previous union and these too are living in the household, recognition is generally granted to them also. Occasionally this does not happen, or recognition may be delayed for a number of years; sometimes within a household some of the children may have recognition and others not.

Respectable men always marry and do not live in concubinage. They are more circumspect in their behavior and seek to avoid scandal. Children they may have outside marriage are avoided, if not ignored, and fatherhood may even be denied. It is exceedingly rare that any of the children of such illicit unions are granted recognition or that any real concern is demonstrated for their future welfare.

In discussing economic life in the *campo*, it was pointed out that particularly in the dry farming areas, relationships are amicable; even in the irrigated valleys, where those of greater resources tend to restrict their recognition of kinsmen to exclude those who might otherwise be an economic burden, there is an absence of conflict among families. Family life shows greater stability than in the *pueblo*; part of the explanation for this lies in the fact that concubinage relationships in any one area are generally formed between members of families that, if not previously linked by ties of real or ritual kinship, more often than not were on terms of close acquaintanceship. Under these circumstances, a man cannot desert his *mujer* or eject her from the house without incurring the censure of her family; when couples do part company, it is usually by mutual consent.

In the *campo* where more than one household is maintained, there is a tendency for a man to grant recognition to his children other than those of the woman who is clearly recognized as his wife, particularly to those children who grow up in homes that are in close proximity. Among these children, relationships are generally amicable. In the *pueblo*, on the other hand, the restriction of recognition to the children of one woman and not of another partly explains the bitterness in family relationships that are characteristic of town life.

In dealing with Negro family organization in San Lorenzo, northwest Ecuador, Whitten has stressed the importance of "personal kindreds." These are Ego-oriented groups that include affinal and fictive kin and ". . . function significantly in child rearing, in economic activities, and in life crises rituals."[1] In the *campo* areas of Constanza, personal kindreds appear to function in much the same way as do those in northwest Ecuador. Moreover, poorer *constanceros*, like the Negroes of San Lorenzo, manifest the same desire to assert familial connections with influential kinsmen, but these kinsmen are frequently reluctant to recognize the connections and at times may deny that they exist.[2] Whitten also refers to the "stem kindred," a concept that is applicable to the wealthier families of *constanceros* who live in the *pueblo*. The stem kindred is defined as ". . . a corporately functioning, self-perpetuating kindred, united by consolidated socioeconomic interests and obligations [that] comes into being in the process of socioeconomic mobility."[3] In Constanza and in San Lorenzo, a family or group of relatives in the *pueblo*

---

[1] Norman E. Whitten, Jr., *Class, Kinship, and Power in an Ecuadorian Town*, p. 140.

[2] "A crucial feature of northwest Ecuadorian kinship structure is that men with status or economic advantage, or both, are more often included in the kindred a person recognizes than men without particular status or economic standing. As a result personal kindreds are easier to recognize from the reference point of an important Ego than from that of an unimportant one." *Ibid.*, pp. 139–140.

[3] *Ibid.*, p. 139. The concept of "stem kindred" employed by Whitten is that formulated by Davenport. See William Davenport, "Nonunilinear descent and descent groups," *American Anthropologist, 61* (1959):565.

that seeks to achieve wealth and status must necessarily sever relationships with those of the kindred who would otherwise be an economic burden, and consolidate relationships with a more restricted group, within which obligations for support will be mutually advantageous.

This chapter will examine relations and the processes of socialization within families, and then how relations are structured between families and individuals of the same and differing socioeconomic levels. In the final section of the chapter, there is a brief discussion of friendships and relationships among neighbors in the *pueblo*. In dealing with socialization and relationships within the family, the "domestic family" will be used as the point of reference.[4] All *constanceros* seem to share certain key values that stem from the manner in which relations are ordered within the household, and from the socialization process itself. This chapter will also discuss relations between families, with reference to Whitten's concept of stem kindreds and how these function in the community.

RELATIONS WITHIN THE DOMESTIC FAMILY

Dominican families tend to be large; those of Constanza are no exception. Particularly among poorer *campesinos*, a woman who has borne a child each year from the age of fifteen or sixteen, when she first conceived, is common. A number of these children die in infancy, and the mother is frequently vague as to the ages of her surviving children.

All those who live in the household take some part in the socialization of the child; particularly in the *campo*, the many visitors who casually move in and out of the home during the late afternoon and early evening also take part in this process. Those in the *campo* who have this close interaction with the domestic family are from

---

[4] The "domestic family" is defined as "a group of relatives and their dependents constituting one household . . . ." M. C. Smith, *West Indian Family Structure* (Seattle: University of Washington Press, 1962), p. 10.

It has already been indicated that membership of this unit may vary greatly among *constanceros* of different levels. In the course of a child's upbringing, some of the key members may change. Further, in describing the life cycle, it was shown that departures from the "normal" are sufficiently regularized as to provide differing expectations for those of different socioeconomic levels. Nevertheless, the range of typical experiences and motivations of *constanceros* who occupy the extreme levels of the socioeconomic hierarchy are not of such an order as to be mutually incomprehensible. This is so because of the common values and understandings all share.

the same locality and compose the personal kindred. Children, likewise, wander freely into the homes of their kindred at all hours, where they may be fed, and where frequently they may pass the night. Any of these adults may take it upon himself to admonish the child for wrong behavior, even in the presence of the child's own parents. *Constanceros,* however, are extremely tolerant of children and are accustomed to their presence and noise.

A baby in the household never wants for attention. If he cries, he is carried; throughout the day he is hugged, kissed, and fondled by those in the household and by visitors who stop by. The great interest shown in babies and very young children is shared equally by both sexes and by children of all ages. It is not at all uncommon to see young boys and men carrying a baby, particularly a baby girl, or kissing and hugging the infant in front of others without any sense of embarrassment.

Notwithstanding the extended group that closely interacts with the growing child, especially in the *campo,* certain individuals stand in special relationship to the child, and appropriate behavior toward these people is learned early in life. The child learns to recognize his godparents and to behave toward them with respect. He also learns to distinguish siblings from half-siblings who may be part of the domestic family and, in better-off homes where there is a child or young woman present in the capacity of a servant,[5] the behavior toward this person imitates that of older members of the family. In the *pueblo,* the attitude toward servants is generally one of contempt and distrust, and exploitation is severe.

Much of the day-to-day care of a young infant is left to an older sibling. Although brothers will play some part in this, it is generally the lot of a sister (or, in some families, a female child servant) to bear the responsibility. Girls as young as seven or eight appear to assume this child-minding role without complaint; unlike girls of wealthier *pueblo* homes, who may be attending the *colegio* or the high school and have more time for leisure, it is expected that they will pass most of the day in or near the home helping the mother with the housework and caring for the younger children. In later years, as was noted before, it is generally one of the daughters who will care for the mother in her old age, although sons too will provide help if called upon to do so.

In most homes it is evident that the mother is the figure most

---

[5] The use of children as servants is discussed later in the chapter. The employment of young women as servants is generally restricted to a number of *pueblo* homes where resources are greater.

held in affection by the children. Among many families of all levels where there is a constant *padre de familia*, it is clear that the father is deeply loved and respected, but he is also feared. Children are rarely thrashed, but it is not uncommon for fathers to assault their grown sons if they are still living in the household of which he is the head.[6] The father, in fact, is a very uncertain quantity and is prone to sudden rages and displays of violence. The mother's relationship to the children is nearly always a warm one. It is the mother who is with the children much of the day and attends to their wants. The father, on the other hand, frequently comes and goes as he pleases without explaining his movements. If he should go permanently, it is generally the mother and not the father who will have responsibility for the care of the children.

In his own eyes and in the view of the community, the *padre de familia* is the figure of supreme importance in the home. All members of the family seek to please him. His moods are catered to and his decisions, in theory, are final. The youngest children, particularly the daughters, generally have an easy relationship with the father; older sons wishing to make some request of him frequently use the mother as an intermediary. In matters of discipline, the mother is expected to side with the father (although this does not always occur); by her example and teaching, the children should learn respect for his position. From both parents and others in the household, and indeed, from all who contribute to the processes of socialization, the child learns *respecto*.[7] Should he not learn this, people will say that he was badly brought up (*malcriado*)—a condemnation that brings shame on all members of the family.

---

[6] In the *campo*, as sons become married and are established on separate *parcelas* of the father's land, it is more common that each work his *parcela* independently, although there is much cooperation among the sons and, when necessary, they combine labor for particular tasks. In the case of Ramón Ornes in El Limoncito, for example, control over the land has not been relinquished and the father continues to direct much of the labor of his married sons, even though each of them lives in a separate house. This is less common and there is a strong feeling, in fact, that when a man becomes a *padre de familia*, he should be master of his house and free to make his own decisions.

Most of the cases of violent father-and-son quarrels that came to notice occurred in the *pueblo*; the reason generally given for the quarrels was failure of the son to show "respect." What *constanceros* meant by respect is described later in this chapter.

[7] Manners' discussion of what is meant by *respecto* in Tabara, Puerto Rico, equally applies to Constanza. He notes that although the word may be loosely translated as "respect," "More properly, *respecto* may be described as behavior or response appropriate to one's age, sex, social and economic status and to the age, sex, social and economic status of others involved in any given situation

Even at the risk of making value judgments, it does strike one that Constanza men are emotionally immature; in large measure, this immaturity stems from the nature of the socialization of the male. Particular attention is lavished on little girls, but from the age when they can be helpful to their mothers, they are expected to be unobtrusive and dutiful. Boys, by contrast, are treated with extreme indulgence and, although they are encouraged to be helpful and are given praise when they accomplish difficult tasks, boys are expected to be rebellious and difficult. More often than not, adults give in to the demands of young children, but there is little consistency in their treatment of male children.

As in other cultures with a strong Mediterranean background, the *machismo* (masculinity) of the male is extremely important. In Constanza, this is expressed in a man's readiness to defend his honor (or that of his family or friends), in bragging and boastful talk, in behavior at the cockfight arena,[8] and in the admiration *constanceros* express for those they consider to be *muy macho* (very manly).[9]

Fathers like to see manliness in their sons; displays of aggression and rage appear to be taken as an indication of this quality, and are sometimes deliberately provoked. When a child goes too far, however, he may be accused of lacking "respect" and struck,

---

marking the interaction of two or more individuals." Robert A. Manners, "Tabara: Subcultures of a Tobacco and Mixed Crops Municipality," in Julian H. Steward, ed., *The People of Puerto Rico*, p. 144.

One who fails to behave as he should is said to lack respect (*falta de respecto*); in Constanza, this expression is commonly used of children when they are disobedient or defiant, and may be used of any adult who does not show to another the respect considered to be his due. Much more serious is the charge of being *sin vergüenza*, which was described earlier in the study.

As noted, *respecto* is primarily learned in the home. In Constanza homes, respect for the father's position as head of the house is instilled from the earliest years of a child's life. The fact that the father's position is an authoritative one from which power is not always exercised consistently may in part explain the readiness of most *constanceros* to accept authority and also their expectation that power will be used somewhat arbitrarily.

[8] Constanza men are immensely proud of their fighting cocks and identify closely with the birds' performances in the arena. The owner of a defeated bird that has fought badly may be ridiculed and insulted, and his humiliation is clearly evident.

[9] In expressing their admiration of Trujillo, many *constanceros* mention this quality, which he apparently had in large measure. Some also recount with great glee an incident that occurred some years ago when Trujillo visited the community and met the *síndico*. According to the story, Trujillo said to the man, "Who are you?" The man, who was supposedly overcome with fear, gave his name and added, "I'm the *síndico* here," whereupon Trujillo laughed at him and said, "You're nothing. You're a coward!"

or further ridiculed and insulted and made to feel completely impotent.

As sons grow older and desire greater independence, they become more difficult to discipline, and violent clashes with the father may occur. The *padre de familia* reserves the right to intervene in any aspect of his family's life. Father-and-son quarrels, especially in the *pueblo*, commonly occur over the company a son may keep, or the amount of drinking he may do, or the political opinions he may express.[10] Nevertheless, until a son leaves the house of his father and becomes a *padre de familia* himself, little responsibility is expected. In the *pueblo*, youths who come from homes where there is more money devote much of their time to amusement. Young men of *los pobres* and most of those in the *campo*, on the other hand, must work, but frequently do so only to earn sufficient money to spend on themselves; they contribute very little to the upkeep of the household. Most *constanceros* seem to feel that in the years before he becomes a *padre de familia* a young man should be free to do much as he pleases; he is not expected to become responsible and "serious" until that time.[11]

To obtain conformity from children, parents rely on threats and promises, sarcasm and ridicule. Threats are rarely carried out, and quite early in life the child learns to be equally skeptical of promises. Parents and others commonly make all manner of promises to the child that they do not feel bound to keep,[12] and they also lie and exaggerate to one another and to children as well.

---

[10] *Constanceros* of the older generation repeatedly say that one of the bad things about Juan Bosch was that he "turned father against son." These men feel strongly that the *padre de familia* should determine the party allegiance of all members of the family.

[11] This attitude undoubtably explains in part why boys tend to leave the *colegio* after sixth grade. In the *colegio*, the accent on discipline and study is difficult for Constanza youths to abide. Another factor is that all the classes are taught by women. Although there are female teachers at the *pueblo* schools, the schools are not run by women.

The belief that youth is a time of irresponsibility probably also partially accounts for the little interest taken in their studies by those who do pursue schooling beyond the elementary level; this appears to be almost as true of girls as of boys. Girls who continue schooling generally aspire to be teachers or "secretaries," both of which are considered to be very desirable occupations for *señoritas*. From the time of puberty, however, the principal preoccupation of girls is making themselves attractive to boys, and this clearly takes priority over attention to study.

[12] Most of the data on this point concern better-off *pueblo* families, although it is probable that making promises and breaking them is characteristic of all Constanza homes. In the *pueblo*, parents may promise children picnics, trips

Constanceros place little value on truth, and at an early age children learn to become adept liars. They also acquire expertise in the employment of ridicule and sarcasm.

Fighting is not approved of and antagonists, whether children or adults, are generally separated by others when blows are exchanged. Rather, there is a reliance upon abuse and name-calling, which always takes a highly personal tone. This is also true of ridicule against children. A child may be taunted because of his stupidity and lack of intelligence or even because of his physical appearance. When other children are doing the taunting, the poverty or reputation of the child's family may also be a subject for ridicule.

It was mentioned before that boys are sometimes provoked into displays of aggression. This is generally accomplished by teasing the child beyond the point of endurance, in which case he may attempt to strike out at the tormentor and be laughed at, or he may dissolve into tears and be called a "cry-baby." While they are very young, boys may respond to teasing with physical retaliation, but as they grow older, they resort only to verbal abuse. Girls too are teased, but from the age of three or four years, when serious teasing commences, girls are expected to learn to answer back, but to do so in an amusing way without becoming sarcastic. If girls do not learn to respond appropriately, disapproval is expressed.[13]

Within the domestic family, relations between siblings are generally harmonious, and sibling rivalry is not particularly evident. This is surprising in view of the frank way in which parents often appear to favor some children over others. In the many households where there are half-siblings present (whether or not all have recognition), a parent can be expected to favor his children of procreation over those acquired through marriage, and this often happens. Yet parents make realistic appraisals of all their children, seemingly with little regard to the sensitivity of the child; children thus become inured to having their strengths and weaknesses openly discussed in their presence. A little girl who is pretty will be repeatedly told so even in front of her less attractive sisters, and parents and other

---

to the capital, evenings at the cinema, and even birthday parties and then, sometimes at the last moment, fail to carry out these promises. It should also be added that physical punishments, which are often threatened without being carried out, are sometimes administered quite violently without warning for offences that at other times have incurred only admonition.

[13] A woman frequently attempted to tease my six-year-old daughter, but the child would only respond with sullen looks and walk away. The woman expressed sympathy and said it was a pity that the child "did not know how to play."

adults do not feel bound to think of compliments that can be made to other children in the household.[14]

A girl who is pretty has a better chance of attracting boys and of marrying well—a matter of no less concern to poor parents than to the girls themselves, whose heads seem to be filled with notions of romantic love. Physical appearance is of less importance in boys and young men. Rather, the importance of intelligence and ability is appreciated, for if the child has these qualities, he may grow up to be *muy astuto* (shrewd, astute)—a quality reckoned most important by *constanceros* because this marks a man out for success.

Astuteness, which develops with age and experience, is essentially a matter of knowing how to manipulate events and people to one's advantage. All the *gente importante* in the *pueblo* are said to be *muy astuto* and so, too, are those who through influence manage to obtain special favors, such as important jobs in government offices. Anyone, in fact, who clearly achieves material success and rises to a position of importance will be reckoned *muy astuto*. It is assumed that in achieving success influential contacts must have been exploited. No one, *constanceros* believe, ever achieves success on his merits alone.

RELATIONSHIPS BETWEEN FAMILIES

Within the household, there is a strong emphasis upon sharing. In the *campo*, where children grow up within the nexus of the personal kindred, constant sharing occurs among all the children who interact closely together.

The bonds established among siblings in the years of dependence are expected to endure for life. Any member of the family

---

[14] A well-off agriculturalist in the Valley introduced me to his two youngest sons and daughter. He embraced the little girl, calling her his "little *negrita*" and explained that she was his favorite but that it was a pity that she was so dark. Then he urged the child to go indoors to her mother and to stay out of the sun. The youngest son, of whom he was obviously also very proud, was said to be "very brave," always playing roughly and hurting himself and having to be washed several times a day. All this was in contrast to the other son, who seemed to have little in his favor at all. He was quiet and had *pelo malo* (bad hair, meaning that it was negroid), but it was possible he did have some intelligence. This was suggested without any great assurance, however.

On another occasion, when visiting a particular *campesino* home for the first time, thinking to please the mother, I admired her little daughter, who was sitting on the floor, and remarked that she was pretty. The mother seemed pleased enough but explained quite candidly that the child was very dark and had *pelo malo* and was not as pretty as her older sister.

who achieves success is expected to help others in the family; family members, it is said, should always support one another, and when help is withheld, criticism is severe. At the same time, it is recognized that when a man becomes a *padre de familia*, his first loyalty is to his wife and children. *Constanceros* also stress that one must look out for oneself; this frequently involves structuring ties, familial or otherwise, in such a manner as to serve immediate and long-term material interests, especially in the *pueblo*.

In contrast to the situation in the *campo*, relationships between *pueblo* families are characterized by distrust and bitterness. To an extent, this is also true of friendships, whether between individuals of a like socio-economic level, or of a dyadic nature involving a status differential. It is only between neighbors, in fact, that *pueblo* dwellers appear to relate to one another in an atmosphere of ease without calculating the cost of the relationship.

It has already been noted that a wealthier family may try to disassociate itself from poorer kinsmen who are too demanding, and that this occurs more in the *pueblo* than in the *campo*. Over the years, certain families that settled in the *pueblo*, where they began businesses or continued as agriculturalists, have become more affluent than many of their kinsmen in the *campo*. They have also become removed from *campo* life, and look upon their kinsmen there as socially inferior and wish to have as little to do with them as possible. Such *pueblo* families have achieved respectability and have validated their position by acquiring various status symbols such as good homes and expensive cars and by sending their children to the *colegio*. The heads of these families are widely respected because, outwardly at least, they lead moral and responsible lives, but more important, they are respected because of their success and the power and influence they can command. In more recent years, other people have moved to the *pueblo*, either as families or as individuals seeking work, and they have not become affluent. Having lost what economic security they enjoyed in living among their kindred, they seek out their familial connections in the *pueblo* for help. Other people in the *pueblo* are relative newcomers to the community and therefore are outside the family system altogether. Nevertheless, they, too, seek to relate to those most likely to be of help; a number of those who are sought out, *la gente importante*, likewise have few or no connections with Constanza families.

Any individual in a position to distribute patronage is clearly expected to distribute it first to his kinsmen. When help is not given, or is given to some but not to others, there is resentment and criticism. But, as Whitten points out in his discussion of stem kindreds in San Lorenzo, those individuals who have achieved some wealth and influence must necessarily limit the number of people with whom reciprocity is to take place. If this is not done, whatever patronage an individual has to dispense (whether in the form of jobs or store credit or various other favors) will soon be dissipated without maximum benefit to himself. Deciding whom to help and whom to refuse, however, depends very much upon the circumstances of the individual whose help is sought. For instance, in seeking election as *síndico*, family connections are of great importance and may be used to advantage. On the other hand, in running a store or any other business, an extensive kin network tends to be a disadvantage because poorer relatives will expect credit, and unless this is very carefully regulated, the business may fail.

Once help has been extended to an individual or family of lower socioeconomic status, there is the expectation that further help will be given and that the *patrón*-client relationship so formed will continue. Those whose help is sought therefore need to be discerning in extending help, and unless the relationship is likely to be of present or future advantage, help is not generally given. Reputation, however, is a very important factor. Generosity is lauded by *constanceros* and meanness is despised; it is therefore important that any man who seeks to exercise influence in community affairs have a reputation for being generous as well as understanding or sympathetic. Help, then, is rarely refused outright; rather, people explain that they would like to help but are unable to do so, and business expenses or the cost of a fine home or a car or the children's education may be given as the reason. The right of any individual of importance to spend heavily on such items is never questioned. In fact, those who are prosperous are expected to engage in conspicuous display.

Much of the tension among *pueblo* dwellers has arisen because of the refusal by many wealthier families to acknowledge relationships or to extend help to legally unrecognized kinsmen. The mother of Juan Conde, for instance, was one of the five *mujeres* of a principal member of the Arafat family who died some years ago. Today, the Arafats have nothing to do with this woman or Juan and his brothers and acknowledge no relationship. Juan's mother was left a small *parcela* in the Valley and a house in the *pueblo*. After the death of her husband, his legitimate sons unsuccessfully tried to take back some of the land, but did succeed in evicting her from the house. In exchange, the woman was given a much smaller house on the outskirts of the *pueblo*. Understandably enough, the Conde brothers and their families are very bitter toward the

Arafats but do not criticize them openly because of the power this family can exercise.

On the other hand, another *mujer* of Arafat and her two daughters and son have managed to stay on good terms with the members of this family and have enjoyed their continuing patronage. This woman was also left a small piece of Valley land and a house in the *pueblo*, and although her children were not recognized, they use their father's name and it appears that they were always accepted visitors in the Arafat home. The woman is addressed as *doña* and the family is counted among Constanza's respectable people. The two attractive daughters attended the *colegio* and in all probability will be married in the church to young men from respectable families. The girls now have positions as secretaries in government offices; they owe these positions to the influence of the Arafats.

Virtually all the older Constanza families have unrecognized branches living somewhere in the community; requests for help are frequently made on the basis of these relationships. Even if occasional help is given, it is unusual for respectable *pueblo* families to recognize these branches as relatives or to relate to them in anything approaching terms of equality. In Constanza society, to a great extent, the sins of the father are visited upon the son. It is significant, for instance, that in 1940, when the casino (then known as the Club Generalísimo Trujillo) was opened in the *pueblo* as a social club for men, a requirement for membership was that individuals be legitimately born or have been granted recognition, and that married members be married in the church.[15] The directive of the club comprised respectable and wealthy men, all of whom lived in the *pueblo*. The desire of these men to restrict membership probably reflected a growing concern with their own status and, perhaps, the need to emphasize the distance they wished to establish between themselves, who closely identified with Trujillo and therefore were close to the sources of power, and others, who were removed from these sources and required to look to them for help.

Poorer families sometimes seek to form *compadrazgo* ties with those who may be of help to them, but deliberate calculation of

---

[15] It was explained that the intention of these restrictions was to keep certain "low" people out of the club, but it appears that the restrictions were rarely, if ever, invoked to bar anyone from membership. Those who were not considered "respectable" were apparently well aware of this fact and did not seek to join. The requirement that members be married in the church was clearly not taken seriously because some of those who were members, including don Alejandro, had been divorced and therefore could not marry in the church.

this kind is more characteristic of townspeople. In the *campo* and particularly in the dry farming areas, the economic security of most individuals rests with the personal kindred, which is primarily a locality grouping made up of real and ritual kin. The *compadrazgo* ties that are formed in these areas serve to reinforce pre-existing ties of kinship and neighborhood although, as was noted earlier, it is also common to form the relationship with those who have greater economic importance and who may, at times, act as *patrón* to those who live in the neighborhood. In turn, these men of local importance are frequently *compadres* to important men in the *pueblo*. When *campesinos* in any area attempt to by-pass the local structure of relationships and tie themselves to individuals of a higher socioeconomic status who clearly stand outside their circle of acquaintances, disapproval and even contempt are likely to be expressed.[16] In these areas where egalitarianism is stressed, it is resented if someone gains a special advantage that others are unable to share. In fact, it is virtually necessary for an individual to move elsewhere if he wishes to break loose from the claims of his kindred and achieve socioeconomic mobility.

In the *pueblo, compadrazgo* relationships are formed between relatives and friends who are of a similar socioeconomic level, but, more so than in the *campo*, there is also a deliberate attempt to form the relationship with those of a higher status who may be in a position to offer assistance. A number of *peones*, town workers, and, until recently, workers in the timber mills who have regular *patrones* seek out these men as *padrinos* to their children in the hope of securing their own positions. Most of those who rely upon manual labor of one form or another, however, are unable to find permanent *patrones* and therefore can only look to one another as *compadres*.

To become *compadres* with one's employer earns no contempt, but contempt is expressed of those who are blatantly selfseeking in forming the *compadrazgo* relationship. For example, harsh things

---

[16] A woman of Los Corralitos, for instance, who earned a little money for her family by selling wood in the *pueblo*, asked one of the well-off storekeepers to be *padrino* to her eighth child. She had been selling wood to this man's family but otherwise had no particular connection with the family or the man himself. With some reluctance, the storekeeper agreed to be *padrino;* when the child died a few months later, the woman complained bitterly because he sent only two *pesos* and did not bother himself in any other way with arrangements for the child's funeral. One of her *campesino* neighbors, however, said that it served her right: "she should know not to expect any help from the people in the *pueblo*." Others said that it was "not right" for her to approach the storekeeper in the first place and that she had shown herself to be *sin vergüenza.*

were said of Enrique Morales when he obtained the promise of don Alejandro to be *padrino* to his second son. This young man has a poor reputation because he leads an irresponsible life and lives largely on the meager earnings of his school-teacher wife. Enrique's wife had been a frequent visitor to the home of don Alejandro and had become friends with doña María, his wife. Apparently, it was through this connection that Enrique was able to approach don Alejandro. Another *pueblo* family let it be known that President Balaguer, with whose family they claimed to have a rather vague association, had agreed to be *padrino* to their seventh child. The father of this family has a minor government post and his wife disclosed that they were hopeful that "their friend, the President," would obtain her husband an advancement. When it became known that the President was to be *padrino* to their child, people reacted with amused contempt.

On the other hand, those individuals who are able to exploit powerful connections within or outside the community are respected and sometimes feared. No one is amused at or contemptuous of Antonio Torres, the agriculturalist in the Valley who boasts that two of the top military figures in the Republic are *padrinos* to his children. This connection is well appreciated by others. Although most of the people in the *pueblo* consider him to be rather stupid, it is recognized that, because of his powerful friends, he is not a man to be trifled with. Antonio Torres has married into the Arafat family, and others of this family also have ritual kin ties with General Wessin y Wessin. It is through these ties that the Arafats are able to exert political pressure and make themselves and their close friends the recipients of so much patronage in the form of jobs in government offices.

The Arafats are not an old family in Constanza; only five brothers and others who are closely related by marriage make up the Arafat stem kindred. These men have formed ritual kin ties with one another. As well, several members of the stem kindred are centers, as *patrones*, of groups of followers, and many of them have been made *compadres*. The Arafats are distrusted and resented by most *constanceros* who stand outside their circle. The importance of the Arafats stems from their wealth and positions as *patrones* and the influential military ties they have outside the community. Along extended family lines, the Arafats are unable to generate much support.

On the other hand, the Espiallat family is one of the founding families in Constanza and has branches in nearly every part of the community. Its two leading members in the *pueblo* are the half-brothers, Pedro and Raóul, each of whom owns a large store. These men are "enemies" because they are business rivals and because Pedro has disgraced his half-brother, a very religious man, by flouting public morality. He openly maintains a mistress and makes no secret of the illegitimate children he has fathered in the *pueblo*. Both of these men are sought out by poorer kinsmen and many others in the hope of obtaining store credit, but it cannot be said that each leads a rival faction of the Espiallat family. Both men, in fact, have lived most of their lives in the *pueblo*, and have discouraged close ties with their kinsmen in the *campo* (most of whom are extremely poor) and with all but a few of their better-off kinsmen who live in the *pueblo*.

In earlier years, when Raóul Espiallat was merely employed as a store hand in the *pueblo*, he made friendships with various people who were in a position to help him. These included Sr. Nashash, his employer, who became one of his *compadres* and lent him money to start his business; Ramón Ornes, the *alcalde* in El Limoncito, who also lent him money; don Alejandro; and his uncle Martín Espiallat, who was then the *síndico*. Apparently it was largely through his uncle that he made valuable friends outside the community; these friendships and his fervid support of Trujillo led to his own election as *síndico* during the Trujillo years. As *síndico*, Raóul Espiallat helped a number of his poorer kinsmen in the *pueblo* by securing them government jobs, but over the years he has largely concentrated his energies on forming friendships with the most important men in the *pueblo* and with other individuals of influence who live outside Constanza altogether. Most of the weekend visitors to the Espiallat home are men from Jarabacoa, La Vega, and the capital. In the countryside, he has managed to avoid alienating his numerous kinsmen, who can be relied upon to vote for him, but he has done little for them. Rather, he has sought to make friends with men like Ramón Ornes in the dry farming areas and with leading men in the *pueblecitos*. None of these is the Espiallat family.

In the case of Mario Rosario, a former timber mill owner who was also an aspirant for the position of *síndico* in 1968 (he briefly held this position during the Council of State), strong family support existed in two sections of the countryside where he had many relatives. Rosario had recently taken up residence in the *pueblo* but he continued to maintain very close ties with his *campesino* relatives, who looked to him for help in a variety of ways. In the *pueblo* and in other areas of the countryside, however, Rosario had only a limited following.

Wide family backing is an important factor, particularly for those seeking election as *síndico*. Of greater importance, however, are ties to key figures in the various sections of the countryside, close association with the most important men in the *pueblo*, and influential contacts outside the community. The establishment of these ties necessarily involves, to a large extent, severing ties with poor kinsmen. The Nashash family, the family of don Alejandro, and a few other influential families, the heads of which are not natives of Constanza, have greater independence in distributing favors because they do not have many kinsmen seeking help. Other than the favors these men can dispense, however, they have no basis on which to enlist community support; such individuals do not, it appears, seek election as *síndico*.

Whether or not familial relationships exist does not inhibit many people from seeking to establish ties with those in a position to offer help. The practice of "giving" a child into service with a better-off family is a means by which a poor family can ensure the welfare of one of its members and also establish some sort of a claim to help. People speak of "giving" a child, but the mother generally explains that she has given the child to a family "to bring up"; the woman who has taken the child simply says that she has been given a child "to help me." Frequently, those who give a child in this way to a better-off family are poor relatives who live in the *campo*, but whether they are relatives or not, no formal adoption is involved and the arrangement may be terminated by either family at any time. If this is done unexpectedly, as is often the case, however, there may be a great deal of bitterness.

Children of both sexes as young as nine or ten years are adopted into service and may continue in this work until the age of puberty, at which time they are strong enough to look for some form of paid work. The adopting family is expected to feed and clothe the child and perhaps give occasional pocket money, and also to be responsible for the child's moral upbringing. *Constanceros* discharge this responsibility by teaching their charges respect and obedience to all members of the family, and by insisting upon attendance at mass on Sunday. In return, the child is expected to be a willing slave and to show gratitude to his benefactors.

Members of the child's family enjoy visiting rights and frequently plan these so that they fall during meal times. There is a tacit understanding that, having accepted a child "to bring up," a family incurs some obligations to the child's family. These may include occasional meals, gifts of food or clothing, and even money in times of emergency, and perhaps work, if they are in a position

to offer this from time to time. Frequently the child's family becomes
too demanding, in which case they may be told to cease visiting
altogether, or to visit less often, but once the relationship is established, it is difficult to break. Many wealthier families prefer to
employ a female servant from outside the community rather than
to adopt a child servant. This relieves them of the burden of training
a servant and there is less likelihood of their being pestered by the
employee's relatives.

Friendships and Relations Between Neighbors

Enough has been said to indicate that those people whose friendship
is sought are often placed in a difficult position. This is no less
true of the storekeeper, who is harassed with endless requests for
credit, than of the *síndico* and the party president, who control
a great deal of the political patronage.

In giving favors to some but not to others, friendships are made
and enmities created. Frequently, in order to win a temporary advantage, promises are made with no intention of keeping them. It
is small wonder then that those of most importance whose friendship
is greatly desired are generally mistrusted and are the targets for
malicious gossip. At the same time, they are envied and admired
for their astuteness and publicly are treated with deference and
flattery. The opportunism in private and public life and the calculating approach to friendship explain much of the brittleness in
interpersonal relations that is characteristic of *pueblo* dwellers.
Further, this brittleness is also apparent in many of the friendships
that are formed among those of the same socioeconomic level.

When two men become friends, they relate to one another with
great intensity and, at a certain point in the relationship, may begin
to address one another as *compadre* or *hermano*. Much affection
and consideration are shown. In theory, friends willingly share with
one another without counting the cost. In practice, friendships commonly break down; when this occurs, there may be considerable
disruption and other people become involved.

Friends generally fall out because one begins to impose on the
other and fails to reciprocate favors, or there is a failure on the
part of one to give support to the other, either in quarrels or in
some crisis when help may be needed. Each maligns the other to
his neighbors and friends and eventually a confrontation occurs,
at which insults and threats are exchanged, although blows are extremely rare. A mutual friend steps in to act as mediator and attempts to restore the relationship in such a way that the honor

of each is satisfied. He sees first the one and then the other; generally a reconciliation is effected. When a reconciliation cannot be brought about, as occasionally happens in the *pueblo*, the permanent rift is recognized and the parties simply stay apart.

The tension and lack of cooperation among many *pueblo* families and the impermanence generally characteristic of friendships are partially compensated by the warm relations that develop among neighbors.

Those who live in the immediate vicinity are *vecinos* (neighbors) and are addressed as such. The women of these homes, more so than the men, spend much time gossiping; there is constant borrowing and giving of small gifts, generally in the form of special items of cooked foods. If a woman needs an egg or a tablespoon of salt, she turns to her neighbor; this may be reciprocated a few days later with a small dish of sweet rice. No clear accounting is kept of these gifts and loans, but reciprocity in some form is expected. When someone is in trouble, the neighbors are the first to learn of it and are expected to help or at least to provide a sympathetic audience. In the *campo*, relations with neighbors are equally strong; for the most part, however, this involves locality groupings of kinsmen. In the *pueblo*, people generally do not live surrounded by kinfolk; the close relations formed with neighbors can best be interpreted as relations of mutual dependence that satisfy certain economic and social needs.

For many *pueblo* households, and particularly for *los pobres*, who are unable to rely upon an extended kin network, neighbors provide the only stable group beyond the household itself. Only among neighbors, in fact, do *pueblo* dwellers appear to relate to one another without calculating the cost and in an atmosphere free from suspicion and mistrust.[17] The next chapter will show that the suspicion and mistrust that characterize interpersonal and family relationships in the *pueblo*, and the absence of any basis on which cooperation can be built, to a great extent explain the impermanence of formal associations that are established in the *pueblo*.

---

[17] Banfield, in his study of Montegrano, a southern Italian village, notes that although all relationships beyond the nuclear family are characterized by mistrust and there is a complete absence of cooperation, relations among neighbors are generally good because people may have urgent need for their neighbors. Edward C. Banfield, *The Moral Basis of a Backward Society* (New York: The Free Press, 1958), Chapter 6.

CHAPTER 8

Formal Associations

This chapter refers to a variety of associations, but few indeed reveal any permanence. Some fail for lack of enthusiasm, others collapse amidst dissention. The temporary nature of certain associations, however, appears to be related to the functions they serve. In a number of cases, associations come into being to meet a pressure emanating from outside the community. Organizations of this type are generally dominated by *la gente mas importante*, who consistently represent the community on the outside. Similarly, on a lower level, many of the political committees that are formed in the *campo* come into being merely to placate individuals of influence in the *pueblo*. Once pressure has been removed, such committees, like many associations that are centered in the *pueblo*, cease to function.

FORMAL ASSOCIATIONS AND THEIR WEAKNESSES

Clubs and associations of various kinds are frequently formed, but the members' enthusiasm soon fades. Only if there is someone of sufficient force to carry the organization will it continue. For instance, stationed at the Agricultural Center is a full-time extension worker who has attempted to organize 5-D clubs among *campesino* young people in various *pueblecitos*. The groups meet fortnightly to discuss agricultural matters and hold social evenings from time to time. The organizer, however, is disappointed at the response. Meetings are poorly attended and there is little doubt that if the organizer were transferred the clubs would not endure.

All schools in the *campo* and *pueblo* on paper have Parents and Teachers Associations, but not one is active. Teachers say there is no interest and that parents will not attend meetings. The Roman Catholic *colegio* has a P and T Association and it too is virtually inactive, but there are occasional parents' meetings that are attended by twenty to fifty parents, mainly mothers. These meetings are called by the Mother Superior, a very forceful woman, who uses these occasions to berate parents for their lack of concern at the poor scholastic performance of their children and the neglect of their moral welfare.

There are a number of religious organizations in Constanza, but only two of these, the Franciscans of the Third Order and the *cursillistas*, are at all active. The Franciscans stress piety and service to others. The organization is perpetuated largely through the efforts of doña Felicia, a highly respected widow who settled in Constanza some years ago. Two other principal members are doña María, the wife of don Alejandro, and Sr. Raóul Espiallat. The Franciscans actually do very little other than meet together for prayer and discussion, but membership earns respect for an individual because of the stringency of the rules concerning conduct. Few of the community's prominent men, other than Sr. Espiallat, are members. The *cursillistas*, on the other hand, include many of *la gente importante* and it is considered, in fact, to be an organization of *los ricos*. Individual members sometimes attend conferences in other *pueblos* and even in Puerto Rico; other than taking part in occasional religious processions through the streets of the *pueblo*, however, the Constanza organization does very little. The obligation to aid the poor is discharged by an annual distribution of clothing to the children of a number of *los pobres* on Three Kings' Day.

All the *cursillistas* and most of the Franciscans are townspeople; so too are most of those who join the few formal associations that exist. Associations are generally centered in the *pueblo;* well-known persons are always involved either as members or as organizers. Whatever group an association is supposedly designed to serve, however, the complaints of the organizers are always the same: enthusiasm is short-lived and the burden of maintaining the organization falls on one or two persons. Constanza, for example, has a scout troop, but technically it has ceased to exist. Its number was given to a troop formed elsewhere in the Republic when, after many months, the Constanza troop had failed to pay its dues. The scoutmaster, who is a well-respected small businessman in the *pueblo*, complains bitterly about the lack of enthusiasm for scouting and the amount of organizing he has to do.

Early in 1967, following the visit of a district organizer from La Vega, a Girl Scout troop was formed. Thirty girls, all of whom came from respectable *pueblo* families, attended the first meeting, at which this decision was made, and enthusiasm ran high. The organizer then returned to La Vega, believing that the movement was under way. At a subsequent meeting two weeks later, which was attended by about half the original number of girls, the meeting still had not commenced an hour after it was due to start; a Constanza woman who had previously offered her services as leader did not appear. The girls played hopscotch and stood around chatting in groups while waiting for something to happen; no one stepped forward to offer direction. At a third meeting, one of the girls announced that the woman who had offered to lead the troop had now said she was unable to spare the time. The girls discussed other possible leaders and later did approach one or two women, but could find no one willing to take the responsibility. This was the last meeting of the Girl Scouts.

The two associations that do function with some efficiency are the band and the baseball association, although the organizers of each complain about poor attendance at practices and lack of enthusiasm. In earlier years, the baseball association was more active and there were many more people wanting to play. The band also used to be "better" and apparently, when it was first formed during the Trujillo years, it did receive more financial support from the *ayuntamiento* to buy instruments and uniforms. The instruments are now very old and need replacing and the uniforms have long since worn out, but there are insufficient funds to provide new ones. The bandmaster and members of the band receive some pay, although they complain that it is very little. Were they not paid, it is doubtful if the band would continue.

When enthusiasm dies, most organizations simply fade away, and their passing is barely noticed. This was so in the case of the Club Generalísimo Trujillo, the directive of which comprised a number of the *gente mas importante*. The principal *raison d'être* of the club was to organize receptions for Trujillo and other visiting dignities who frequently appeared in Constanza during earlier years. In the late 1950's, fewer such visits were made and key members lost interest. Subscriptions were no longer paid and the club gradually ceased to be effective. Today, although most *constanceros* remember the Club Generalísimo, very few are able to recall what it did or what its objectives were.

Like many other Dominican communities of any size, Constanza has a Red Cross Association. A few of the *gente mas importante* are numbered among committee members. When the Association was first formed, the central organization in Santo Domingo gave it an ambulance and various other kinds of help. In 1966, in response to a national appeal, the Association held money-raising functions in the *pueblo* to assist the victims of hurricane Inez, which had devastated part of the country. Since then, there have been one or two poorly attended meetings, but no functions are planned for the future. Members have lost interest and most *constanceros* are unaware that the organization exists. The Red Cross Association still exists on paper and there is no doubt that should the need arise, it could be made to appear active.

In 1967, following a public meeting, a visiting Roman Catholic nun began adult education classes, which were broadcast over Radio Constanza in the early evenings. A committee was formed that comprised the visiting nun, the Mother Superior, and doña Felicia, the woman mentioned above in connection with the Franciscans. Several groups of pupils were organized in the *pueblo* and in the colonies around volunteer teachers, each of whom was supplied with a book. When the organization was established, the nun left Constanza to continue her good work elsewhere. Initially there was some enthusiasm, but numbers soon dwindled as people lost interest; all but two of the groups had ceased to meet a few weeks after the plan was put into action. Radio Constanza, however, which appeared to have an unending supply of taped lessons, continued to broadcast instruction long after the groups had ceased to meet, much to the annoyance of most people, who preferred to listen to *merengue* music and were at a loss to explain what the programs were all about.

Other organizations break up because some crisis develops, as the following cases show. In 1965, the nuns of the Roman Catholic church organized cooking and sewing classes for poor women of the *pueblo*. These were run voluntarily by doña Felicia and another respected woman. Initially, there was much enthusiasm but it was not lasting. Doña Felicia, who was teaching the cooking class, gave up in disgust when there were objections to her giving the nuns a cake made in class. Some of the women were agreeable to this, but others argued that because they had each provided the ingredients, the cake should be shared among them all. The sewing class lasted a little longer, but attendance fell and the instructoress became embittered at the constant difficulty she was having extracting the 25 *centavos* fee, which went toward the cost of sewing materials. Classes ceased altogether when someone stole the sewing machine from the *colegio*, where the classes were being held.

In 1966, a club known as the Club Enriquillo was organized among young people of the *pueblo* by the Community Development field worker stationed in Constanza at the time, but it lasted only a few months. Some people say there was little interest in the sports and cultural activities the club tried to promote, but others say it failed because the organizer permitted certain PRD men to take leading positions in the club. There is probably some truth in both these accounts, but the actual incident that brought about the downfall of the club was of quite a different order. Someone stole the club's funds, which were kept in an unlocked money box; the box as well was taken but was later found. People could not agree on whether the individual incriminated was actually the thief and, if so, what should be done, or whether someone else was the thief and had merely planted the box to divert suspicion away from himself. There was much argument about the matter. Members failed to pay their dues and stopped attending the club, which then ceased to exist. Some people point out, however, that at the time this incident occurred, most people had lost interest in the club and the theft of the money only precipitated its collapse.

ASSOCIATIONS FORMED IN RESPONSE TO OUTSIDE PRESSURE

Constanceros are anxious to demonstrate their willingness to cooperate, particularly when dealing with outside officials. The *gente mas importante* always play a leading part in these encounters, and associations or committees may be formed and commitments given without any real sincerity of purpose.

In August 1967, an evening meeting was called in the public school to discuss adult education. Present was an official from the Education Department in Santo Domingo and five other individuals: the *síndico*, the school inspector, don Alejandro, and a Spaniard and a Japanese who were referred to as "representatives" of the foreigners. The visiting official talked at length about the need for adult classes. All decided that volunteer teachers would be called for and evening classes in a variety of subjects would be commenced in the *pueblo* and in the colonies. There was to be another meeting in two weeks, at which the classes and teachers would be organized; at some future time, the organizer was to return and give further guidance. Nothing in fact happened. The meeting was not cancelled, it simply did not take place; probably none of those present seriously thought that it would. The organizer from Santo Domingo was not heard of again.

Yet another program in adult education was begun shortly before my field work ended. A group of adult education experts from Venezuela, on loan to the Dominican government, appeared in Constanza and, in great detail, explained to a captive audience of teachers and *alcaldes* how the program was to be operated and the benefits that would be derived. Certain individuals publicly thanked the visitors and spoke enthusiastically of the plan and everyone applauded. Later, in private, several of the teachers confessed that they considered the whole thing an unfair imposition because they were not going to be paid for the extra work that would be involved; they predicted that, in any case, the plan would fail.

In November 1967, the *síndico* hurriedly assembled over one hundred young people of the *pueblo,* who were to be addressed by the President of Reformista Youth, who was visiting from the capital. At the meeting, the visitor and then the *síndico,* the school inspector, and the President of the *ayuntamiento* all spoke with great concern of the responsible role youth had to play in the future. With much enthusiasm, they decided to form a Reformista Youth Association of Constanza. Office bearers were elected; there was a president, a vice-president, a secretary, a treasurer, a secretary for *campo* youth (no one from the *campo* had been invited to the meeting) and another for *pueblo* youth, a person in charge of publicity, one for discipline, and another in charge of correspondence. It was believed the general secretary alone would be unable to handle the volume of work involved. Don Alejandro and Sr. Nashash, who were present at the meeting, were elected "guidance men" for the Reformista Youth. The meeting was then adjourned and lunch was served. Most of the later comments about the meeting concerned the lunch, which was totally inadequate for the number present, and the fact that the *síndico* and one or two of his cronies drank most of the rum that had been provided before others had had a chance. Reformista Youth has never met, and only one individual has been at all active.

Toward the end of 1967, an American working for the Liga Municipal officially met with the *síndico* and *ayuntamiento* to discuss problems of municipal government and to advise them on how its quality could be improved. Later, he was enthusiastic about the capacity of some of the men he had met and their understanding of community problems. In particular, he was impressed by don Alejandro and Sr. Nashash, unaware of the fact that other than the *síndico* and a newly appointed president, none of the men he had met was still a member of the *ayuntamiento.* After a series of violent clashes with the *síndico,* the *regidores* had resigned one by one; the group that impressed the American had been hastily assembled to deal with his visit. Don Alejandro, who apparently organized this group, had not been a member of the *ayuntamiento,* nor had Sr. Nashash.

Interestingly enough, the deception leading *pueblo* figures perpetrate against outsiders through the formation of short-lived organizations is to some extent practiced on themselves by the *campesinos,* who generally make up local political committees. This was certainly true in 1962, when Juan Bosch was elected president of the Republic. Toward the end of 1962, the assistant *alcalde* and the school teacher in the *paraje* of Los Corralitos were approached by members of the PRD committee in the *pueblo* and asked to form a local party committee to organize people to vote for the Bosch candidates in the coming national elections. They agreed to do so and, without bothering with the formality of organizing a meeting of *paraje* residents, these two men permitted their own names to be recorded and submitted the names of two other men to make up the local committee. Shortly afterward, the Union Civica representatives appeared in the *paraje* with the same request, and the same names were recorded to form the Union Civica committee. Before the June elections of 1966, following the revolution in which Juan Bosch was overthrown, these men of the *paraje* were approached once more in turn by representatives of the PRD and of the Reformista Party, which was more or less heir to the loosely organized Union Cívica. On this occasion, however, they declined to form a local PRD committee.

The teacher and the assistant *alcalde*, both of whom were born in the area and are related to most of the families around, told the following story against themselves to show, as they put it, that they have no interest in politics, but are not as stupid as many in the town believe. In 1962, some time after the election campaign was under way, they had made up their minds to vote for Bosch because they believed his promises and were persuaded, mainly on the basis of talk in the *pueblo*, that he was going to win the coming election. At what point they made this decision is not clear, but it appears to have been almost immediately prior to the election, when many important figures in the *pueblo* realized that Bosch was likely to win the national election and therefore ceased to be active supporters of the Union Cívica. Rather than argue with the Union Cívica representatives, the Los Corralitos men had agreed to form a committee for them also, and they claimed that, had the PRD people come demanding to know why, they would simply have explained that it was a mistake on the part of the Union Cívica organizers or that they had not understood. In the later elections, however, they wanted nothing to do with the PRD because they had been told that Bosch was a communist and were convinced by Ramón Ornes and opinions expressed in the *pueblo* that he would not win. Further, the things Bosch had promised had not materialized.

In Los Corralitos, all those who voted in 1962 voted for Bosch; in 1966, they all voted for Balaguer. On neither occasion did the local committee act in any formal way, but the people did talk over matters with three of its members at various times and these men told them how they thought they should vote. They, in turn, were largely influenced by what people in the *pueblo* were saying about the rival candidates. They simply voted to be on the winning side.

What occurred in Los Corralitos is an isolated case only to the extent that exactly the same men formed what were supposedly rival committees; such a thing could occur only in very small localities. It commonly happened both in 1962 and 1966 that some men were on more than one party committee, but most of these committees existed only on paper. Individuals give promises of support and political committees are formed with great ease, but frequently the promises are meaningless and the committees never become active.

In most areas of the *campo* people prefer to appear to conform to what is demanded rather than to risk antagonizing those who are influential or may be influential in the future. Thus, the people of Los Corralitos tried to please both sides in 1962 when there was some doubt as to the final outcome. When, in 1966, they were fairly certain that Bosch's party could not win, they declined to form a local PRD party in their area for fear they would antagonize the *reformistas*, who clearly had the upper hand. Also, and they say this themselves, they did not want to be labeled communists; to appear to support Bosch's party at this time was to invite such a label.

THE IMPERMANENCE OF FORMAL ASSOCIATIONS

The *gente mas importante*, who stand between the community and the outside, are men of influence who have some contacts with the outside; the *campesinos*, who play this role in the countryside, are respected men in their localities who are better able to interpret *pueblo* sentiments to their fellows and to tell them in what direction they should go. *Constanceros*, in fact, have had considerable experience in dealing with the outside and in placating those who hold power, both within and outside the community. Throughout the 31 years of Trujillo, the *campesinos* voted as directed and formed their local committees when required, knowing that if they did these things, and paid their taxes, they would be left alone; on occasions benefits even flowed from the top. In the *pueblo*, there was never any open dissent; each year, much the same men held public office and, by their membership in various organizations, represented the community to the outside.

Many organizations that were formed gave the appearance of serving the public good in some way or other, but when it was no longer necessary to present this image, they faded away. In the middle 1950's there was a Progress Association, a Tourist Association, and a Constanza Beautification Committee, which seem to have been associations of this type; today, there is the Red Cross Association. The Beautification Committee did organize park benches (it was suggested to certain wealthier individuals that they should each contribute one) and the Red Cross has had one or two social functions. It seems fairly clear, however, that when such associations come into being, there is an inevitability about their demise. They come into being to answer some outside pressure or perhaps to anticipate one, and they enable the people of most importance to go through certain motions that are likely to be pleasing to the outside. Once the pressure has been removed, the associations cease to exist.

It is tempting to attribute the impermanence of many associations to fickleness and to a lack of real concern with community progress on the part of leading *constanceros*, but at best this is only part of the explanation. The pressure that is exerted on the community from time to time is intermittent and *constanceros* have come to expect that little lasting effort will be required of them. Few of the promises made by outsiders materialize, and most of the programs initiated from outside peter out for lack of sustained pressure or resources as much as for waning enthusiasm within the community. Over the years, *constanceros* have become thoroughly inured to seeing programs and associations of one sort or another fail within a short time of their initiation,[1] and, although the announcement of any new program is greeted publicly with a great show of enthusiasm, privately there is apathy and cynicism as to the likelihood of success. There is cynicism about motives involved, whether programs or associations are initiated by individuals within or outside the community. It is axiomatic to the thinking of most *constanceros*

---

[1] The list of failures is considerable indeed. From the time of Trujillo's death, there have been no less than six separate programs in adult education (one of these was organized by the U.S. military and another by Peace Corps volunteers), three attempts to organize cooking and sewing classes, and, in addition to the agricultural cooperative and the 5-D clubs, there have been two agricultural associations concerned with "educating" growers and providing assistance in marketing. Twice clinics have been opened with much publicity and then closed for lack of medicine or trained personnel. As well, Peace Corps volunteers and, later, community development workers initiated what were supposedly self-help projects in various locations of the *campo*, such as breeding rabbits, raising chickens, building bridges and canals, and installing pumps. From what can be learned, virtually all of these projects failed and served to generate suspicion rather than enthusiasm and self-reliance.

that anyone (except possibly those connected with the Church) launching any activity or association supposedly for the public good must have some private motive, no matter how laudable the aims may appear to be.

Two further questions arise. To what extent are outsiders deceived when the community appears to be responsive to demands, and are *constanceros* consciously practicing deception? No absolute answer can be given to either question because the motives of the actors involved on each occasion may differ.

We cannot know whether the Vice-President of Reformista Youth seriously believed that his visit had led to the creation of a permanent organization with active committees, but in political matters, those who stand to gain will do whatever organizing work is necessary when the time comes. Only one of the Reformista Youth committeemen played any part in the 1968 municipal election campaign. This was a young high school graduate without full-time work who was believed by many to have been a Bosch supporter.

Deliberate deception was probably intended when what purported to be the *ayuntamiento* met with the American. He assumed, however, that the men he was dealing with were the *regidores;* because he represented a likely source of material help to the community, it was hardly expedient to disclose the true state of affairs.[2] Much of the trouble being experienced at that time stemmed from personality clashes and therefore was not considered a matter of concern to outsiders. Relatively few in the *pueblo*, in fact, knew of the crisis that had developed in the *ayuntamiento;* like many other conflicts among those of political importance, it never became common knowledge.

When associations formed for some community endeavor simply fade out of existence after having accomplished little or nothing, it strikes no one as being particularly strange and there is no question of fixing blame. On the other hand, the collapse of associations that are formed to meet the needs of a particular group, e.g., the Church sewing and cooking classes, the Club Enriquillo, or the agricultural cooperative, is frequently marked by bitterness and violent

---

[2] It was hoped that through the American the *ayuntamiento* might gain access to American funds and, when it was learned that he bore only advice and not gifts, there was some disappointment. The American was asked whether he could secure a distribution of CARE food and clothing for Constanza's poor; apparently he undertook to look into this possibility. At a later date, when I was to visit the capital, don Alejandro asked me to speak to the American about the food and clothing he had "promised" but to stress upon him that the distributions must be made through the *ayuntamiento* and not through the Church, as had once previously occurred.

argument, and individuals or groups are blamed for the failure. The reason associations of this type seem doomed to impermanence (unless, of course, there is very strong leadership or an enthusiast prepared to do all the organizing) lies in the nature of group life and in the quality of interpersonal relations.

With two possible exceptions, there is virtually no permanence in the composition of the informal groups that form at particular places from time to time; in view of this alone, it is not surprising that associations also show little permanence. At a more basic level, however, the mistrust and brittleness that characterize relations between families and individuals in the *pueblo* would seem to explain the inevitable transience of groups that may begin to form, whether merely informal gatherings of a number of close acquaintances who regularly drink or play pool together, or on the formal level of an association with all the trappings of elected offices and written constitutions. Structurally, much of the behavior described in this chapter is explicable if examined against the background of the system of political patronage as it operates within the community; this will be discussed in Chapter 9.

CHAPTER 9

Power Structure and Patronage

This chapter and the one that follows will show how, by dint of the power or influence they command, *la gente mas importante* are able to maintain their own positions and also to control the public affairs of the community. Much of the material in the present chapter deals with patronage, with how positions in government offices and various other favors are obtained, and with how favors are repaid. It also deals with the part played by the military and police in Constanza's affairs. These forces represent relatively independent sources of power that certain people, on occasions, are able to influence. Attitudes toward the use and abuse of power are discussed, particularly the expectation that those with power will use it primarily for their own ends.

Because patronage is limited and the claimants for favors are many, conflict is frequently generated among the people of maximum importance. Chapter 10, which deals with the recent *municipio* elections, shows by an "event analysis" how conflict may arise and how, in this case through the mediation of don Alejandro Gonzales, resolution can be achieved. The broker role that this man in particular plays is also referred to in this present chapter.

PATRONAGE

Weingrod has argued that what anthropologists have generally meant when referring to patronage is increasingly becoming a thing of the past.[1] He argues that ". . . patron-client ties can be seen

---

[1] Alex Weingrod, "Patrons, Patronage and Political Parties," *Comparative Studies in Society and History, 10* (July 1968):337–400.

Weingrod discusses various meanings that have been given to "patronage" and concludes that, whereas political scientists tend to restrict the term to an aspect of political support, anthropologists perceive patronage as a particular kind of interpersonal relationship. It is ". . . the analysis of how persons of

to arise within a state structure in which authority is dispersed and state activity is limited in scope, and in which considerable separation exists between the levels of village, city, and state. Party-directed patronage, on the other hand, is associated with the expanding scope and general proliferation of state activities, and also with the growing integration of village, city, and state."[2] As state power expands throughout the countryside, political parties become closely linked within the state structure and party patronage becomes more important. "The new men of influence are thus likely to be the political men, and it is their ability to deal effectively with the wider system that gives them their power."[3]

Weingrod's analysis can be applied to the present situation in Constanza, but it was in the early years of Trujillo, when economic and political ties to the capital became firmly established, that party-controlled patronage became important. This fell into the hands of a small group of economic and political power seekers, some of whom were born in Constanza and therefore had wide family contacts throughout the community; others were outsiders. These men were "nation-oriented," to use Wolf's phrase,[4] and whether they actually held political office or not, they endeavored to maintain close ties with Trujillo and his political party and on every possible occasion sought to demonstrate their loyalty.

Traditional patron-client ties continue to function in Constanza; but because of the economic changes that have occurred, the number of *patrones* has decreased. In fact, the decline in importance of these ties is as much due to changes in economic life as to increasing penetration by the state and the proliferation of government agen-

---

unequal authority, yet linked through ties of interest and friendship, manipulate their relationships to attain their ends." *Ibid.*, p. 379.

It is in this wider sense of an enduring social relationship that patronage has so far been considered in this paper.

[2] *Ibid.*, p. 381.

[3] *Ibid.*, p. 384.

[4] Eric R. Wolf, "Aspects of Group Relations in a Complex Society: Mexico," *American Anthropologist*, 58 (December 1956):1065.

In describing such groups as they have emerged in Mexican communities, Wolf notes that they follow ways of life that are different from that of their community-oriented fellow-villagers and often in fact are ". . . the agents of the great national institutions which reach down into the community . . . ." *Ibid.*, p. 1065. The government party is the principal organization through which these people mediate their interests and the party provides ". . . a channel of communication and mobility from the local community to the central power group at the helm of the government. Individuals who can gain control of the local termini of these channels can now rise to positions of power in the national economy or political machine." *Ibid.*, p. 1071.

Cock fighting is very popular in Constanza. A man poses with his favorite cock outside the cock fight arena in the *pueblo*.

Above: Children of La Zanja outside their home.

Opposite: A scene at the birthday party of a three-year-old child in the *pueblo.* The celebration of each successive birthday is common among better-off people of the *pueblo.*

Left: Those who have the right to own revolvers are seldom seen without them. They are even worn on such social occasions as dances in the bars.

Below: Peones and laborers drinking in one of the *pueblo* stores that also serves as a bar.

cies. Even though the opportunities are fewer, for the present at least *constanceros* continue to be disposed to form such contracts.

PARTY-DIRECTED PATRONAGE

Mayer, in describing how political support may be enlisted, has distinguished between "diffuse" and "specific" transactions.[5] Diffuse transactions are promises given publicly to an electorate by party leaders, whereas specific transactions are private agreements made with particular individuals to win their support. This section describes only certain specific transactions; a number of examples illustrate the various connections or linkages *constanceros* may utilize in securing party-directed patronage.

Mayer refers to two types of specific transactions—those of patronage, whereby the "transactor" himself bestows favors, and those of brokerage, in which the broker promises favors that must come from a third party to whom he has access.[6] Both patrons and brokers face difficulties that are peculiar to their position,[7] although in practice there is a good deal of overlap in the two types of transactions. In Constanza, most of the party-directed patronage is concerned with securing government positions, and both types of transactions may be involved.

With the exception of the police and military, and supposedly education, agriculture, forestry, waterworks, electricity, and public health, the heads and staffs of all other government offices in the *municipio* change with a change in government. Except for the *alcaldes*, their unpaid assistants, and a few other posts appointed directly by the *ayuntamiento*, these appointments are made from Santo Domingo; the heads of offices, the office personnel, and their works do not come under the control of the *ayuntamiento*. Many of these office heads are not natives of Constanza. Office personnel

---

[5] Adrian C. Mayer, "The Significance of Quasi-Groups in the Study of Complex Societies," in *The Social Anthropology of Complex Societies*, Michael Banton, ed. (London: Tavistock Publications, 1966), pp. 113–114.

Mayer's concepts of action-set and quasi-group are not utilized here, but are referred to in the next chapter.

[6] *Ibid.*

[7] Patronage resources, Mayer points out, are always limited and even the most influential patron will be unable to satisfy everyone. "He must therefore husband these direct patronage transactions so that they produce linkages with key people who can bring followers with them." *Ibid.*, p. 114. The broker, on the other hand, can blame his contact if promises are not fulfilled, but if there are too many failures, his reputation as a broker will be lost. Nevertheless, ". . . the broker can enter into more transactions, in relation to his resources of power, than can the patron." *Ibid.*, p. 114.

of all these offices, however, are Constanza people; to gain such an appointment, an individual must have a sponsor who will make a recommendation for the appointment to the director of the department concerned in Santo Domingo. The director generally acts upon the recommendation and authorizes the appointment. Frequently the party president or the *síndico* plays this broker role.

When Tulio Moya, an eighty-dollar-a-month clerk in one of the government offices, sought his appointment, he personally delivered a letter of recommendation written by the Reformista Party President in Constanza to the director of the department in Santo Domingo. This was to ensure that the letter would get there safely and be acted upon promptly. The director then sent a telegram to the head of his office in Constanza, authorizing the appointment. Tulio seems to be well qualified for the position he now holds; he is a high school graduate and is able to type. Qualifications or experience, however, are of very secondary importance in gaining appointments; friendships and party allegiance outweigh all other considerations.

Although the *ayuntamiento* has little direct patronage to distribute, some people in Constanza are able to influence key appointments in a decisive way. One of the Arafat brothers is the Labor Inspector (he is also believed to be with the secret police) and another is the head of the Colonies Office, a position of particular importance because, without his recommendation, aspirants for colony land that becomes vacant have little hope of securing *parcelas*. These two appointments were made from Santo Domingo; apparently Rafael Arafat, the wealthiest and most influential member of this family, serves as the principal broker in securing favors for the Arafats and their friends. The Arafats are able to exert pressure through their ties of ritual kinship to military figures to extract patronage both locally and in Santo Domingo. Because of these ties, the Arafats are feared and mistrusted by many *constanceros*. Although Rafael Arafat seeks no political position for himself, the influence he exerts is used to advance the interest of the Arafats alone.

Raóul Espiallat has long been in a position to influence appointments, either because of positions he himself has held or through his uncle. His re-election as *síndico* in May 1968 placed him in a key position to distribute patronage. It was generally assumed that he would use the post to further his own interests and that of his family and friends just as he had done previously and as his uncle had done before him. Don Alejandro, on the other hand, has no family interests in Constanza to serve, and he neither holds nor seeks political office. Yet, because he has the ear of the President (people say that he can walk into the President's office any time he wishes, which is undoubtedly an exaggeration) and is able to pretend a disinterest, he is in a key position to secure positions for various people and to mediate conflicts that may arise among key aspirants for patronage. Others like Sr. Nashash and the professional men referred to earlier, who have frequently served on the *ayuntamiento*, are also in a position to help their friends by playing the role of broker. As well, the *commandante* on occasion has approached the head of the Colonies Office and secured land for *campesino* friends.

Notwithstanding the influence of some of these men, individuals sometimes are appointed to posts or gain special favors over the heads of other local aspirants and their sponsors because they have important contacts in Santo Domingo. For instance, a man who had gained title to a *parcela* of colony land through the intervention of a government friend in the capital later, through this same friend, obtained a position in one of the offices in the *pueblo*. This office is not of the government department to which his friend belongs and it was explained that his friend had approached yet another individual in the government to secure him the position. This man cannot type and has had no high school education, yet the job is supposedly a clerical one. In taking the post, he did not have to surrender his colony land, which he proposed renting. This, of course, is illegal.

Having influential friends in Santo Domingo not only greatly assists an individual in gaining positions or in obtaining other favors, but also places him in a powerful position vis-à-vis local patrons or brokers. Sr. Martínez, for instance, who is a close friend of the head of one of the smaller government departments in Santo Domingo, claims that a municipal office of this department was established in Constanza principally so that he might be employed as its head. After this appointment, a *parcela* of colony land on which Sr. Martínez had long had his eye became vacant, but the head of the local Colonies Office insisted that it was to go to another individual and not to Martínez as had been promised because he now had a government position. Sr. Martínez protested and demanded the land, arguing that his government job offered no permanent security and that the individual to whom the colony *parcela* was to be given already had a large private holding; he apparently implied that graft was involved.

To restore this quarrel, don Alejandro and Rafael Arafat came from the *pueblo* and discussed the problem with Martínez and the head of the Colonies Office. The disputed *parcela* in the end went to a different man altogether; subsequently, Sr. Martínez was given another *parcela* of colony land that became available soon after. Just how, if at all, the land owning claimant was appeased is not known, but according to Sr. Martínez, Rafael Arafat and don Alejandro sided with him against the head of the Colonies Office, arguing that it was not right that a man who already had land of his own should be given colony land. They did not, apparently, seriously challenge the right of Sr. Martínez to have colony land, because he is obviously a man with a powerful friend who could possibly stir up trouble at a higher level.

Once in office, some people consider it their prerogative to exploit the position to their own personal advantage. The judge and other court officials are open to bribery and the poor do not expect to receive justice. In those offices that can withhold or grant favors, graft is believed to be rife; there is a good deal of foundation for this belief. Yet people who frequently express their disgust at stories about corrupt officials at high government levels do not see parallels in their own behavior. One young man in several conversations piously deplored corruption in high places; when appointed to take charge of a timber inspection station, however, he promptly took advantage of the position to acquire a considerable quantity of timber for himself and his father-in-law. This, he admitted, was not altogether honest, but it was not corruption because no money changed hands. This man and at least one other individual who was employed in the forestry office owed their position to the influence of don Alejandro. Many people believe that they expressed their gratitude by not always carrying out the duties of their offices too rigorously.[8]

All groups are extremely cynical toward those individuals who hold public positions of influence; people expect that those who are able to do so will take advantage of their situations. For instance, in 1968 the principal of the *pueblo* public school was relieved of his post following an investigation conducted by people from Santo Domingo, who were looking into the mishandling of CARE food. There was no public outcry and, in fact, little comment about the matter at all. A relative of the principal said that he lost his job only because someone else was after his post, the implica-

---

[8] In the months before the timber mills closed down completely, mill owners attempted to cut as much timber as possible. Only trees that had been marked by forestry workers were supposed to be cut, and inspection stations were set up on the highways to check the timber lorries to ensure that only legally cut timber was being carried out. Under this system, there were many opportunities for graft; in some cases, there was collusion among mill owners, forestry people, and the individuals in charge of the inspection stations.

tion being that selling food intended for children was not a sufficiently serious matter over which to lose one's job. Most people were of the opinion that the man should only have been warned and the matter left to rest. This was also the view of the district education inspector, but because outsiders were investigating the case, it could not be hushed up as usually occurs in such scandals.[9] The attitude commonly held is that no one should be dealt with too severely for using his position to his own advantage, since this is the expected behavior. *Constanceros* do not find it particularly surprising to see a government vehicle clearly marked *"para uso oficial solamente"* (for official use only) setting off on a Sunday afternoon grossly overcrowded with a load of picnickers; or that a vehicle so marked should be seen parked outside the brothel, even during government office hours. People look upon these abuses as something to be expected and accept them with much the same kind of resignation as they accept repeated electricity and water failures and the enormous potholes in the streets.

Only when graft becomes too flagrant does it arouse indignation, but even then little will be said if enough people are benefiting. People laugh about the activities of a former *síndico* who quite blatantly set about enriching himself, but they add that during his time in office he obtained many things for the people of Constanza and tried to help as many as he could. By contrast, people were disgusted at the behavior of a later incumbent who talked much but produced little and, by all accounts, operated in the manner of a petty extortionist.[10]

---

[9] When a public scandal occurs or appears to be in the making, the official concerned is not, as a rule, prosecuted, but simply transferred elsewhere. The position of head of the Colonies Office, for instance, which is one of the most lucrative in terms of the opportunities it offers for graft, has changed hands several times when graft has become so flagrant as to cause public comment.

On the other hand, officials are sometimes transferred against their will because of maneuverings at higher levels. For instance, when a district inspector of education in Constanza was suddenly transferred against his will, people said it was the work of "political enemies" and the transfer was interpreted as a "punishment." The inspector also viewed his transfer in these terms, but could ·not (or would not) say what he had done to offend.

[10] The attitude of *constanceros* toward graft and corruption among public officials appears to be much the same as that of the people of Sonora, Northwestern Mexico, described by Erasmus. Erasmus recounts a comment made about a former mayor: "He not only did nothing for the town, he was too stupid to do anything for himself." "This," says Erasmus, "not only illustrates the general tolerance of graft in spite of the fact that it is publicly disapproved of, but it also demonstrates the ambivalence with which graft is viewed." Charles J. Erasmus, *Man Takes Control* (Indianapolis: The Bobbs-Merrill Company, Inc., 1961), pp. 225–226.

People are conditioned to a system of graft that operates at all levels; when money is not involved, they expect that help beyond the ordinary will be given only to particular friends or relatives or to individuals who will reciprocate in some way or other in the future. A person's failure to get what he wants is almost invariably attributed to his being unable to offer the price, or not having an influential friend in the right quarter. When officials do appear to be acting in an impartial and consciencious manner, they are still suspected. The notion of disinterested public service is in no way prevalent.[11] One thing people repeatedly say of President Balaguer is that he is honest and has not used his position to enrich himself or to benefit his family, as if this were an extraordinary thing, and indeed, perhaps it is.

Constanceros constantly stress that to get anywhere a person must have a *cuña*—a supporter or helper on whom to depend—and those unable to exploit local contacts sometimes make direct appeals to the President himself. When Juan Conde wanted to obtain a small business loan from a government source to expand his business, he not only wrote to the administrators of the fund in the capital but also wrote a personal letter to Balaguer asking that he might receive this help. In this letter he explained his need for the money, pointing out that he wanted to expand his business so that he could adequately feed and clothe his large family. He added that he was a member of the Reformista Party and greatly admired the President for the leadership he was offering the country and the progress that was being achieved. Neither of these letters was replied to; Juan believed this was only because his letter to the President had been diverted in some way and had not reached him. He was sure that if the President knew of his need, he would have received the help he had asked. Some letters, however, do get results. A *campesino* woman who had been deserted by her husband and was destitute wrote to the President explaining her plight. Some weeks later, she received a personal letter from the President that expressed his sympathy; included with the letter was a check for RD $25.00.

Writing such letters is not at all uncommon, although replies are unusual. Apparently many such letters were written to Trujillo; each time he visited Constanza, the poor crowded around him trying

---

[11] When in 1968 the head agronomist at the Agricultural Center resigned, it was immediately assumed that he must have been involved in graft and was resigning to avoid an inquiry. Various people enumerated his supposed crimes, which included selling government seeds, selling tractor parts, falsifying the payroll, etc. In actual fact, it is almost certain that none of this was true. The agronomist was conscientious and enthusiastic about his work and had merely resigned to accept a better-paying position with a private company.

to present letters appealing for help, or in the hope of receiving some of the banknotes he at times gave out.

Generosity is a key virtue to *constanceros* and giving is a theme that is manifested at all levels. The degree of adulation and approval accorded to those at the highest level is largely commensurate with the amount of help that is given, whether this is in the form of handouts of food, clothing, money, or jobs. The *campesinos*, in particular, say that Balaguer is a good man and a fine president because he is trying to help them, but it is very clear that many are becoming impatient because few benefits have filtered down to them. Trujillo, many of them say, was a good man because he always tried to help the poor and gave them many things; the Americans, too, are good because in times past they have given them food and clothing, although people add that nothing has been forthcoming for some time. Bosch, on the other hand, is an anathema to most of the *campesinos* because their expectations of receiving were not fulfilled. In the 1968 *municipio* election campaign, however, very little of a concrete nature was promised to the *campesinos;* the political chiefs had apparently learned the folly of making wild promises that could not be kept.

Frequently, things that one would be more inclined to see as a right are turned into acts of giving. The *síndico* "gives" work when the *ayuntamiento* has the funds to pay for it and he personally distributes the jobs; at the Agricultural Center, the head agronomist "gives" day work to laborers and personally pays them, even though there is a pay clerk employed in the office. The first time President Balaguer officially visited the *pueblo,* long lists of things that the President had "given" to the people of the Dominican Republic were read out; these were various public works projects in progress throughout the country and it was announced that the President would soon be "giving" Constanza the hospital and better roads. When Balaguer came to open the hospital some six months later, a huge sign placed outside the building read, "Constanza gives thanks to Dr. Joaquin Balaguer," and large letters painted on the road announced, "Welcome to President Balaguer from his people of Constanza." At both the hospital and the market center, which was also opened that day, speeches thanked the President for his gifts and assured him of the loyalty of his people of Constanza.

Those with more education repeatedly stress how much the country needs help to overcome the problems of widespread poverty and economic backwardness. Without such help, they say, the country will very likely go communist; they are adamant that the United States must provide this help without delay. Don Alejandro and Raóul Espiallat, who spoke at length of the country's needs, both own ostentatious motor cars, have considerable wealth, and pay taxes on a level that in most advanced countries would be considered low. Many young people with some education also look to the United States, but for different reasons. Their hope is that someone will help them obtain a visa to enter the United States or Puerto Rico, where they believe they would have no difficulty in obtaining highly paid work.

THE USE OF COERCION

Coercion is at times employed against the political opposition for what may be construed as the public good. Frequently, but not always, the military or the police are involved. At the extreme undisguised intimidation is employed, with the military as the main instrument of force.

Any outbreak of violence or threat of violence in the capital is the signal for a number of local arrests. Generally, these arrests are made by the military alone, but at times the police as well take part. On two occasions during 1967 when there was minor rioting in the capital and again in February 1968, when there was a great deal of trouble at the Autonomous University of Santo Domingo, police and military patrolled the streets in force; several arrests were made both on the streets and in people's houses. The PRD people, or anyone else who is considered leftist, are arrested; these periodic arrests have continued ever since the outbreak of violence some months after Trujillo's death, except during the presidency of Juan Bosch. Such men as don Alejandro and Raóul Espiallat claim to deplore these arrests and point out that the number of people arrested decreases each time, which is true. Most of those who were prone to arrest have managed to remove themselves from this category. They have either declared for Balaguer or made it very clear that they are no longer PRD supporters and have completely withdrawn from all political activities. Immediately after the elections in June 1966, and on at least one other occasion that year, a considerable number of PRD people were arrested. In September 1967 ten were arrested; in February 1968, however, there were only six arrests. Some of these men were detained at the police station, others in the garrison. Apparently none was beaten and all were released within a few hours of or on the day following the arrest.

The military, in particular, take it upon themselves to be guardians of political opinion and in some cases feel it is their duty to stamp out any political dissent that they consider to be of the left. In a conversation with two young officers from the garrison, one of them expressed his political philosophy quite succinctly by saying that in all matters there is a right and a wrong and it was the same in politics; two sides cannot both be right. Bosch and the PRD are communists or at least leftists—there is no real difference. The point is they are wrong and must be stamped out. He added that the Americans would understand this quite clearly because they are fighting the communists all over the world. What the officers could not understand is why the United States, which intervened once to stop the communists in Santo Domingo, would not permit them to destroy the leftists once and for all. Rightly or wrongly, many people in the *pueblo* believe that the United States is exercising some restraint on the present government in this area.

On occasions, the local military unit certainly does its best to harry those considered to be leftists; they clearly are not always acting on orders from above. In October 1967, a group of Community Development workers attending a course at the Nueva Suiza hotel were stopped in the town one night by soldiers who demanded to know if they were for Bosch or Balaguer. They were permitted to pass only when they assured the soldiers they were *balagueristas*, which, in fact, was not entirely true. Some individuals in the *pueblo* consider many of the Community Development people to be communists; but one of their workers, who at times carries a pistol, is said by some people to be a police spy. Individuals who are considered to be leaders of the left have been subjected to particular harassment by the military and by the police as well.

Like the military, the police are independent of the *municipio* administration, but to a far greater extent they are amenable to manipulation and are not feared in the same way. Important individuals have an easy relationship with the police, as the following incident illustrates. Enrique Morales, the ne'er-do-well who managed to secure don Alejandro as *padrino* to his infant son, recounted how on one occasion when he was passing the police station, don Alejandro told the police to arrest him, which they promptly did, and marched him inside. He was released a few moments later, however; his *compadre* was only enjoying a little joke, which he had arranged with the police when he saw Enrique approaching. Important individuals are greeted respectfully and are not subjected to the petty annoyances that others must endure. They are not constantly asked to show their drivers' licenses and are generally waved through the checkpoint outside the entrance to the *pueblo*. Nor do the police and military come to them with requests to borrow their vehicles, as sometimes happens to others. It is evident that the law works in their favor.

One of the visitors to the *fiesta* in El Limoncito was the new Chief of Police, who was taken there by the judge so that he might meet Ramón Ornes, the *alcalde*. Illegal gambling was in progress at the *fiesta*, but this was not interfered with in any way. In more serious matters, some are favored by the law; this apparently has long been the case. Some years ago, for instance, one of *la gente mas importante* was involved in a particularly ugly incident when he was stabbed by an enraged relative after he had sexually assaulted one of his own daughters. The would-be killer was jailed, but the other man, who was a *compadre* of Trujillo and one of his most ardent supporters in Constanza, was not charged or required to testify. More recently, another leading citizen seriously wounded his wife in what was apparently an attempt at premeditated murder; he was not even arrested.

The friendship of some of *la gente mas importante* is highly valued for the degree of protection it may provide. For instance, Eduardo Santana, a member of an extremely wealthy and well-known Dominican family that strongly supported the PRD, lives in the *pueblo*. At the time of Bosch's overthrow Eduardo Santana withdrew from political activity, but he has never been subjected to the same degree of harassment by the military or the police as have other PRD supporters. Even though Sr. Santana has never declared for Balaguer, people well appreciate that he has influential friends in Santo Domingo. In Constanza, he has a strong friend in don Alejandro, who is his *compadre*.

On at least one occasion in 1967, don Alejandro secured the release of an individual who was arrested by the police for political reasons; in Trujillo's time, Sr. Nashash assisted several individuals who were arrested by the military. Today, however, very few, if any, people are able to exert direct influence on the local military, although many people believe that the two or three who are said to be spies for the military or secret police have such influence and at times order arrests. This is probably untrue, but it is clear that the Arafats, because of their close ties with military figures in the capital, which places them in high standing with the local *commandante*, are free to act against particular individuals in what are clearly cases of political oppression and therefore more the concern of the military than of the police.

One evening in the summer of 1967, Felipe Arafat, who was the Labor Inspector and also believed to be with the secret police, entered the public school at night and ordered a group of students out of the building in the name of the *commandante*. The pupils had been given permission to study there in preparation for their examinations, but the *commandante* (or Arafat, it is not clear which) believed they were discussing communism.

Reference was made above to a group of young rightists who have carried out acts of violence. The group is centered around a member of the Arafat clique; one of their principal targets is a Spaniard who has taken Dominican citizenship and who claims to be a close friend of Juan Bosch. This man has suffered a great deal of persecution, not only at the hands of this group, but from the military, the police, and the court as well. He has been threatened with assault, his property has been damaged, he has repeatedly been arrested by both the police and the military, and he has had to face trumped-up charges in court. Yet, if this man is to be believed (and his persecutions are real enough), he has only to recant, as it were, and his sufferings would cease. This brings us to the more subtle forms of coercion that are employed, the forms that seem to be favored.

When Balaguer visited Constanza in June 1967, one of several people who publicly delivered eulogies in favor of the President and the Reformista Party was a woman teacher from the high school, well-known as a firm supporter of Bosch. Supposedly the woman was informed that her job would be in jeopardy if she did not make the speech. Whether this was true or not, the woman's public declaration for Balaguer caused much comment and was seen as a triumph for the *reformistas*. Another incident concerned Ricardo Sánchez, who was the party president during the Bosch administration. The Sánchez family is one of the oldest families in the *municipio;* Ricardo, a small agriculturalist, although he owns no land himself, is well known to all. After the defeat of the PRD, key Bosch supporters suffered repeated arrests. Ricardo Sánchez, like the Spaniard mentioned earlier, was singled out for persecution to the point where he was virtually deprived of his livelihood—no one would lend or rent him land. In return for a promise of a *parcela* of land in the colonies, Sr. Sánchez made a statement over the local radio denouncing Bosch as a communist and renouncing his membership of the PRD. No land was forthcoming; instead, he earned the contempt of all. Since the broadcast, however, he has been left alone. Another incident concerned a professional man who likewise suffered greatly; for reasons that are not altogether clear, however, his persecution abruptly ceased during 1967. In April 1968 he received an invitation to dine with President Balaguer and a few of the most important men of the *pueblo*. Peace apparently was made. Finally, the Spaniard who has been much molested by the rightists claims that he was told by one of the Arafats that he would not be troubled further if he would denounce Bosch and the PRD as communists.

Many supporters of the PRD and other defeated parties who

were active before the 1966 elections have been able to avoid trouble simply by making it clear that they have withdrawn completely from all political activity, or by becoming *reformistas*. Some say rather contemptuously of the few PRD men who are still considered active that they, too, would gladly become *reformistas* were it not that they would be subjected to ridicule. Whether this is true or not, it does illustrate the attitude of the majority toward politics. Political convictions are of little importance; people simply ally themselves with those in power. This is not the attitude of everyone, but it certainly is true of the vast majority. *Constanceros* believe that an individual must look out for himself, especially in political matters.

Those people who do not align themselves with the party in power (and suffer as a result) earn no particular respect and, if anything, are considered foolish. This is equally true of those individuals who have been unwise in their choice of *patrón* (whether or not much choice was involved) and of those who themselves are *patrones*. For instance, the family of Eduardo Santana (referred to earlier in this chapter) owned two large timber mills in the *municipio*. The workers in these mills, like their *patrón*, were PRD supporters. When the mills closed, permanent workers were promised compensation by the government, to be made in two payments. All workers received the first payment, but when the second payment was made some weeks later, the Santana workers received nothing. The officials from the capital who had come to the *pueblo* to make the payments explained that these men would be paid at some future date; this still had not happened some months later when my field work ended. Timber mill owners had also been promised compensation, but by July 1968 supposedly only six men in the entire country had received any preliminary payment, and these men were firm *reformistas*. One of the six was don Alejandro, who has ready access to the President. Verily, he has his reward.

In the various instances of coercion that have been described above, the object is not merely to punish, but also to bring recalcitrants into line with the majority. Once a public confession is made persecutions cease and there may even be the hope of reward. Some of the Arafats clearly favor outright intimidation, and there is no doubt that the military and probably the police would act with less restraint were they more free to do so. Others who exercise political influence favor more subtle forms of coercion, but they are equally anxious to achieve a political consensus in the community.

CHAPTER 10

Crisis, Campaign, and the Municipio Elections of May 1968

This chapter deals with a series of crises that preceded the municipal elections of May 1968 and with the campaign itself, which led to the election of an unopposed Reformista candidate. The crises directly involved relatively few individuals—those who made up the "political fields" at that time—and most *constanceros* were in ignorance of the struggle for power that was being played out among the principal actors. The crises were of such an order, however, as to threaten to disrupt the entire community—the "arena" of political activities with which this study has been concerned.[1]

A political field does not imply anything static, for it changes over time in both personnel and organization. In considering the political events that occurred before the May elections, this chapter will show both how the various political fields underwent change and the bases on which particular individuals sought to recruit support. For some of the principal actors, the political fields extended outside the community and, in fact, events that occurred outside triggered the crises within the *municipio*.

Turner has formulated what he terms "political phase develop-

---

[1] The term "political field" comes from Swartz. A field is made up of specific persons and ". . . is defined by the 'interest and involvement of the participants' in the processes being studied and its contents include the values, meanings, resources, and relationships employed by these participants in that process." Marc J. Swartz (ed.), *Local-Level Politics* (Chicago: Aldine Publishing Co., 1968), p. 9.

Swartz refers to "arena" as ". . . a social and cultural space around those who are directly involved with the field participants but who are not themselves directly involved in the processes that define the field." *Ibid.*, p. 9. The first chapter of this study set forth the justification for examining political activity within the confines of the community; the community therefore is the arena of political activity in this study.

ment"—a schemata of related processes that are particularly useful for describing political conflict and its resolution.[2] Although he stresses that the phases may be of variable duration and under some circumstances may even appear "out of order," Swartz believes that the phases ". . . are the basic modes in the politics of a great many—perhaps all—groups when examined over time."[3] In the following section, Turner's phases have been utilized to order the events of a political nature that preceded the elections.

Turner's first phase is "mobilization of political capital," during which the groups and persons to be concerned in the struggle attempt to build up support and to undermine rivals.[4] Then follows "breach of the peace," which leads to "crisis" when conflict becomes open and ". . . in which the contenders are ultimately arrayed in two camps or two factions."[5] In societies where basic values are held in common and where relationships are multiplex, however, complete cleavage is likely to be inhibited by "countervailing tendencies"; from these will follow the next phase, "deployment of adjustive or redressive mechanisms," in an effort to resolve the conflict and to lead to the final phase, the "restoration of peace."[6]

POLITICAL PHASES PRIOR TO THE MUNICIPIO ELECTIONS OF MAY 1968

Background to the Events

Well before the elections of May 1968, it had become apparent that many people in the community were dissatisfied. Much of the blame for this was placed on the *síndico*, Roberto Molina, a rather brash young man with little presence, who had managed to antagonize many people, both in the *pueblo* and in the *campo*. During 1967, all of the *regidores* had resigned after a series of quarrels with the *síndico*, and no one wished to serve on the *ayuntamiento* with him.

The *síndico* was also blamed by many people for the lack of public works that had been undertaken in Constanza during his term. Many people believed that the community was being discriminated against in the allocation of funds because officials in Santo

---

[2] M. J. Swartz, V. W. Turner, and A. Tuden (eds.), *Political Anthropology* (Chicago: Aldine Publishing Co., 1966), pp. 32–39.

[3] Marc J. Swartz, ed., *Local-Level Politics*, pp. 18–19.

[4] M. J. Swartz, V. W. Turner, and A. Tuden eds., *Political Anthropology*, p. 32.

[5] *Ibid.*, p. 34.

[6] *Ibid.*, p. 37.

Domingo had little confidence in the Constanza administration so long as Roberto Molina remained in office. In the election campaign, after which Bosch had been so decisively defeated, Sr. Molina, in particular, had made all sorts of promises to obtain votes for the *reformistas. Campesinos* had been promised roads and bridges in their localities, as well as land. *Pueblo* dwellers were led to believe that various public works would be commenced that would provide employment; permanent government employees, including office workers and teachers, had expected substantial salary increases to follow the austerity of Bosch's administration.

Very few of these things happened; conditions, in fact, became worse. The timber industry closed down, causing much distress; government employees complained that they actually earned less than before. There had been much talk of land reform, and there was some action in certain parts of the country, but no new *parcelas* were made available in the Constanza *municipio* and the ban on clearing land made it virtually impossible to squat on unclaimed land. Work on the canal system within the main Valley had progressed; in the months prior to the election the hospital was renovated and opened, a market center was built in the *pueblo*, and work was begun on resurfacing the main road between El Río and El Abanico. But many people complained that much of the work these projects provided went to people outside the community, and the poor complained that the hospital did not give free medicines as it had in the days of Trujillo.

Perhaps more important was the feeling of uncertainty and frustration shared by a number of the *gente importante* of the *pueblo* and some of the *campesino* leaders, who look back to the days of Trujillo with nostalgia. These men are fearful of the future. They say that the President is weak and is permitting communists to gain positions of influence in the government; they see communist influence at work in the growing restlessness of *los pobres* and in the demands for land. Moreover, they complain of the present government's inefficiency and corruption and believe that under a military regime there would be more work for everyone, more money for themselves, and their positions would be thoroughly assured. They pine for a restoration of the old kind of order. The Arafats emerged as the spokesmen for this sentiment, and the rapid support they were able to gather in some quarters is largely explained by the failure of the *reformistas* to make good their many previous promises, by the growing restlessness throughout the *municipio*, and, to a lesser extent, by the failure of the PRD to emerge as an effective opposition.

In January 1968 the PRD supporters held a meeting in the house of one of their members. It had been announced on the radio that the meeting was to decide on a plank for the coming elections and to organize committees to work for a PRD victory. Five PRD organizers from La Vega and Santo Domingo were present; apparently the meeting had been organized at their behest.

At 3:30 p.m., when the meeting was due to commence, there were only fifteen people present, other than the visitors, and several of these stood at a distance from others who were waiting on the porch and within the house, as if they did not wish to identify too closely with the group. When the meeting finally got under way some forty minutes later, there were 28 present, but some individuals remained outside the house throughout the proceedings and a few left the room when nominations for various positions were called for. A number declined to accept because of lack of time. Most of those present at the meeting were *pueblo* dwellers and none of them had any importance in the community.

One of the visitors spoke at length of the need for courage among PRD supporters and of the importance of making their voices felt whatever the consequences, but it was very evident that the PRD had little strength; many of the people at the meeting, understandably enough, were afraid. Most of those who had previously been involved in the PRD organization did not appear at the meeting, and although a number of organizing committees were elected, it was quite evident that the PRD would amount to little. When, in April, a decision was made by the PRD in the capital to withdraw from the campaign, the Constanza organization faded away, none of its committees ever having met.

Toward the end of 1967, groups supporting General Wessin y Wessin appeared in many parts of the country. These groups were to work for the election of Wessin sympathizers in municipal elections and then to organize support to elect Wessin as president in the 1970 presidential elections. This new party—the Partido Quisqueya Dominicano (PQD)—did not materialize in Constanza until early in 1968, only to disband almost immediately. But the supposed secret activities of the Wessin supporters in Constanza during this time caused considerable dissention within the community.

Mobilization of Political Capital

Apparently the guiding spirit of the Wessin group was Rafael Arafat, but exactly what part he played in organizing the PQD is not known. Throughout January and February, some of the

Arafats and their friends sounded out various individuals who might lend support; this was not done openly, but in secret, and very little could be learned of their specific activities. The key supporters of the PQD are known, however, and the potential support some of these men were able to generate can be described.

Mayer's concepts of "quasi-groups" and "action-sets" are particularly applicable in the analysis of the system of linkages that are exploited by various people to generate political support.[7] In the action-set to be described, Rafael Arafat was a key actor and almost certainly he recruited most of those who make up the linkages in the set. Yet it appears that this was done primarily through intermediaries, and Rafael Arafat himself was able to stay in the background. Other individuals were largely considered responsible for the split that threatened the community.

It was mentioned above that the Arafats are not popular in Constanza but are respected for their wealth, and their influence is appreciated. The Arafats and their affines own more land in the main Valley than any other family; because they offer much employment to *peones* who live in the *pueblo* and in the colonies, they are in a position to influence their thinking. This is particularly true of Antonio Torres, who has a very strong following among those *peones* to whom he regularly offers employment. As well, he and another agriculturalist, Sr. Baez, are popular among many of the *peones* and small agriculturalists of the Valley because they agitated for the expulsion of the Spaniards and the distribution of their colony land among poor Dominicans. These two men are close friends and both were Wessin supporters. They are considered *muy macho* and were previously strong *trujillistas*. They have little influence in the *pueblo*, but their combined influence in the Valley is considerable and there is no doubt they could have built up strong support for Wessin.

Felipe Arafat, the Labor Inspector who was apparently also working as an informer for the secret police, is distrusted by nearly all of the people in the *pueblo* (except the other Arafats and their friends), but he had much influence among the older *campesino* leaders who, like himself, were strong *trujillistas*. He is a welcome

---

[7] Adrian C. Mayer, "The Significance of Quasi-Groups in the Study of Complex Societies," pp. 97–122.

An action-set is a bounded network but cannot be considered a group, for although there is a central ego who stands at the center of a network of linkages, ". . . the basis of membership is specific to each linkage, and there are no rights or obligations relating all those involved." *Ibid.*, p. 109. An action-set has no permanency but, "To the extent that the same linkages remain in use in successive contexts of activity, a quasi-group is formed. . . ." *Ibid.*, p. 110.

visitor in the homes of these men and in the early months of the
year visited some of them a great deal, presumably to enlist their
support. The influence of such leaders is strongest in the dry farming
areas, where personal kindreds are readily definable in terms of
locality and economic cooperation and where egalitarian sentiments
generally prevail. Several times Felipe boasted that these leaders
could easily be persuaded to support Wessin and that he himself
could accomplish this merely by telling them that Balaguer was
permitting communists to infiltrate the government and that the
times called for a strong military man as president if another revolution was to be averted.

The Almost certainly Felipe Arafat did not have the degree of influence he claimed, but Antonio Torres and Sr. Baez respected his
opinion highly, and so did Ramón Ornes, the *alcalde* of El Limoncito.
These men regarded Felipe as an authority on what was going on
in the highest circles of government in Santo Domingo and what
future political developments were likely to be. Ramón Ornes and
other *campesino* leaders gave as much if not more weight to the
opinions of Raóul Espiallat, Sr. Nashash, and don Alejandro,
however.

One individual who provided an important linkage in the Wessin action-set was Mario Rosario, who commands wide support in
two sections of the *municipio* where dry farming is practiced, and
where he has particularly extensive family ties. Rosario had been
appointed *síndico* for a brief period during the Council of State;
during that period, he achieved a good deal of popularity, even
though he used the post to enrich himself and to help his friends
and relatives. Rosario wished to be *síndico* again, and it was primarily for this reason that he made overtures to the Wessin men.
He was on good terms with the Arafats, and was known to be an
extreme rightist and a former *trujillista*. He was not a member
of the Arafat clique, however, and tried to avoid involving himself
too closely with the Wessin supporters—presumably so that he
would have a way out if strong Wessin support did not emerge.
In the bars and in the *campo*, where Rosario conversed with various
people, he let it be known that he did not favor Wessin as president
but only as vice-president. Wessin's strength, he argued, was needed
in the government but is was "not right" that a military man should
be president, as in the days of Trujillo. This attempt to straddle both
sides proved to be only partly successful.

The Arafats, as it turned out, had their own potential *síndico*
candidate; this brings us to an analysis of their strength in the
pueblo. The individual around whom the group of right wing ex-

tremists centered was Marco Ríos, the son of Edmundo Ríos, the former mill owner who distributed parcels of food to poor families each *día de Altagracia*. Marco had wanted the nomination for *síndico* in 1966, but the Reformista Party directive had decided on Roberto Molina, who at that time had more popular appeal. The Ríos family were comparatively recent arrivals in Constanza and through ties of ritual kinship were closely connected with the Arafats. Unlike his father, however, Marco was not popular in the community; in fact, he was largely unknown outside the *pueblo*. His following was limited within the *pueblo*, and it was unlikely that he would have generated much enthusiasm throughout the *municipio* as the *síndico* choice of the Wessin supporters.

Edmundo Ríos was deeply respected as a religious man. As a former *patrón* who practiced generosity, he had the approval of a number of *los pobres* and therefore was of some importance in the Wessin action-set. This importance derived more from the status he held in the community than any political organizing he was likely to undertake, however. Edmundo Ríos had no deep political interests; he was drawn into the Wessin action-set only because of his close ties with the Arafats. This was also largely true of one of the Arafat brothers and of another former mill owner who had married into the Arafat family and, like Edmundo Ríos, came from outside the community.

One *pueblo* dweller of some renown who was outside the Arafat clique but who became an avid Wessin supporter was Pedro Espiallat, the half-brother of Raóul, who was elected *síndico* in the election that year. Pedro owned one of the most successful stores in the *pueblo* and it was principally because of business rivalry (so people said) that strong enmity existed between the half-brothers. At various times during the Trujillo years, Pedro had been a *regidór* and was known to have been a firm supporter of Trujillo. Whatever influence he may have exerted previously had largely been forfeited, however, because of the way he publicly flouted moral conventions. Pedro, in fact, was considered somewhat strange; many people were convinced that he joined the Wessin camp only to embarrass his brother and to display his contempt for other leading citizens, whom he regarded as cowards. It does seem certain that Pedro Espiallat was likely to exert no great influence on the voting of others.

As it turned out, the Wessin men had very little direct support in the *pueblo* from those people with most influence, but many individuals remained uncommitted until they were certain that the PQD was not going to amount to anything. A number of government servants, for instance, were concerned that if they did not show some enthusiasm for the Wessin movement at this time, they were likely to lose their jobs in 1970 if Wessin became president, even if prior to those elections they were able to make a sudden switch in party allegiance. The judge, an outsider in the community who had fallen out with the Arafats some time before, explained this dilemma to me and said that even though he admired Balaguer, if it looked as if the Wessin movement was going to prove popular, he would have to join the PQD "out of necessity" because he was, after all, a *padre de familia* and had his responsibilities. Tulio Moya, a lowly government clerk, was also fearful for his future and tried to protect himself by being friendly to the key Wessin men without actually committing himself in any way.

Those people who wanted government jobs but had no hope of gaining these so long as the *reformistas* were in power (the fact was that virtually all the patronage available to the *reformistas* had already been dispensed) were ready recruits for the PQD. So far as is known, none of these individuals formed significant linkages such that they in turn would be able to recruit further supporters for the party.

Potentially, the greatest strength of the PQD lay in some of the *peones* and small growers of the Valley and in the dry farming areas, where leadership had long been asserted by men who had been strong *trujillistas* and who had extensive family connections in their areas. In the more populous areas, where intensive agriculture was followed and leadership was more diffuse, the degree of support was less clear. Notwithstanding the boasts of Felipe Arafat, it was unlikely that even former *trujillistas* like Ramón Ornes, who saw Wessin as an heir to the Trujillo tradition, were likely to give support to the PQD unless there was a clear certainty of victory. For victory to be certain, the Wessin supporters had to win the allegiance of *la gente mas importante* in the *pueblo*. This they failed to do.

Thus far, I have described only some of the key linkages in the Wessin action-set and have indicated the kind of support each was able to generate. The actual recruiting of support was carried out secretly and it was only those who themselves were in a position to influence others who were approached. There was nothing in the nature of a public campaign and no attempt was made to reach those who occupied the terminal positions of the various linkages. Yet a great deal of uncertainty and speculation developed, particularly in the *pueblo*, as to where various people stood; rumors abounded and tension built up. In large measure, this was the work of Roberto Molina, the *síndico*, and of Mario Rosario.

Roberto Molina was well aware that he had lost much support and that both Mario Rosario and Marco Ríos were contenders for his position. There was every likelihood that even if the Wessin movement came to nothing, Mario Rosario would still want the Reformista Party nomination as the *síndico* and this, in fact, proved to be so. Roberto Molina wished to retain the post and sought to protect his own interests by building up antipathy toward his rivals. Throughout January and February, he spent a great deal of time in the bars, in the park, and on street corners holding private conversations with various individuals, in which he would hint of a plot by *los ricos* (or the *"trujillistas"* as he often referred to them) to take over the *pueblo* so that they could exploit the poor. These men, he said, were dangerous and would destroy all the gains that had been made by the democratic government of Balaguer. Molina rarely indicated any of the plotters by name, but it was rumored that Raóul Espiallat, Sr. Nashash, and even don Alejandro secretly favored Wessin. This was possibly true in the case of Nashash but almost certainly untrue of the other two men. There was no question, of course, that the Arafats and their friends were numbered among the "plotters" and so, too, was Mario Rosario, whom, much more so than Marco Ríos, the *síndico* regarded as his most dangerous rival.

Outside his own close circle in the *pueblo*, Ríos did not appear to make any attempt to publicize his interest in becoming *síndico*. Mario Rosario, on the other hand, who was an "enemy" of the *síndico*, had been building up support for his own candidacy since the latter months of the previous year. He had even visited distant parts of the *municipio*, where he talked to *campesino* leaders and, without naming the *síndico* directly, managed to convey the impression that Molina had been grossly derelict in his duties, was merely a self-seeker, and had no real sympathy for the plight of the *campesinos*. Everywhere he went he made it clear that he was available to serve if called upon to do so; by the earliest months of 1968, there were very few persons of influence in the *campo* or *pueblo* who were unaware that Rosario wanted the position.

In the second week of February, at a function organized by the high school, the *síndico* issued what almost sounded like a call to arms. Speaking in his capacity as the president of Reformista Youth in Constanza, he said that there were some individuals in the Republic and even some in the *pueblo* who wanted to overthrow the democratic regime and restore a military rule. He warned the youth of Constanza not to let this happen. A few days after this speech, the PQD party was formed in the *pueblo* following a private

meeting that was held in the house of Edmundo Ríos. It was the
secrecy surrounding those who had attended the meeting and what
had transpired as much as the formation of the party that constituted
a breach of the peace and led to a crisis in which the community
all but split into two camps.

Breach of the Peace and Crisis

The PQD meeting was not publicly announced; those who attended did so by invitation. Almost certainly, the meeting was organized by Rafael Arafat, but the fact that it was not held in his house
absolved him from much of the criticism that followed, when it
became general knowledge that the meeting had occurred. Sr. Ríos,
however, was criticized widely, and some believed that, because the
meeting had been held in his house, it was he who had initiated the
Wessin movement in Constanza.

The PQD meeting was attended by some forty to fifty men;
the exact number was not known, nor was it possible to ascertain
exactly what transpired. Many of those present were influential
campesinos who had been contacted by some of the individuals mentioned earlier. Eighteen committees were organized at the meeting
to begin campaigning in various parts of the *municipio*. A significant
number of the people at the meeting, however, showed little enthusiasm because they believed the PQD could not succeed without
the support of some of the most influential men of the *pueblo*. Another meeting was scheduled to take place in the near future; before
this meeting could be held, however, the principal organizers decided
to disband the party. The reasons for this decision are discussed
below, but the leading PQD supporters may also have been influenced by two serious incidents that occurred in the *pueblo* and
brought the impending crisis to public attention.

A few days after the PQD meeting, the *síndico* became involved
in a violent quarrel with Pedro Espiallat in the bar. Pistols were
drawn and the *síndico*, who was drunk, had to be forcibly disarmed
by two military officers who were also in the bar at the time. News
of the quarrel soon became public; supposedly the quarrel had
erupted because the *síndico* accused Espiallat of being in league
with the Arafats to restore the *trujillistas* to power. This was the
first time, in fact, that Pedro Espiallat's association with the Wessin
people became public knowledge.

On the Sunday following this incident, another quarrel broke
out in the bar—this time between the judge and a member of the
young Arafat extremist clique. There were some blows; the judge
ran to the street and then backed away slowly, arguing the whole
time, followed by several young men who were trying to restrain

one of their number from striking the judge. In this way, the group progressed along the street before a large crowd of *pueblo* dwellers who stood in the park watching. The *síndico* and some others then appeared on the scene and led the judge away to safety.

According to the judge, this quarrel arose because he had had an account of the PQD meeting published in the Santo Domingo newspaper, *El Caribe*,[8] which gave the names of the principal office holders and details of the speeches that had been made. This was probably untrue, but there was no doubt that even after the meeting most of the Wessin supporters were concerned with keeping their identities secret—presumably so that relations with various others who were firm *reformistas* would not be disrupted if the PQD proved to have no future in the community. That this is the most likely explanation is borne out by the fact that in the weeks following the disbanding of the movement, even some of those who were key linkages in the action-set denied that they had played any real part in sounding out support. At that time virtually all *constanceros*, in fact, were anxious to forget that a pro-Wessin group had ever emerged.

The organization of the PQD party in Constanza made no immediate impact on the wider community because initially relatively few knew of the meeting that had taken place. The two incidents in the bar, however, brought the issue into the open and caused considerable agitation among many people in the *pueblo*. Even then, the crisis did not reach down to the lowest levels of the community, but inevitably it would have done so once campaigning commenced, and the disruption would have been considerable. People would have been forced to choose between the PQD and the *reformistas*, with no certainty as to the final outcome, and, as has been indicated before, this is the kind of choice *constanceros* prefer not to make. The PQD disbanded, however, thus averting an absolute break. The decision to disband was made because the PQD men of key importance had conflicting loyalties and also, it seems, because pressure was exerted from outside.

Countervailing Tendencies

Turner has pointed out that even in large-scale societies, ". . . multiple cross-cutting conflicts of loyalty and allegiance (if there

---

[8] A part-time activity of the judge was reporting Constanza news for this paper. He was paid for each item that was published. He declined to provide the details of this supposed account on the grounds that it could be read in the newspaper. No such account appeared in *El Caribe* or in any other newspaper. It is known that the judge did attend the meeting but in what capacity is not clear.

is agreement on basic values) tend to inhibit the development of dichotomous cleavage."[9] Previous chapters have described the role of real and fictive kinship, how friendships of various kinds are formed and the duties and obligations these entail, and the obligations incumbent upon the recipient of patronage. Here I will do no more than to indicate how, in a few cases, ties of these various kinds served to inhibit complete disruption.

Ramón Ornes in El Limoncito respected the opinion of Felipe Arafat and was very friendly with Mario Rosario, whom he hoped to see become *síndico*. He was also very friendly with don Alejandro, however, to whom he frequently went for advice; economically, he was closely tied to Raóul Espiallat. Sr. Ornes did a great deal of business with Espiallat and, in fact, had lent him money to open his store. If Ornes had to choose between supporting Rosario or supporting Raóul Espiallat, almost certainly he would be bound to side with the latter.

Mario Rosario owed a debt of gratitude to don Alejandro, Raóul Espiallat, Nashash, and other people of importance, for it was these men who had made possible his earlier appointment as *síndico* (from which he had made sufficient money to set himself up in the timber business), and if the Wessin movement failed to take hold or if he was not successful in gaining the PQD nomination as *síndico*, it was quite apparent that his political future rested in the hands of these men. Mario Rosario, therefore, was bound to act with restraint; in rendering partial support to the PQD, therefore, he tried not to offend the Reformista chiefs nor to cut his ties with these men.

Roberto Molina had been chosen as the Reformista *síndico* candidate in 1966 in order to detract from PRD support. He owed his nomination principally to don Alejandro and, consequently, was in his debt. Despite his extreme youthfulness, Roberto was an eloquent speaker, but, what was more important at that time, he was considered an ardent revolutionary; for a brief time he had been a member of the 14th of June Movement. Many people believed that his candidacy would allay the fears of those who identified the Reformista Party with the old Partido Dominicano of Trujillo. Raóul Espiallat, who is an uncle of Roberto, was chosen as the president of the *ayuntamiento;* people hoped that in this capacity he would be able to exert a strong influence over the young man and more or less direct his activities. This was not to be the case, however,

---

[9] Marc J. Swartz, V. W. Turner, and A. Tuden (eds.), *Political Anthropology*, p. 35.

and Espiallat himself was one of those who resigned from the *ayuntamiento* when the *síndico* proved to be so intractable.

In explaining this matter to me, various individuals pointed out that Espiallat could not really take firm action with his nephew because if, for instance, he had attempted to force Molina's resignation, it would have led to a serious conflict between the two families and Espiallat would have been much criticized. In this case, then, fear of causing inter-family conflict inhibited an individual from taking a strong hand, even though firm action could possibly have prevented a serious situation that indirectly threatened the peace of the entire community from arising. Moreover these same familial ties made it impossible for Raóul Espiallat to declare his own interest in becoming *síndico* in 1968 as long as his nephew made it clear that he wished to continue in the post. Such a conflict could only be resolved by someone who stood outside the arena of family loyalties and, at the same time, had the necessary influence to compel the acceptance of a compromise solution. This was a role don Alejandro was able to play.

A number of people in the *pueblo* believed Sr. Nashash was pro-Wessin because of his previous close ties to Trujillo and was merely waiting to assess the strength of the PQD before committing himself. This was probably more true of other *los ricos* than of Nashash. Since Balaguer's election in 1966, Nashash had made a strong commitment to the *reformistas* in an effort to regain some of the influence he wielded in the days of Trujillo. With don Alejandro, he was elected one of the "guidance men" for Reformista Youth; he appeared on welcoming committees on both occasions when President Balaguer had visited Constanza. Moreover, although Nashash enjoyed good relations with Rafael Arafat, there was some enmity between Nashash and Felipe Arafat, and he had no particular ties with the other Arafats or their friends. On the other hand, Nashash and Raóul Espiallat were friends of long standing, and Espiallat was fully committed to the *reformistas*. Like Ramón Ornes, Nashash had helped Espiallat to establish his business; recently, Espiallat's son had become engaged to one of Nashash's daughters. In short, Nashash could have sided with the Wessin men only at the cost of his long standing friendship with Raóul Espiallat; this he would not be likely to do unless there was a clear certainty that the PQD was going to succeed.

More important were the ties of friendship between don Alejandro and Rafael Arafat. On one occasion, Sr. Arafat expressed his admiration for don Alejandro and claimed that he did not question his opinions. "If he walked into my house right now and told me to put that table around the other way," he said, pointing to a small coffee table in the middle of the room, "I would do it because I know he would have his reasons."

Whether Arafat invariably accepted don Alejandro's opinions on more serious matters is questionable, but there is no doubt that the two men were close friends and were in the habit of conversing frankly. In the dispute concerning the head of the Colonies Office and Sr. Martínez, the public servant who was denied a *parcela* of colony land to which he believed he had claim, don Alejandro accompanied Rafael Arafat to the Colonies office to settle the matter. Whether don Alejandro played any part in persuading the principal PQD men to disband their movement (albeit, possibly only a temporary disbandment) is not known. But in the transactions that were made with various individuals to restore peace, don Alejandro almost certainly acted with the foreknowledge and approval of Rafael Arafat.

The PQD in Constanza was formed in imitation of such groups in other *pueblos*. It is probable that the organization in Constanza would not have disbanded and more support would have materialized had it been apparent that the movement was sweeping the country. This was not the case, however. In the capital, the principal military figures remained either uncommitted or favorable to the *reformistas*, and there appeared to be little likelihood of a military coup in favor of Wessin. In fact, rather than receiving encouragement from events and individuals outside the community, it seems that the PQD in Constanza came under pressure from some quarters to disband.

A few days after the party had been formed in Constanza, Felipe Arafat was suddenly transferred from the local Labor Office to the capital. Some people said that the secret police, for whom he was working, learned that he was also in the pay of Wessin, ordered him to cease activities for the PQD, and transferred him to the capital, where he could be placed under surveillance. Whether this was the real reason for the transfer, his removal from the *pueblo* meant the loss of a key figure to the Wessin supporters.

Some time after the PQD had been disbanded, Antonio Torres confided that he, personally, had come under pressure from General Perez y Perez (one of his *compadres*) to quit the PQD; he hinted that Rafael Arafat had come under similar pressure. It is not unlikely that Sr. Torres invented this story to explain what may have been a sudden loss of enthusiasm on his own part. The man had an exaggerated sense of his own importance and the extent of his influence in the *pueblo*. He also was considered to be an unmitigated liar. Nevertheless, various PQD people probably did come under pressure to desist their activities. It was strongly rumored, for example, that the *síndico* and the Reformista party president had been instructed to forward the names of the Wessin sympathizers employed in the various government offices so that they might be dismissed after the May elections and their jobs given to loyal *reformistas*.

Once the PQD was disbanded, a need arose to present some sort of rationalization acceptable to the community to explain why the movement had commenced in the first place, and why it had disbanded so soon thereafter. Many people in the *pueblo* believed that the Arafats had initiated the party in Constanza merely as a gesture of loyalty to Wessin because of the ties of ritual kinship that linked the two families. Many people said that the Arafats and others were well aware that there was insufficient support to challenge the *reformistas* in the elections and that they had had no serious intention of doing so. Consequently, the movement was disbanded after one meeting. This story, it appears, was circulated by the Arafats themselves, and for all its implausability, it found ready acceptance. This was indicative of the desire of the Wessin supporters themselves and of the leading *reformistas* to seek a rapprochement and heal the breach as quickly as possible.

Deployment of Adjustive or Redressive Mechanisms

Turner's discussion of this fourth phase of power struggle notes that ". . . various mechanisms of redress—jural, ritual, arbitrational, etc.—may be tried in order to produce a settlement or to restore the semblance of a peaceful state of relationships so that individuals and groups may once again pursue their ordinary lives and nonpolitical goals."[10]

The mechanisms of redress considered here are those of arbitration, or, more properly, to follow a distinction made by Turner, those of mediation.[11] The particular concern in this section is the part played by don Alejandro in restoring peace; transactions of brokerage played an important part in mediating the conflict.

"Mediation," Turner points out, "involves the sustained intervention of the mediator, who must be concerned with more than

---

[10] *Ibid.*, pp. 36–37.

[11] "If the decision of the third party *must* be accepted, we may speak of 'arbitration' . . . . If negotiations are conditioned on voluntary acceptance by both contestants of the settlement proposed by the third party, we may speak of 'mediation'." *Ibid.*, p. 36.

the legal issues at stake and must utilize a variety of pragmatic techniques—ranging from friendly advice and pressure to formulation of new terms—to bring about a reconciliation of the interests of the opposed parties."[12] Swartz, in a discussion of the various techniques that may be used to gain compliance, states that "influence," which is one form of persuasion, ". . . involves bringing those who comply to believe that the course proposed to them is genuinely for their benefit." He continues: ". . . but another form of persuasion is based upon threats and bribes, and . . . [this] depends upon its intrinsic effectiveness more than upon shared values."[13]

Swartz has also noted the many functions the political "middleman" may fulfill,[14] but states that "the diversity and multiplicity of the middleman's roles are often combined with and operate primarily through the social ties of friendship and kinship (including ceremonial kinship) while avoiding or at least not seeking formal office."[15]

The previous chapter, where some reference was made to the role of don Alejandro, noted that he is in the confidence of the President and therefore in an ideal brokerage position; because he seeks no office for himself and has no family interests in Constanza to serve, he is also ideally situated to mediate in disputes that arise among other people. In a conversation with me, don Alejandro described himself as the "planner and pacifier" of the *pueblo* and insisted that he had no political interests but sought only the good of the *pueblo*. Other people have described him as the "arbitrator" or "councillor of the *pueblo*," and explain that he is able to play this role because he has no enemies, enjoys much popularity, and is able "to speak with authority."

Don Alejandro has no "authority," in the sense that he cannot command unquestioned obedience.[16] Rather, he must rely upon

---

[12] *Ibid.*, p. 36.

[13] *Ibid.*, p. 23.

[14] "Depending on the various prominence of his activities as translator, arbiter, 'fixer,' and so forth, the status might reasonably be labeled intermediary, interpreter, mediator, or broker. . . ." Marc J. Swartz (ed.), *Local-Level Politics*, Part III, "The Political Middleman," p. 203.

[15] *Ibid.*, p. 203.

[16] In Easton's view, it is this factor in particular that distinguishes "authority" from "persuasion" as a means of exercising power. "The power relationship of authority arises (1) when a person receives an explicit message from another; (2) when he then adopts it as the basis of decision or action; and (3) when the grounds for doing so are that messages received in this way ought or must

friendly persuasion, or what Swartz has called "influence." On occasions, however, persuasion takes the other form to which Swartz refers—namely, that based upon threats and bribes—and this is possible because of the powerful position of brokerage that don Alejandro occupies.

The events that transpired in the *pueblo* from the time when the PQD was disbanded until the official acceptance of the Reformista plank can now be examined in the light of this preliminary discussion. The particular focus will be on the part played by don Alejandro in restoring the peace.

With the disbanding of the PQD, it was apparent that the *reformistas* would have no opposition in the coming municipal elections. Much uncertainty remained over the question of who was to be *síndico*, however; it was evident that neither Mario Rosario nor Roberto Molina, each of whom continued to build up support on his own behalf, was a satisfactory candidate.

Rosario had a strong following in two sections of the *campo*, where his family connections are extensive; he was also the more acceptable candidate to the former Wessin men. His connection with the PQD and his Wessin sympathies made him completely unacceptable to the directive of the Reformista Party in the capital, however. As well, a number of people critcized him because he had a reputation for graft; it was assumed that he would use the *síndico* office to benefit his family and friends.

Sr. Molina had the support of those whom he had directly or indirectly helped as *síndico;* for the most part, these were family or friends living in the *pueblo*. As well, a number of the younger people of the *pueblo* preferred him to Rosario. Because of his rash promises to the *campesinos* and subsequent total neglect of their interests, however, Molina had forfeited virtually all support in the *campo;* the influential *reformistas* in the *pueblo* and the party directive in the capital apparently were adamant that Molina not be permitted to remain in office.

In short, it was imperative that the *reformistas* find a new candidate who could rally all sectors of the community behind him. To accomplish this, Molina and Rosario not only had to be induced to waive their own claims, but also had to lend their support to

---

be obeyed without subjecting them to independent evaluation in terms of one's own criteria of judgment." David Easton, *A Theoretical Approach to Authority* (Stanford, Calif.: Department of Economics, Stanford University, 1955), p. 28.

In the case of persuasion, the party whose response is desired by the power holder will evaluate such messages "according to his own standards of judgment." *Ibid.*, p. 27.

such a candidate. Further, it was highly desirable that some key Wessin figure be included among the *regidores* who, together with the *síndico*, would make up the Reformista Party plank. This would be a proof to the community that the breach caused by the appearance of the PQD no longer existed, and the *síndico* candidate could then better pose as the head of a unity party pledged to serve all sections of the community.

A few days after the *síndico*'s quarrel with Pedro Espiallat in the bar, the two men had become reconciled and were now friends. Don Alejandro had visited each of the men in turn and then brought them together in the bar, where they had talked over their differences and then publicly embraced. The judge was not reconciled with the Arafats (the quarrel here was a longstanding one), but the judge himself let it be known that he would soon be leaving Constanza to take up another post in the capital.

In the first week of March, in what was really the only frank conversation I ever enjoyed with don Alejandro, he hinted that the political problems of the community would soon be resolved. Roberto Molina, he said, would be "placed" in a position outside Constanza that was "more mechanical and better suited to his abilities," and Mario Rosario would "soon be given a position in Constanza very much to his liking." The position, as it turned out, was that of judge, which he assumed in June, after the incumbent had left to take another post in the capital. In return, both Molina and Rosario agreed to support the new *síndico* candidate actively; the candidate was to be Raóul Espiallat. Rafael Arafat had also agreed to having his name placed on the list of proposed *regidores*, which otherwise comprised basically the same men who had resigned from the *ayuntamiento* during the previous year. Don Alejandro was not among those proposed (to have become a *regidór* would have weakened his position as mediator), and neither was Sr. Nashash, who apparently had declined nomination for reasons unknown.

Most, if not all, of these transactions were carried out by don Alejandro in his capacity as broker; in winning the acceptance of those concerned and in obtaining promises to cooperate, he acted as mediator. In the few days prior to the conversation mentioned above, don Alejandro was frequently seen conversing on street corners and occasionally in the bars with Raóul Espiallat, Srs. Nashash, Molina, Rosario, the party president, and a few others who made up the directive of the Reformista Party. As well, he paid several visits to the home of Rafael Arafat.

For the most part, don Alejandro conversed with only one

individual at a time. Some of the other men mentioned above were seen conversing together, but because of enmities that had arisen, certain of them did not come into direct contact until the transactions previously referred to had been arranged. Rafael Arafat, for instance, did not associate with any of the others; his agreement to serve as a *regidór* probably was won by don Alejandro alone.[17] The *síndico* and Rosario kept apart, for had the two men come together at this time, a quarrel would very likely have erupted. Likewise, the *síndico* avoided Raóul Espiallat. There had been tension between these two men from the time Espiallat had resigned his position on the *ayuntamiento;* now that he was to become *síndico,* Molina resented him all the more.

Molina, in fact, was the one individual who was left unsatisfied by the turn of events, and indeed he had the most to lose. The exact position in which he was to be "placed" was not specified; because it was obvious that he had been judged incompetent and was being removed from his office, his pride was hurt. He remained a potential source of trouble.

The full details of the transactions that were made at this time could not be learned, although rumors abounded. Some people said that Espiallat had been pressured by don Alejandro and others in the *pueblo* into accepting the position, whereas others attributed this pressure to President Balaguer or the Vice-President, Francisco Augusto Lora. A popular belief, in fact, was that Raóul Espiallat had been ordered to accept the position "to save the situation in Constanza." In the view of one of the Arafat brothers-in-law, however, Espiallat had deliberately sought the nomination because he wished to advance the interests of his own family and had political ambitions that went beyond the position of *síndico.*

Whatever pressures were brought to bear on Espiallat and whatever his private motives may have been, the likelihood of his accepting the nomination was not made public until after the event itself had occurred. All the transactions, in fact, were handled in great secrecy; only those individuals who were most intimately concerned and a few of their closest associates were aware of what was transpiring. Only when a clear consensus had been reached was the party

---

[17] Some people believed that the agreement involved an understanding that the judge would be transferred and replaced by a local man more amenable to the Arafats, but this is highly improbable. The judge, who himself was not without influence in Santo Domingo, had for some time been trying to secure another position in the capital, and it was quite fortuitous that the position he sought became available at this time. There is little doubt that don Alejandro was instrumental in securing the position of judge for Mario Rosario; in this, he may have acted with the approval of Rafael Arafat.

plank made known to those individuals who stood outside this inner-most circle in the *pueblo;*[18] and then the plank was officially communicated to the community.

On the evening of March 14, the directive of the Reformista Party held a private meeting in one of the hotels in the *pueblo*.[19] The purpose of the meeting was to decide upon the *síndico* and *regidores* who would make up the Reformista plank in the coming elections; this plank was to be presented to the Reformista supporters for ratification a few days later at a public meeting in the party building. I was present at this meeting of the directive, having been invited by the *síndico* that same day. It was at once apparent that my presence was embarrassing to the others, although I was told that I was very welcome and urged to stay when I offered to leave.

At the meeting, the president of the *ayuntamiento* read out the names of the proposed *síndico* and the *regidores* (all of whom, of course, had been decided upon previously) and then asked if all those present were in agreement with the plank. Roberto Molina immediately objected to the inclusion of one man, whom he said was not a true *reformista* because until recently he had been involved with another party. He demanded that this man be replaced by a representative of Reformista Youth, and then spoke at some length on the importance of youth in the Reformista Party. The future of democracy and of the Reformista Party, he said, rested in the hands of youth.

It was obvious that the *síndico* was objecting to Rafael Arafat, but throughout the entire discussion that followed, Arafat was not referred to by name, nor was the PQD specifically mentioned. Everyone, including the *síndico* himself, was anxious to keep the discussion as impersonal as possible, lest it degenerate to the level of personal

---

[18] Two days following a closed meeting of the Reformista Party directive, at which the party plank was decided, I attended a political meeting in one of the sections, at which the local Reformista committee was to confer with the *síndico* and other political leaders from the *pueblo*. While waiting for the *pueblo* men to arrive, I asked the *campesinos* what they thought of the choice of Raóul Espiallat as *síndico* candidate. At the time, this seemed a harmless question, as it had been assumed in the *pueblo* that Espiallat would be nominated and this had been officially decided at the directive meeting two nights before. The *alcalde* of the section, in whose house the meeting was being held, looked alarmed and put his finger to his lips. He whispered that it was still not certain and added that they were waiting to be told who the *síndico* would be.

[19] Those present at the meeting included don Alejandro, Srs. Nashash, Rafael Arafat, Rosario, two of Constanza's doctors, the School Inspector, the *síndico*, the party president, the president of the *ayuntamiento*, and three other men who were to serve as *regidores*. There were no representatives from the *campo* at the meeting.

quarrels. When the chairman asked others for their opinions, they merely said that all the *regidores* were well known and respected men and that the plank was a good one. Don Alejandro's opinion was called for; he repeated the opinion of the others and added that the times called for "mature men" as *regidores* who "understood the problems of the *pueblo*."

The *síndico*, however, continued to argue, although it was clear he had no support. He grew more excited and insisted that he should have his way; he finally lost his temper when he shouted, "I am still the *síndico* here and it is my right!" At this point, don Alejandro stood up and curtly ordered Molina to follow him outside. When they returned a few moments later, the *síndico* was visibly shaken and had nothing more to say. The plank was then put to a vote and passed unanimously; the *síndico* voted with the rest.

Almost certainly Molina's protest was not spontaneous but had been planned; in retrospect, it is not unlikely that I had been invited to the meeting to witness it. Molina's intractibility threatened to undermine the careful work of mediation that had preceded the meeting and to make consensus impossible. Being entirely without support, the *síndico* could have been outvoted, but to have put the matter to a vote before complete consensus had been achieved would have been tantamount to recognizing that valid grounds for dissent existed. In the thinking of all those present at the meeting, the *síndico* would have been relieved of the responsibility for rendering full cooperation in the campaign that was to follow. Moreover, there was every likelihood that the lack of unanimity would have become known outside the closed circle of the party directive.

In F. G. Bailey's terms, the party directive was an "elite" council[20]—a corporate body with interests that separated it from the

---

[20] F. G. Bailey, "Decisions by Consensus in Councils and Committees With Special Reference to Village and Local Government in India," in *Political Systems and the Distribution of Power*, Michael Banton, ed. (London: Tavistock Publications, 1965), pp. 1–20.

Bailey has cut through the mystique surrounding the "need" for consensus frequently attributed to committees and councils, and rightly points out that, "To say a council strives for consensus because its members value consensus is evidently a circularity." *Ibid.*, p. 5. His distinction between "elite" and "arena" councils has application to the present case. Bailey argues that decisions by consensus are characteristic of elite committees, in which membership is small and the individuals meet in a variety of situations that call for mutual support and the exchange of favors. *Ibid.*, p. 11. The use of some mechanical means to resolve conflict, such as the majority vote, is more characteristic of arena councils, in which councillors represent segments in the public and compromise is difficult ". . . because each councillor . . . is steered by the heavy rudder of those . . . to whom he is answerable." *Ibid.*, p. 10.

public. As was indicated in Chapter 8, these men have always striven to present a consensus to the outside. In short, it was not enough that the *síndico* merely be overruled; rather, in the interests of all present, his concurrence had to be obtained. To this end, don Alejandro apparently found it necessary to depart from friendly persuasion and to resort to threats.

After the plank had been approved, the chairman called for names to make up what was described as an "alternative plank."[21] The names submitted were those of young men who were known to be *reformistas* but who were without any particular influence. The meeting of the directive then ended.

The Reformista meeting that was called a few days later was attended by some two hundred people from the *pueblo* and the *campo*. Representatives of the local party committees, whose task it would be to activate the voters, were present, but many who crowded into the small party building were merely curious *pueblo* dwellers who were not party workers.

The meeting was by no means a solemn affair; if anything, the mood was one of levity. In part, this was contributed to by the party president, who again chaired the meeting and inadvertently began by addressing the gathering as "Brothers of the Partido Dominicano!"—much to his own embarrassment and to the amusement of the crowd.

The chairman explained the purpose of the meeting and then presented those who were seated at the official table: the *síndico*, the president of the *ayuntamiento*, Srs. Rosario, Nashash, Raóul Espiallat, and don Alejandro. The men who had been nominated as *regidores*, including Rafael Arafat, sat close to the front facing the official table. Sr. Nashash and don Alejandro were introduced as the "guidance men" of Reformista Youth. Rosario was referred to as a "strong *reformista* and a friend of you all."

The first plank that had been decided upon by the directive was read out; after each name, the chairman made a brief comment in support of the individual concerned. Espiallat was described as a "son of Constanza," a successful businessman known to all in the *municipio*, and a man of political experience who had served Constanza well in earlier years, whose capabilities were recognized by the President himself. His moral qualities were also mentioned.

---

[21] It was explained that the practice of submitting an alternative plank to the party supporters was an "old democratic custom" of the Dominican Republic. At the party meeting that followed a few days later, voters were asked to approve one plank or the other. The alternative plank was in no way taken seriously.

He was a good Catholic, a *padre de familia*, and a man without enemies who would faithfully serve all in the community, not merely one group. Rafael Arafat, whose name followed that of Raóul Espiallat, was described as a "son of Constanza" and a man of much ability known to all in Constanza.

After this first plank was read, the alternative plank was read without comment. The meeting was then called upon to vote verbally for or against each plank; the first plank was approved unanimously. The voting was followed by short speeches by the *síndico* and by Rosario, both of whom sang the praises of Espiallat and urged all to "vote red" (the Reformista color) in the coming elections. Espiallat then gave a short speech of thanks in which he pledged to serve the interests of all *constanceros* and "not just one group." The meeting closed with a series of *vivas* for the *síndico* candidate, the Reformista Party, President Balaguer, and the Vice-President. The crowd dispersed with a great deal of jubilation.

The public declaration by Molina and Rosario in support of Raóul Espiallat and the presence of Rafael Arafat's name among the *regidores* signified the restoration of peace. Further, the *reformistas* had found in Espiallat a candidate who was widely known and respected throughout the *municipio* and who could appeal to all sectors of the community. He enjoyed a reputation for fairness and restraint such that even the hard-core PRD people viewed him with approval; because he had been *síndico* in Trujillo's day, the *trujillistas* (who considered him to be one of themselves) associated him with what they considered to be happier times. Espiallat was a successful businessman, and *campesinos* and *pueblo* dwellers alike spoke admiringly of his "astuteness" and were impressed by the influence he was believed to command in the capital. People hoped that under his administration benefits once more would flow into the community. In fact, Raóul Espiallat, more so than any other leading figure in Constanza at that time, was able to pose as a unity candidate.

Two weeks after the meeting in the party building, a Reformista rally was held in the park, which marked the beginning of the election campaign. The Secretary of Police and Interior arrived from the capital to attend the rally; his lavish praise of Espiallat and of the men who were slated to be *regidores* gave official blessing to the *reformistas'* plank.

THE MUNICIPIO ELECTIONS OF MAY 1968

With a unified front and no opposition, the *reformistas* were able to concentrate their energies on strengthening their hold over the *municipio* without the necessity of having to outpromise others or to deal with openly conflicting loyalties among electors. The only options opened to those who opposed the *reformistas* were either to refrain from voting or to render their votes invalid. But this was a decision of individual conscience and those of the opposition were not required to declare themselves one way or the other. Nor had they any effective way to counter Reformista propaganda or to preserve their organization against further inroads by the Reformista Party.

Most of the linkages that made up the Reformista action-set were already well established; in theory, nothing more was required to activate these again shortly prior to the elections to ensure a good turnout of voters. On the surface, in fact, there was no necessity for the *reformistas* to conduct a campaign in the normal sense at all. That they saw fit to do so and that the Reformista chiefs of the *pueblo* carried the campaign to the *campo* was indicative of the need they felt to counteract the damage that had been done by the brief appearance of the PQD, and of the need to revive enthusiasm for the Reformista Party, which had clearly waned during the incumbency of Roberto Molina. Perhaps more important was the personal desire of Raóul Espiallat to assert leadership; this could effectively be accomplished only by actively campaigning in the *campo*.

The key linkages of the Reformista action-set in the *campo* were men with extensive kin ties who owned more land than most and on occasions acted as *patrones* in their area. These men had long been influential and were accustomed to exercising authority, just as those in their area were in the habit of looking to them for direction. During Bosch's administration, some of them had sided with the PRD to preserve their own authority, but even where this had not occurred, as in El Limoncito, the influence of these men was not supplanted but only temporarily diminished by the appearance of new figures who suddenly achieved political importance in those areas. The originators of these linkages in the *campo* were *la gente mas importante;* in the *pueblo,* they were the *trujillistas,* who, like the *campo* figures, had long exercised influence. In other words, the Reformista action-set, better described as a quasi-group,[22] was basically a revival of the Dominican Party of Trujillo. Notwithstanding a number of changes in the personnel who made

---

[22] Adrian C. Mayer, "The Significance of Quasi-Groups in the Study of Complex Societies," pp. 97–122. Mayer's distinction between action-set and quasi-group was referred to earlier in the chapter; see footnote 7.

up the linkages, most of those who stood at the center of the set in the *pueblo* and those who provided the key linkages in the *campo* were the same men who had had the strongest influence in the days of Trujillo. As one informant put it, "It is the same team, only the jerseys are different."

In 1966, when the *reformistas* came to power, these key *pueblo* figures stayed in the background; the work of campaigning was largely left to Roberto Molina and other younger men, who were not tainted by having had a close association with Trujillo. In 1968, in the political climate then prevailing in Constanza, this was much less a factor, and it was in the interests of the *reformistas* to stress the identity of their principal supporters in the *pueblo*. Further, it was in the personal interests of Raóul Espiallat to conduct a vigorous campaign in the *campo* to tie the key linkages to himself so that the machinery might once more become his.

In the campaign, the *reformistas* made use of Radio Constanza, which each afternoon broadcast a program of political speeches and comments by various citizens, and of a truck with a loudspeaker, which traveled throughout the *municipio* urging all to vote for the *reformistas* and informing people when a political rally was to take place in their area.

Rallies were held in most of the major centers of population throughout the community; the procedures were the same on most occasions. The arrival of the main visitors, who generally came by car, was heralded by a series of *vivas* called for by a young man of Reformista Youth who traveled about in the truck. The visitors greeted the *alcalde* of the section and other leading men and then separated to listen to requests and complaints, which were made in private. During the speeches, these local leaders (and sometimes one of the *pueblo* men) would act as cheerleaders and initiate applause with remarks like, "Well said!" or "That deserves applause!" Other than to offer a few words pledging support, however, the *campesino* leaders rarely made speeches. In the opinion of Juan Suriel, the young man of Reformista Youth, this was because, as *campesinos*, they "lacked the capacity."

There were four principal speakers at the rallies: the *síndico*, Raóul Espiallat, Mario Rosario, and Marco Rojas, who had been president of the *ayuntamiento* and was to continue in that post. Other individuals from the *pueblo* accompanied the speakers; when they were particularly well known, their presence was drawn to the attention of the crowd. Invariably the speeches involved reading the Reformista plank; when the *regidores* were announced, the name of Rafael Arafat was always read first. Neither Arafat nor don

Alejandro took any part in the campaign, but on two occasions Sr. Nashash accompanied the speakers to the *campo*.

The contents of the speeches varied somewhat from place to place, and it was not always the same individuals who spoke. In the dry farming areas, where crowds were smaller, the speeches took on a more paternalistic tone than they did in the main *pueblecitos*. Little of a concrete nature was promised to voters, however, because it was evident that the party had already been brought into some disrepute because of the rash promises Roberto Molina made in the 1966 campaign.[23] The failure of many benefits to materialize since the election of President Balaguer was attributed to the opposition, who were said to have brought the country to revolution and bankruptcy, leaving it to Balaguer to rescue the country from ruin.

For the most part the appeals made to the voters were highly emotional. Not to vote in the coming elections, it was said, was to side with the forces of the left, who were anti-Christ and communists, seeking only selfish ends and not the good of the country. Religious symbolism was employed to identify the Reformista Party with Christ. Voters were told to "Vote red! Red as the color of Christ on Calvary!", and President Balaguer was represented as God's instrument, who was predestined to lead the country out of backwardness and misery. His name was linked with Duarte, Mejia, and Sanchez, the three great heroes of Dominican history.

The strength of the Reformista Party was constantly stressed. It was referred to as "the party of the great majority of the Dominican people," and *constanceros* were urged to "be on the winning side." The fact that in Constanza there was no opposition was used as evidence of the popularity of the *síndico* candidate and the unity for which he stood. In praising Raóul Espiallat, speakers emphasized those qualities likely to be most appealing to *constanceros*. It was stressed that he was a son of the *pueblo*, a friend of all, the father of a family, a good Catholic, and a successful businessman, who had accepted the nomination not because he needed the salary, but only out of desire to serve the community. For his part, Espiallat promised that he would be a friend and a brother to all *constanceros*,

---

[23] The only incident that marred an otherwise successful campaign was a consequence of these promises. In Tireo Abajo, after the *síndico* had finished speaking, a *campesino* commandeered the loudspeaker and told the audience not to be deceived because previous campaign promises had not been fulfilled. Raóul Espiallat was able to reassure the crowd that everything possible was being done to honor the promises and that Tireo Abajo had not been forgotten.

and he pledged to devote himself to the interests of the entire community, not to those of any one group.

Various people said that the crowds attending the rallies were much smaller than those in 1966. This was attributed to a lack of interest because of the absence of any opposition. Nevertheless, the campaign was evidently effective. In the voting, which took place on May 16, 1968, 7,160 votes were cast for the *reformistas;* there were only seven invalid votes. This compared very favorably with the 7,642 votes the *reformistas* gained in 1966, which at that time represented 87.7% of the total votes cast.

Conclusions

Those who dominate political life in Constanza are men who, through friendships, familial connections, or ritual kin ties, are able to exploit powerful connections outside the community. These sources, however, whether they rest in the military, in government functionaries, or in the President himself, are not constant but are subject to change.

In Trujillo's day, there was but a single ultimate source of power; it appears that whatever rivalries and discords may have existed among *la gente mas importante* were not brought into the open. The interests they had in common always prompted them to find a consensus and to present a front of unanimity. Since the death of Trujillo, two significant changes have occurred on the national scene that are clearly reflected on the local level: the emergence of opposition parties and the relative independence of the military from civil control. In short, the sources of power emanating from outside the community have become more diverse and less certain and, as a consequence, the position of *la gente mas importante* in Constanza has been rendered more tenuous. Consensus has become increasingly difficult to achieve.

Constanza has always sought to appease the outside; it was to be expected that with the election of Bosch in 1962 *la gente mas importante* would show some ambivalence. Only two men of any importance actually declared for Bosch, but it was rumored that some others secretly gave money to the PRD organizers in Constanza. Publicly, however, there was no open split among the *trujillistas* and, despite whatever overtures some of them may have made to the PRD as individuals, they were considered to be opposed to Bosch and known to have welcomed his overthrow. On the other hand, the appearance of the Wessin group in Constanza in 1968 was of great significance for the political future of the community because it represented a split in the ranks of the *trujillistas.*

Turner, in discussing his final phase of political development, "the restoration of peace," points out that the restored peace is likely to entail drastic changes in the field boundaries and the ". . . nature and intensity of the relations between parts and the structure of the total field, will have changed."[1] The Arafats failed in their bid for power but the restored peace is an uneasy one; the political and economic unrest, which largely accounted for the support the Arafats generated, remains.

The importance of the powerholders has rested in the fact that through the contacts they have outside the community, they are able to distribute a great deal of party-directed patronage locally; but equally important has been their position as patrons. As store owners or as employers they have been in a position to offer credit or employment to a large number of people, and consequently *constanceros* seek to form relationships of dependence with these men in order to extract favors. Today, however, the demands for land and employment have placed an impossible strain on patronage resources, both traditional and party directed. With ever increasing population pressure, these problems are likely to become worse.

Constanceros have long been conditioned to following the directions of those who hold power. Throughout the Trujillo years they attended rallies and voted as directed by their leaders in the *campo* and *pueblo;* and this pattern is still largely followed today. But, just as those who direct affairs have at best been subjected to only intermittent pressure from the outside, traditionally they have not had to be responsive to the demands of those who vote. There has always been the expectation that power will be used arbitrarily; once in power, individuals have been free to do much as they pleased, so long as the wrath of those in power outside the community was not incurred. With the emergence of opposition parties, this pattern appears to be changing, and the political chiefs have been confronted with the necessity of actively campaigning to hold allegiance. Inevitably, it seems, those elected to public office (and those who engineer their election) will have to become more responsive to the demands of voters. The vigorous campaign conducted by the Reformistas in the *municipio* elections, and the caution exercised in refraining from making rash promises, would seem to indicate that this realization has already been brought home to these men. In short, if rival political parties survive in the Dominican Republic, politics in communities like Constanza is likely to become less the province of the few, and more the concern of the many.

---

[1] M. J. Swartz, V. W. Turner, and A. Tuden, eds., *Political Anthropology,* p. 37.

Bibliography

Arensberg, Conrad M.
  1961 "The Community as Object and as Sample." *American Anthropologist* 63:241–264. Reprinted as Chapter 1 in *Culture and Community*, Conrad M. Arensberg and Solon T. Kimball, eds. New York: Harcourt, Brace and World, Inc., 1965.

Bailey, F. G.
  1965 "Decisions by Consensus in Councils and Committees with Special Reference to Village and Local Government in India." In *Political Systems and the Distribution of Power*, Michael Banton, ed., pp. 1–20. London: Tavistock Publications.

Banfield, Edward C.
  1958 *The Moral Basis of a Backward Society*. New York: The Free Press.

Bredemeier, Harry C.; and Stephenson, Richard M.
  1962 *The Analysis of Social Systems*. New York: Holt, Rinehart and Winston, Inc.

Chappel, Eliot Dismore; and Coon, Carleton Stevens.
  1942 *Principles of Anthropology*. New York: Henry Holt and Company.

Clarke, Edith.
  1957 *My Mother Who Fathered Me*. London: George Allen and Unwin, Ltd.

Concepcíon, J. Augustín.
  1958 *Constanza*. Cuidad Trujillo: República Dominicana.

Davenport, William.
  1959 "Nonunilinear Descent and Descent Groups." *American Anthropologist* 61:557–572.

Deschamps, Enrique.
  1907 *La República Dominicana, Directorio y Guía General*. Barcelona: Vda. de J. Cunill.

Easton, David.
  1955 *A Theoretical Approach to Authority*. Technical Report No. 17. Prepared under contract for the Office of Naval Research. Stanford, California: Department of Economics, Stanford University.

Erasmus, Charles J.
   1961   *Man Takes Control.* Indianapolis: The Bobbs-Merrill Company, Inc.

Freilich, Morris.
   1961   "Serial Polygyny, Negro Peasants, and Model Analysis." *American Anthropologist* 63:955–975.

Manners, Robert A.
   1956   "Tabara: Subcultures of a Tobacco and Mixed Crops Municipality." In *The People of Puerto Rico,* Julian H. Steward, ed., pp. 93–170. Urbana: The University of Illinois Press.

Martin, John Bartlow.
   1966   *Overtaken by Events. The Dominican Crisis from the Fall of Trujillo to the Civil War.* New York: Doubleday and Company, Inc.

Mayer, Adrian C.
   1966   "The Significance of Quasi-Groups in the Study of Complex Societies." In *The Social Anthropology of Complex Societies,* Michael Banton, ed., pp. 97–122. London: Tavistock Publications.

Mintz, Sidney W.
   1956   "Cañamelar: The Subculture of a Rural Sugar Proletariat." In *The People of Puerto Rico,* Julian H. Steward, ed., pp. 314–417. Urbana: The University of Illinois Press.

Redfield, Robert.
   1955   *The Little Community.* Chicago: The University of Chicago Press.

Schomburgk, R. H.
   1852   "Una Visita al Valle de Constanza." In *El Alpinismo en la República Dominicana,* Ml. de Js. Tovares, ed., Sucs., C. por A., pp. 115–130. Santiago de los Caballeros: Editorial el Diario, 1948.

Smith, M. G.
   1962   *West Indian Family Structure.* Seattle: University of Washington Press.

Steward, Julian H. (ed.).
   1956   *The People of Puerto Rico.* Urbana: The University of Illinois Press.

Swartz, Marc J. (ed.).
   1968   *Local-Level Politics.* Chicago: Aldine Publishing Company.

Swartz, Marc J.; Turner, Victor W.; and Tuden, Arthur (eds.).
   1966   *Political Anthropology.* Chicago: Aldine Publishing Company.

Walker, Malcolm T.
   1970   *Power Structure and Political Behavior in a Community of the Dominican Republic.* Ph.D. dissertation, Columbia University. Ann Arbor: University Microfilms.

1971   "Foreign Colonists in a Dominican Rural Community: The Costs of Economic Progress." *Caribbean Studies* 11(3):88–98.

Weingrod, Alex.
1968   "Patrons, Patronage, and Political Parties." *Comparative Studies in Society and History* 10 (No. 4):377–400.

Whitten, Norman E., Jr.
1965   *Class, Kinship, and Power in an Ecuadorian Town: the Negroes of San Lorenzo.* Stanford, California: Stanford University Press.

Wolf, Eric R.
1956a   "Aspects of Group Relations in a Complex Society: Mexico." *American Anthropologist* 58:1065–1078.

1956b   "San Jose: Subcultures of a 'Traditional' Coffee Municipality." In *The People of Puerto Rico*, Julian H. Steward, ed., pp. 171–264. Urbana: The University of Illinois Press.